DEFENSE OF THE REALM

BRITISH STRATEGY

IN THE NUCLEAR EPOCH

DEFENSE OF THE REALM

BRITISH STRATEGY

IN THE NUCLEAR EPOCH

R. N. ROSECRANCE

COLUMBIA UNIVERSITY PRESS
NEW YORK AND LONDON
1968

R. N. Rosecrance is Professor of Political Science, University of California at Berkeley, and for the 1967–68 academic year is a Member of the Policy Planning Council, Department of State.

For Harvey A. DeWeerd

PREFACE

UNTIL QUITE RECENTLY British strategy has been a neglected field of study. There has been a frequent assumption that British notions have somehow been asymptotic to American conceptions, only several years behind. Most analyses have concentrated on the period since Suez, and the most typical conclusion has pointed to British weakness in military affairs. Since Britons themselves have been wont to criticize their defense posture, it is not surprising that Americans have also taken up the cudgels. This work, centering on the period from 1946 to 1957, aims partly to redress the balance.

Achievements are not measured only in terms of successful weapons systems, nor are they a function of total diplomatic prescience. Britain has certainly made mistakes in her postwar military policy, but they do not, on balance, seem greater than those made by the United States. If British influence is currently at a nadir, it need not be so for all time. Most importantly, strategic position is not simply a matter of military power, but of political credibility. Britain's military influence was greatest, paradoxically, when its military power was less than it is at the moment. Its influence was greatest when British purposes in Europe and overseas were both clear and unvacillating, and when Whitehall formed the necessary bridge linking Washington with the continent.

Two things follow from this: first, that Suez was a greater disaster than has yet been imagined; second, that it is more easily erased than has yet been conceived. Britain is now back at Square 1 in international terms, but her progress in the game of international strategy could be surprisingly rapid. Most of the arguments concerning her diminished international role have dealt with partial causes, and the remedies suggested are unlikely to cure the disease. If this book succeeds in providing a fuller account and an analysis of the British position in strategic affairs it will have achieved its purpose.

The research for the study was largely accomplished during a year's tenure at Kings College, University of London, and supported by the Rockefeller Foundation. It was enormously facilitated by the press files of Chatham House and the collections of the Royal United Service Institution and the Institute for Strategic Studies. Professor Michael Howard and Alastair Buchan kindly aided me with sources. My colleagues Hedley Bull and Raymond Dawson contributed greatly, though sometimes unwittingly, to the approach and content of what follows. At the University of California I received grants from Ford Foundation funds which permitted interviewing in Washington and the employment of several research assistants. I am indebted to Hasu Patel, Richard Verchick, Michael O'Hara, and Stanley Rosen for the abstracting of materials. Susanne Spence, Xenia Tanayevsky-Ordovsky, and Belle Horwitz assisted my survey of defense debates. Nina Bertelsen, Sara Pedersen, Rachelle Barber, and Eva Klercker did the necessary typing.

Without the guidance of principals in British and American defense policy-making, the study could not have been completed. It benefited greatly from interviews with Dean G. Acheson, F. J. Bellenger, David Bendall, Sir Frederick Brundrett, Rear Admiral Sir Anthony Buzzard, Sir John Cockcroft, Sir Maurice Dean, Admiral Sir Michael Denny, Desmond Donnelly, Air Chief Marshal Sir Alfred Earle, Air Chief Marshal Sir William Elliott, Lord Franks, Lord Gladwyn, Mrs. Margaret Gowing, Admiral Sir Guy Grantham, John Hall, Sir Robert Hall, W. Averell Harriman, General Lord Ismay, Lt. General Sir Ian Jacob, Brigadier Sir Fitzroy Maclean, Air Chief Marshal Sir George Mills (Gentleman Usher of the Blackrod, House of Lords), Paul Nitze, Michael Palliser, Sir William Penney, Lord Plowden, General Sir Nigel Poett, James T. Ramey, Lord Sherfield, Marshal of the Royal Air Force Sir John Slessor, Gerard C. Smith, Sir George Strauss, C. W. Wright, Kenneth Younger, and Sir Philip de Zulueta. None of the information or perspectives lent in interviews has been attributed in the text.

My most important debt is to Dr. Harvey A. DeWeerd, who first interested me in the study of British defense problems. He provided invaluable insights and analysis; his interest and enthusiasm offered a constant inspiration. As teacher, friend, and colleague over the years it is most fitting that I dedicate this book to him.

CONTENTS

CHAPTER ONE

MAJOR ISSUES OF BRITISH DEFENSE

AMONG MODERN NATIONS the United Kingdom occupies a unique military position. Ranking behind the United States and the Soviet Union in physical power, she has nonetheless disposed a multiple defense capability, comprising forces for both thermonuclear and conventional war. At the same time the military self-sufficiency of the two nuclear giants was not the goal of British efforts. Far more than the United States or Russia, Britain relied upon allies for a large budget of military tasks. Indeed, in the generation since World War II, British defense policy has in no small measure been alliance policy. The partial dependence which ensued, however, was not that of the second-rate power. For Britain alliance has not been a simple military necessity; it has been a matter of decision and choice. Her experience since 1945 invalidates oft-asserted French dictims that in a world of nuclear deterrence and vulnerability, no state will rely on allies in a crisis. Britain has frequently done so, sometimes to her discomfiture, but generally to her benefit. And there is evidence that alliance connections will endure. Somewhat surprisingly, perhaps, as NATO cohesion declines, the Sino-Soviet accord ruptures, and nuclear weapons spread, Britain remains unmoved by vistas of nonalignment or dreams of nuclear autarchy.

In other respects Britain's postwar defense policy holds special interest. Before World War II the United Kingdom carried more colonial responsibilities than any nation in modern history. After the war she laid these down, one by one, as formal commitments. Until very recently, however, past obligations helped to define the contours of current interests. Erstwhile colonial territories demanded her military presence. Until the changes set in train by the Defence Review of 1965–66, a very large proportion of Britain's military resources were devoted to the defense of political entities of her own creation. In the Far East, the Indian Ocean, the Middle East, East Africa, and elsewhere, these burdens helped to explain why other defense tasks were hard to bear. North Atlantic defense and the nuclear deterrent program were additional to the obligations deriving from empire. And in this respect Britain's defense has been distinct from that of other Western states. America had only a small colonial preoccupation, and very substantial strength to indulge it. France and the Netherlands parted from their colonies on such bad terms that future defense links were generally ruled out. In contrast Britain's very success in emancipation engendered problems. Conceding independence before it could be taken, the United Kingdom left frail political structures around the globe. The first requisite for new states was usually British military assistance against external and internal challenge.

These tributes to British political acumen, however, have had their strategic and financial costs. Other Western nations —France, Germany and the Low Countries—had only national and European defense to consider and national and European interests to defend. In addition to these, Britain had both international interests and an internationally dispersed force. Aside from Korea and Vietnam, Britain has sent more troops to Africa, the Middle East, and Asia in the past twenty years than has the United States.

Three arenas of commitment—strategic, European, and worldwide—together comprise Britain's financial problem. If any one of them could be dropped or substantially reduced, the other two could be sustained with continuity and vigor. For the past generation, however, the United Kingdom has striven to fulfill all three, and the result has been a limitation on industrial progress and a chronic balance of payments deficit. If we exclude the two super-powers, no nation over time spent a greater proportion of its Gross National Product on arms, and in the first five years of the cold war, no Western nation spent as much. The British public's internal sufferings have been testimony to the preeminence of state-craft and external defense in the allocation of national re-sources. They remain so today. New nations emerging on the threshold of international politics, and old states with colonial heritages or world ambitions long relinquished or discredited, can have no conception of the present British predicament. The new power can undertake enhanced responsibilities with the zeal of inexperience. The old may launch novel enterprises because its past is no longer an encumbrance. Britain has not been able to indulge such luxuries; her interests have been those of a world power.

Equally distinctive, Britain is the one major victor of World War II who lost influence in succeeding years. In most respects British military and political power attained its apex during the war. Her rank at its close was higher than it had been as one of the five Concert Powers of the nineteenth century. In an odd twist of fate, her international and diplomatic efforts were most successful when national autonomy was being undermined. The alteration in fortunes was not easy to acknowledge. Defeated powers, like Germany and Japan, suffered humiliation but also obtained Western largesse and support. They emerged in the 1950s with buoyant economies and few foreign responsibilities. France's tenuous nationalism was shattered in 1940, and her governmental system had to undergo practical revolution before new confidence could be gained. But even France, a vanquished nation, recognized that entirely new measures, politically and internationally, were necessary to regain world status. In one sense a British disadvantage was continual success. Never suffering a cataclysmic reverse, Britain never was forced to rethink her patterns of foreign involvement. The imperial obligations of the nineteenth century could be seriously entertained in the twentieth. Fundamentally, Britain's reduced status was economic, not strategic; the need for a major national reorientation was not fully apparent. And thus, the British public, skating on the veneer of international achievement, have year by year supported military commitments which they could not indefinitely maintain.

The internal implications of British adequacy abroad were striking and largely unique. To begin with her economic incapacity went unperceived for a considerable time. Success in the atomic program, in NATO, in the V-bomber force, and in the maintenance of overseas garrisons helped to beguile the electorate. Britain would continue to be a Great Power. Aside from Suez, there were no major international setbacks; in Africa and Asia the devolution of authority was orderly, and Britain remained on good terms with previous client-states. In external terms British efforts were crowned with success: British victories in Greece, Kenya, and Malaya contrasting with French failures in Indo-China and Algeria. In the Middle East, British efforts were less well rewarded, but the CENTO Pact, and informal connections with Saudi Arabia and Jordan survived other defeats. Nor could Cyprus be accounted a total failure. The inability of the British government to carry all the responsibilities of world power was only gradually revealed, and then against a backdrop of attainment. It was in this sense harder to understand and accept than in the case of other countries. The challenge was great enough to cause concern, but not crucial enough to compel abandonment. Perhaps as a result, the government continued to champion a pattern of worldwide interests, and the failures emerged piecemeal.

The cancellation of Blue Streak and TSR-2, the reliance on American-provided Skybolt and then Polaris, the dependence on U.S. nuclear components—all these questioned British eminence in the field of strategic weapons. But the deductions drawn in Britain were not so radical as might have been the case elsewhere. Major surgery on the many-limbed tree of British interests did not appear necessary; the basic soundness of the plant declared against amputation. Ultimately, finance argued in favor of paring certain commitments so that others might be better cared for. But in the shorter run it seemed possible to nourish them all, though on meager fare. The British public was confronted only with apparent ineptitude at the governmental level; no major national crisis was presented as the fundamental cause of changes in defense plans. Often the new, reduced programs were claimed to provide the same security as the old.

That these claims could not be sustained may have artificially magnified the eventual *crise de confiance*. A nuclear progam on the modest scale of the French strategic force was certainly not beyond British means. But it could not be carried on while Britain had major physical commitments in Asia, at Aden, in the Mediterranean, and on the Rhine. The failure of important weapon components of the deterrent, then, had a misplaced significance. If certain sectors of the British electorate underplayed these reversals, others saw in them the collapse of British power in world affairs. Since Britain could not do one thing well, some presumed she could do nothing well. If, under the pressure of far-flung defense burdens, she evinced minor failures, defense policy as a whole was at fault, and the Campaign for Nuclear Disarmament reached its apogee after the failure of Blue Streak. But these conclusions were unwarranted. A nation which did not do three things well might still do two things well; the prerequisite for high performance was readiness to cut one of the commitments.

In addition to the gradual development of a financial crisis, there was the concrete political defeat at Suez. The second as much as the first was responsible for British political revaluation. Until Suez Britain had a record of accomplishment. She had developed nuclear weapons independently, sustained a major post-Korea rearmament, and most importantly, her diplomacy had met with almost unrivaled success. Britain and the United States worked together most of the time, but when they diverged, Britain seemed in the right. She recognized China and acted to restrain American policy at the time of the Korean War. More than any other influence she prevented the United States from intervening militarily in Indo-China in April, 1954. When the European Defense Community failed later in the year, Anthony Eden personally negotiated a solution which admitted Germany to NATO without restriction and yet brought French acceptance of German rearmament. Churchill and Eden were primary advocates of summit talks with the Russians and helped to arrange the Geneva meetings of 1955. Though Britain operated on an admittedly narrow power base, it seemed in the mid-1950s that she was one of the most influential factors in international diplomacy.

Then came Suez. It was not only the sharp defeat which mattered, but the way it was administered. In the first place Britain sought to do battle with a minor adversary, a country which could not expect to stand up to British arms. Assuming normal divisions among outside powers, one could expect the Suez invasion to succeed in short order. This did not happen. Second, Britain's humiliation was accomplished not at the hands of her enemies, but through the intervention of her friends. Nor was the frustration of British efforts strictly military. There was no major obstacle impeding the bombings, the landings at Port Said, or the projected occupation of the canal. The problem was political and financial. The Anglo-American alliance was jeopardized, and there was concrete pressure on the pound sterling which would have forced devaluation in a matter of days. The British failure at Suez was not military; it was social. Political and economic resources were insufficient to bring it off.

The conclusions drawn again were dual. There were those who, against the background of prior success, asserted that Britain should aim even higher. She should enhance her military prowess and seek a more independent role in foreign affairs. Others reached an opposite conclusion. The British blunder at Suez did not simply reflect deficient national resources, it represented a lack of national vision. The inadequacy which Suez revealed was linked with ideological sentiment. Britain not only failed at Suez, she should have failed. The war was an atavistic return to nineteenth-century imperialism. Modernity, in contrast, should play down military force and emphasize peaceful relations with the developing countries. Unlike Dunkirk, Suez split the British nation. Defeat in France in 1940 rallied both nationalists and ideologues. Defeat in Egypt in 1956 divided them, the first plumping for an even larger and more independent capability, the second supporting a complete redirection of national efforts. A consensus failed to crystallize, and the common deductions from Suez were as fragmentary and incomplete as before. The national response to challenge was ambivalent.

Taken as a whole the British reaction to military stimuli since 1945 has been a very special one. In general, British defeats went unrecognized; success overshadowed failure. But when specific rebuffs could not be ignored, public attitudes were contradictory. Economic constraints did not mean that Britain could not be a formidable military power. The Suez disaster did not suggest that British forces were impotent or British purposes malign. The French reaction to Suez, after all, was altogether different. But Britain emerged uncertainly. Because of success, she is only now beginning to trim military expenditure in certain sectors in order to do a better job in others; because of failure, she is diffident about her abilities and purposes in world affairs. The crisis of confidence has been great enough to incur doubts; it is just beginning to foster change. For all these reasons, Britain is a greater nation than she seems in the third decade of the nuclear epoch.

At the end of World War II, Britain's readjustment in the face of Soviet hostility was probably more rapid than America's. Publicly, a semblance of cooperation was maintained until December, 1947, when the Council of Foreign Ministers finally expired. And it is true that Ernest Bevin was embarrassed by Mr. Churchill's Fulton speech in March, 1946.[1] The latter complicated the British Foreign Secretary's dealings with his own party and prompted a formal disavowal. At the same time the British military had come to identify Soviet Russia as their main enemy, even though the USSR was not explicitly mentioned as the probable foe in a defense staff paper until the end of 1946. There were simultaneous frictions with the United States over atomic policy, Palestine, the cessation of lend-lease, and future world economic arrangements. Despite these, official Britons were convinced that an unwritten Anglo-American alliance should remain the basis of British security.[2]

That this should be true was by no means a reflex response to the facts of the postwar period. There were many good reasons for *not* allying with the United States. Differences in concrete political attitude, now that the Labour Party had ascended to power in Britain were not inconsiderable. British imperial interests would not be supported by the United States, and British socialism was distrusted by the American Congress. On the atomic issue, Britain quickly learned that she could expect little if any help with her national nuclear effort. In economic matters, the liquidation of vast British foreign investments in the common war effort entitled the United Kingdom to no special treatment in postwar financial arrangements. President Truman's policy on Palestine nearly drove Bevin to distraction. And even if a favorable temporary

[1] See C. R. Rose, "The Relation of Socialist Principles to British Labour Foreign Policy, 1945–1951," pp. 104–20. Unpublished dissertation, Nuffield College (Michaelmas Term), 1959.

[2] Max Beloff, *New Dimensions in Foreign Policy* (New York, 1961), pp. 17–20.

relationship with the United States were attained, it might not be permanent. The United States might revert to its interwar policy of isolation. Many members of the ruling Labour Party believed that socialist foreign policy should accompany socialist internal construction and reform. Yet no prescribed foreign policy was more quickly jettisoned than that of the Labour Party after it had attained to power in 1945.[3]

Even the Soviet threat did not seem to make a connection with America automatic. Given Soviet hostility, policymakers could not be sure how far Russian opposition would be carried. One could still harbor the notion that the Russian problem was political and economic, not military. But if it was military, the proximity of threat was again unclear. Although British defense spending did not decline as rapidly as that of the United States, a ten-year no-war planning assumption was adopted in the winter of 1946.[4] At much the same time, Prime Minister Attlee was proposing to the Defense Committee that Britain aim at disengagement from areas where conflict with the Russians might occur.[5] In addition the decision had been made to produce military-grade plutonium.[6] The atomic bomb, once attained, could be expected to provide a considerable degree of security for Britain acting alone, but even the bomb program did not have an overriding priority on British resources.[7] Nor did other British military

[3] See Rose, *passim.*

[4] Alfred Goldberg, "The Military Origins of the British Nuclear Deterrent," *International Affairs* (October, 1964), p. 601.

[5] Hugh Dalton, *High Tide and After* (London, 1962), p. 105.

[6] Sir Leonard Owen, "Nuclear Engineering in the United Kingdom —the First Ten Years," *Journal of the British Nuclear Energy Society* (January, 1963), p. 23.

[7] Sir Christopher Hinton, "British Developments in Atomic Energy," *Nucleonics* (January, 1954), p. 6.

perspectives suggest a near-term conflict with the Soviet Union. When the V-bombers were designed in 1947, a conscious decision was made to concentrate on long-term development, not short-range production. If Britain had anticipated a Russian military challenge in the near future, she might have built bombers with existing jet engines.[8]

In short there was no preparation for an immediate military contest with the USSR. An unwritten military alliance with the United States, then, was not an absolute and immediate prerequisite for postwar British policy. The wartime relationship might have been allowed to languish; it might have been pursued in a much more forthrightly egalitarian vein; it might have been resumed only when a Soviet military menace loomed. In fact, however, the informal Anglo-American relationship preceded the revelation of Soviet military hostility.

Once developed (and there is evidence that America was the more reluctant partner initially), the Anglo-American alliance became a crucial reference point for both countries. Military strategy came to be considered within the context of alliance, and it cannot now be understood outside it. For Britain particularly, later military developments and strategies were not to be taken as ambitions for strategic self-sufficiency. Even in the design and manufacture of the atomic bomb itself, Britain offered a true pooling of national resources with the United States. This is not to say, as some writers have done, that Britain would not have sought the bomb if she had obtained full nuclear cooperation and exchange with America.[9] Even during the war it was perfectly apparent that the United Kingdom was thinking not only of a

[8] Goldberg, p. 605.
[9] See Elizabeth Young, "Arms and Strategy in American View," *Bulletin of the Atomic Scientists* (June, 1965), p. 53.

bomb which could defeat Hitler, but also of bombs for the postwar period.[10] The exchange of information and the pooling of production facilities would not only have given Britain knowledge, it would also have made a British stockpile grow more rapidly.

The bomb program and the alliance, however, did not reflect radically different policy alternatives. Even after the British bomb had been developed, one still had to decide how to use it. Even more important, how much reliance was to be placed upon it as compared with support from allies? Here alliance purposes were largely governing. The British bomb was not apparently intended to provide the required security by and of itself. It was an enormous fillip to the British posture, but it was not conceived as a real surrogate for the Anglo-American alliance. The justification for the decision to reequip the Royal Air Force with V-bombers was not that the United States and Britain might some day go their separate ways, it was that certain targets, vital to Britain, would not be hit in the first round of Strategic Air Command retaliation on the Soviet Union.

Britain, moreover, made occasional economic, political, and military sacrifices to maintain the American alliance. After the arrangement for the division of nuclear ore supplies expired at the end of 1949, London might have held up further allocations to the United States until she had obtained a satisfactory agreement on nuclear sharing. She refrained from doing so. In 1950–51 it is clear that British rearmament in response to the Korean War would not have approached its awesome magnitude had it not been for U.S. prompting. Britain thought not only about the Soviet military menace; she thought also

[10] Margaret Gowing, *Britain and Atomic Energy: 1939–1945* (London, 1964), p. 323.

of the danger of U.S. retrenchment or withdrawal in Europe. In the end she spent what she had to spend to ensure increased American commitment and support. The sacrifices imposed were real. Economic shortages and a balance of payments crisis followed, and Labour lost power in October, 1951.

In other respects the alliance proved its resiliency. By all precedents Suez or the 1962 Cuban confrontation should have put an end to the alliance bond with the United States. The first not only manifested diametrically opposed military and political interests, it also saw U.S. pressure call a halt to the occupation of the canal. Russian threats and Egyptian resistance had little to do with the British decision to accept a ceasefire. Of greater importance was the danger that India might desert the Commonwealth and, more significantly still, that America would force a devaluation of the pound and perhaps end the alliance.

In the Cuban crisis the British government was skeptical about the "quarantine" and angry at not having been consulted. The British public was even more critical, exhibiting a patently neutralist attitude on the Cuban issue.[11] The successful termination of the conflict no doubt served to allay British concern, but the affair *in toto* reminded both nations of their different approaches to international questions. Even the *Times* would have conceded the Turkish missile facilities in return for a withdrawal of Soviet missiles from Cuba. How, it might be asked, could two nations which had such divergent perceptions of international reality remain allied?

Yet, in each case the alliance attained a greater vitality shortly afterward. Within five months of the Suez venture, the United States was planning for a radical broadening of

[11] See John Mander, *Great Britain or Little England?* (London, 1963), chs. 1 and 2.

nuclear exchanges with the United Kingdom. With the passage of the 1958 amendments of the McMahon Act, the exchange of bomb information became virtually complete. In making these concessions, the United States was informally assuming that the nuclear technology revealed would never be used against her. Implicitly she avowed that there could be no difference of interests on central nuclear questions. But the difference of interests at Suez had approximated contrariety. The Cuban crisis also lent substance to division in the alliance, and this time it related to issues of strategic nuclear war. To some Britons it was the purpose of the British strategic force to require consultation on just the questions posed by Soviet missiles in Cuba. That consultation did not occur was a tacit admission of communication failure, both political and strategic. Within two months, however, the United States had agreed at Nassau to furnish its most sophisticated strategic weapons system to Britain at moderate cost. Again, the connection had withstood fundamental strains. In 1966, and despite the protests of the left-wing, the alliance seemed even more soundly based.[12] For a generation the Anglo-American alliance has been a fundamental reference point for British defense policy.

The British nuclear program is one facet of British strategy for which different justifications have been provided. Original objectives had to do with Great Power status and the need for the bomb to guard against a series of future contingencies. In this context it should be observed that if an informal Anglo-American accord preceded the full revelation of the Soviet

[12] See Raymond Dawson and Richard Rosecrance, "Theory and Reality in the Anglo-American Alliance," *World Politics* (October, 1966).

threat, the U.K. bomb program in turn antedated resumption of the informal alliance. Basic decisions on nuclear production were taken at a time when the future of Anglo-American relations was unclear. A U.S. reversion to isolation was still possible; concrete frictions were dividing Britain and America around the globe. A nuclear capability was particularly necessary in case Britain had to stand alone against formidable opponents in some future clash.

When a modern delivery capability was decided upon in 1952, the rationale for a bomb was somewhat different. By this time the Anglo-American alliance had been formalized and extended to nuclear matters—American atomic bombers were operating from bases in the United Kingdom. The U.S. capability, however, was not yet overwhelming. Since a war of attrition, economic blockade, and strategic recuperation was anticipated after the exhaustion of stocks in an initial nuclear exchange, the British believed it imperative to hit Soviet submarine pens before their vessels could put to sea. These targets apparently did not have such a high priority in American calculations, and the V-bomber force could be seen as a useful addition to the total nuclear capacity of the West.

Later on, however, a period of "broken-backed" war was no longer envisaged by Western strategists. The initial exchange of strategic thermonuclear weapons would be decisive. The United States possessed nuclear capabilities more than sufficient to destroy all militarily relevant targets in the Sino–Soviet bloc. In the mid-1960s it was acknowledged that British nuclear weapons had become dependent on U.S.-provided components: the Polaris missile, essential technology for the missile-firing submarine, and fissionable U-235. Even after 1968 (when U.K. Polaris submarines would begin to become operational) the Prime Minister pointed out that warhead components would have to be obtained on a continuing basis from the United States. There could be, therefore, no "independent" British deterrent in the sense that British nuclear forces were both indigenously developed and sufficient for all strategic tasks. It might still be insisted, however, that those forces could be used "independently." Britain would have "independent" powers of decision even if the capabilities employed partially owed their origin to the United States.

In purely formal terms this justification had something to commend it: there would be no physical restraint on separate British use of nuclear forces if the occasion demanded it. Such use against the USSR, however, would almost certainly implicate the United States. The Soviets would require conclusive proof of U.S. neutrality to spare America on a retaliatory mission. The British deterrent in other words probably possesses the capacity to "trigger" U.S. strategic forces against the Russians. This possibility has not altogether escaped British officials in discussions with continental counterparts. If America might seem incompletely committed to the protection of European interests in a future crisis, the British force could provide an additional reassurance. If the United States was not involved initially, she could theoretically be committed through British action.

The "triggering" capability of the British deterrent has received little attention, and is discounted in public statements. Only the most tortured scenarios provide justification for an independent British use of strategic weapons against the Russians. A recent writer speculated that a Soviet conventional attack upon Britain afforded the only realistic case for separate use, and this in turn rested upon a prior Russian ground absorption of Western Europe.[13] Since existing NATO strategy predicates use of nuclear weapons to prevent such an eventuality, it is scarcely conceivable that Britain would be faced with a traditional air–sea invasion. It is equally inconceivable that British strategic forces would themselves represent the difference between deterrence and defense.

From the Russian point of view a similar conclusion would be drawn. Acknowledging that the United States could not stand by while Europe was being occupied by ground forces, the Soviets would undoubtedly attack Europe and the United States in tandem if they opted for war. In the context of a major ground offensive, to spare the United States would merely be to hand the nuclear initiative to the Strategic Air Command. Since American forces would be involved as a consequence of Soviet actions, British "triggers" would be wholly redundant.

This is not to say that the British strategic force has no utility in the context of Western strategy. The cohesion of the Atlantic alliance is not a function of the *actual* credibility of an American nuclear response; it is rather a function of the *perceived* credibility of that response. The United States may actually be more willing to escalate a conventional conflict than Europeans believe. Since security for Western Europe under prevailing conditions depends upon a willingness to employ nuclear weapons, Europeans must be convinced that such a defense will in fact be used. Cohesion in this sense is determined by credence. A British trigger on the U.S. strategic force adds marginally, if at all, to the range of situations in which the deterrent would be called into action; it adds more significantly to the perception of alliance credibility. In

[13] E. J. de Kadt, *British Defence Policy and Nuclear War* (London, 1964), p. 50.

the net, British strategic weapons may contribute more to NATO political solidarity than they do to its actual quantum of security.

There are at least three other justifications for British thermonuclear weapons. First, it is theoretically conceivable that Britain might become engaged with a smaller power outside of Europe while the United States and the USSR stood aside. When, in 1963, it was first mooted that Britain could best provide a nuclear guarantee of Indian territorial integrity, such evolutions were foreshadowed. The United States would not be involved in the guarantee, as that might bring the USSR to the support of China. It was argued, however, that the Soviets would not back the Chinese if Britain was the sole Western guarantor. In other cases an ingenue nuclear state not linked to the Soviets or the United States might use a bomb in defiance of British positions or interests. The United Kingdom should be ready and able, it was held, to respond to such attacks. Such occurrences could not be ruled out, particularly if the spread of nuclear weapons induced both Russia and America to dissociate themselves from minor power conflicts.

Finally, Britain might need independent nuclear force if the alliance with America was interrupted or discontinued. The British were conscious of previous U.S. isolationism and disinclination to become involved in security commitments throughout the globe. At the time of Korea there was danger that the United States would be so drawn into Asian tempests that it would neglect its primary task in Europe. Where isolation and intervention were two sides of the same coin, there was always the possibility that the failure of the second would provoke the first. In one sense, at least, the British strategic force represented itself an admixture of alliance and autonomy. Not content to rely on the British deterrent alone, the United Kingdom had developed extensive nuclear and basing relationships with the United States. Not content to rely on the Anglo-American alliance alone, the British deterrent was a hedge against political failure. Britain's force was potent, but needful of U.S. nuclear support. It was that measure of "self-defense" which would bring "mutual aid."

Final judgments of the British nuclear deterrent await strategic reformulations that are only now in train. As a contribution to European defense, the British force could be even more important in the future than it has been in the past. As a contribution to equilibrium in a world of nuclear diffusion, it might undertake certain tasks neglected by the two superpowers. As a contribution to national defense, U.K. weapons might partially substitute for alliance guarantees. The difficulty is that each of these possible strategies rests on purely theoretical formulas. Forces are only as useful as the disposition to employ them. If British bombs will not be used to trigger a U.S. strike, if they will not be employed in third area conflicts, if they cannot be regarded as replacement for alliance, their direct military utility declines. British arguments concerning the dangers of the spread of nuclear weapons have helped to underscore these dilemmas. One cannot at the same time deplore the spread and praise the security devolving from nuclear capability. This operation was difficult enough for the United States where major capacities were already in hand. Britain, disposing a much smaller capability, could strengthen its position only by postulating a doctrine of early or unlimited use. But it was this doctrine that London found most unsettling when asserted by potential nuclear countries in other realms. In the end the case against the nuclear tyro became a case against the British deterrent: if *Nth* country forces had to be used vigorously or not at all, they should not be used at all. Other means of security were preferable, not only to world society, but to the nation itself. In this way the British depreciated the value of their own arms.

Future evolutions will move along one of three paths: toward nuclear renunciation, internationalization, or national retention. The third is most likely, but most difficult to justify. The first is least likely, but probably most defensible. The second is least explored, but holds possibilities for future development. Britain will probably remain a nuclear military power, but the integration of her forces with those of others may take forms at present largely unforeseen.

British nuclear strategy has evolved forms somewhat differently from that of other countries. Certain American writers have seen British military doctrine developing more rapidly than that of the United States, and notably more speedily than that of Soviet Russia.[14] This has been due, it is argued, to the clearer economic constraints in the British context: Britain could least afford to delay the impact of the nuclear revolution. While the United States talked of deterrence through balanced military capabilities and the Soviets of "constantly operating factors," the United Kingdom was already formulating the world's first doctrine of nuclear deterrence. If doctrine evolved most rapidly in Britain, however, the same writers claimed that technological realization of the new weapons has been gradual at best. Both the United States and the Soviet Union were able to develop nuclear weapons and delivery systems more rapidly, though

[14] See Samuel P. Huntington, *The Common Defense* (New York, 1961), p. 118.

they were slower to elaborate novel strategies for their employment.

These judgments appear to be only partly sustained by the British record on defense. If Britain was the first to stress nuclear deterrence, she also continued to emphasize it when other powers had turned to more limited strategies. In pursuit and further development of the deterrent, the decision to abandon conscription entailed continuing reliance on nuclear strength to the detriment of conventional capability. At a time when even the Soviets were becoming more enamoured of limited war, British forces and strategies stressed rapid escalation. While the Defence Review took full cognizance of the need for additional conventional forces if overseas commitments were to be maintained, it moved to cut those commitments.

In these circumstances it seemed as if Britain had been early to seize upon the advantages of a nuclear strategy, but late to recognize its disadvantages. Economic limitations failed to bring strategic reorientations. In fact, if in 1952 nuclear capabilities could be defended as an economical substitute for large ground forces, by 1957 conventional forces had to be trimmed to make the independent nuclear deterrent possible. In terms of costs and benefits, a nuclear strategy seemed a cheaper option for NATO than conventional strength in 1952. In the same terms conventional strength was a better solution to Britain's overseas problems ten years later.

If British doctrine was not continuously in advance of that of other great powers, its rate of technological development has not been uniformly behind. To be sure, British missile development was leisurely, and the Blue Streak would have been outmoded long before it had become operational. British nuclear weapon development, on the other hand, apparently kept pace with American designs, and in the naval field innovations in British carriers were sometimes in advance of those achieved abroad. British jet engines were not only a stimulus to improvement of an initially inferior American product, they laid the basis for the entire Russian effort. In their day, procurement of the Canberra, the Centurion tank, and the Hunter, represented significant advances in the state of the military art. The V-bomber designs were exceedingly impressive for their time (1947), but quantity production was long delayed. In general Britain was most able to keep abreast of military technological advances in the immediate postwar years. This suggests that American strategic analysts have erred in two respects: they have failed to discern a growing inflexibility in British doctrine since 1957, and they have omitted to credit Britain with some really outstanding technological successes in the period before 1954.

British strategy was important not only in comparison to that of the Soviet Union and the United States, but also because of its lessons for future nuclear countries. The United Kingdom was the third nation to develop an atomic bomb, but it was the first to decide to do so without a specific enemy in mind.[15] The British program, moreover, was carried to fruition in the context of an already powerful nuclear alliance with the United States. Aside from prestige and security against a series of unforeseen future contingencies, there was no compelling reason for a British bomb; yet, the program went inexorably forward. British doctrine, in addition, underwent several unique transformations. The British Global

[15] See Gowing, p. 323, and R. N. Rosecrance, "British Incentives to Become a Nuclear Power" in R. N. Rosecrance ed., *The Dispersion of Nuclear Weapons: Strategy and Politics* (New York, 1964), p. 58.

Strategy Paper of 1952, predicated on realization of the hydrogen bomb, contained the first enunciation of strategic nuclear deterrence, and it marked the first step away from American notions of "balanced" deterrence. The Soviets, the United States reasoned, would be deterred only if each possible move could be countered in its own terms. The vast ground buildup in NATO, 1951–53, was testimony to the latter theory. When the British talked of the efficacy of strategic bombing, they did not intend to substitute air strikes for ground warfare, but they did believe that divisional goals in Europe could be considerably reduced.

By 1957 the argument had been carried a step further. A major attack on the alliance in Europe would produce nuclear retaliation. Conventional forces had prewar and limited war roles, but they were unlikely to be of much use in general war. Eight years later, Britain contended that the conventional forces in West Germany should deal only with minor Russian thrusts, miscalculations, or accidental encounters. For attacks of greater magnitude, the alliance would rapidly escalate to all-out war. Even tactical nuclear war could not be waged for more than a straitly limited period without degenerating into strategic attack and retaliation. Strategically, British emphasis upon a thermonuclear doctrine had grown with time.

Concomitant with the development of a nuclear deterrent strategy for Britain, however, was a burgeoning uncertainty about British willingness to use weapons of mass destruction. In one sense this evolution was logical. Smaller British forces would "deter" only if doctrines of employment were both rigid and immediate. Britain would have to initiate use of nuclear weapons. But such notions presumed an almost inhuman *élan;* they demanded too much resolve. Indeed, the

United States and the Soviet Union had burked at anything approaching automaticity of nuclear employment. British doctrines seemed to imply a deliberate courtship of suicide. Hence, the very insistence upon doctrinal credibility may actually have helped to undermine its realistic counterpart. In the end, British nuclear strategy was appropriate for only the most improbable of contingencies, and these were not the ones envisioned in doctrinal pronouncements.

The lessons to be drawn for future nuclear countries were tentative, but at the very least, they seemed to involve caution in formulating rules of nuclear engagement. Countries do not lightly resolve their own annihilation, and strategies which cause them to do so are vain and inefficacious. Doctrines must accord with realistic interests. U.S. doctrines of "flexible or controlled response" probably understate the actual American commitment to Europe; British notions of immediate escalation may suggest the opposite. In a context in which great powers may be involved, *Nth* country forces may lose influence in the system. Their doctrines, perforce, claim too much.

Not only have British strategic doctrines raised ambiguities, the areas of doctrinal application have varied from case to case. At least three geographic foci have held British attention: the New World as the core of the Anglo-American alliance, continental Europe, and overseas realms of the Commonwealth and empire. In a measure these influences have individually competed for British resources and concern. In practice, however, the European emphasis has usually been regarded as alternative to the world and the United States. While the Anglo-American alliance and the Commonwealth might proceed hand-in-hand, neither of these was believed fully consistent with concentration upon Europe. That this should be so is not altogether surprising. The resources involved in a major European commitment were deemed so substantial, and the political and economic identification required so complete, that a choice of the European option seemed to impinge upon the solidity of other ties. The United States and the world, on the other hand, were not polar alternatives. Devotion to the Commonwealth and to far-flung interests did not weaken the link with the United States. The Commonwealth did not really impose limitations on British freedom of action, and though its defense requirements were heavy from time to time, these burdens might be adjusted or redistributed by British initiative and action. Nor did the Anglo-American link involve such magnitudes of expenditure that the British world role had to be sacrificed. The connection with America was at least partly sentimental; it did not depend upon fixed patterns of British resource allocation. Europe involved a British commitment; Britain involved an American commitment.

In the past generation, then, the major question for Britain has traditionally been how far to go into Europe. British interests in Europe have been central enough to rule out mere reliance on the Commonwealth and the United States. After World War II, notions of tentative or temporary connections with European states were abandoned, as were ideas that the formulation of alliance combinations could await a crisis. British security could no longer depend upon *ad hoc* links with the continent. A hostile power might dominate Europe unless Britain were committed and in peacetime. Such deductions, however, left unclear the requisite degree of British involvement. Ideally, London might have the best of both worlds: a relationship with Europe which in no way restricted her freedom of action in North America or overseas. In 1948 there seemed little conflict between arenas of British interest. By 1952, with the inauguration of the Schuman Plan and the proposal for a European army, Britain was forced to a decision, and she chose "association" instead of "participation." Integration with the continent would impinge upon her military links with the United States and her economic links with the Commonwealth.

This choice, reflected in other British policies until Prime Minister Macmillan decided to join the Common Market in 1961, rested on two assumptions: 1) that sufficient European cohesion to deter aggression would be possible without British participation in schemes of integration; and 2) that Europe would not, in any event, move toward full economic and political integration. The first meant that Europe would not become too weak; the second that Europe would not become too powerful. A weak Europe would need British support, regardless of its form, and the weaker Europe was, the more necessary would be a comprehensive integration to restore its strength. A strong Europe would not need Britain, but it would be able to displace the United Kingdom as the primary partner of the United States. Again, Britain could not afford to abstain.

As time proceeded, both of these assumptions were successively challenged. In 1954 the failure of the European Defense Community necessitated a much stronger pledge of British forces to aid in continental defense. The Paris Agreements of 1954–55 involved British commitment of four divisions and a tactical air force to the continent for the indefinite future. Aside from two specified contingencies, the troops were to remain there at the pleasure of a majority of the members of the reformulated Brussels pact.[16] The pledge reassured France and made possible West Germany's entry into NATO. British material support helped to rebuild European solidarity.

Later, after 1957, an opposite condition briefly emerged. The Treaty of Rome held the prospect of a six continental-state integrated community. Britain first countered with a free-trade zone plan, which, had it been accepted, would have diluted continental unity and allowed Britain to participate on equal terms. When that overture was rebuffed, she formed a free trade area among seven other trading partners, hoping to force the Six to compromise. It was not until 1961 when all other tactics had failed, and when it seemed that the Common Market had an irreversible forward momentum, that she applied for full membership in the group. The very success of the European "pillar" was anticipated to lead to European supplanting of Britain in American estimations. If Britain did not join, she would lose her influence in Washington.

Today the situation is quite different. While some of the major economic crises within the Community of the Six have been resolved, political divergence is more characteristic than ever. De Gaulle's veto on British membership has apparently become conditional. Because of divisions among the Six, British adhesion is less necessary than before. There is less likelihood that a cohesive political-economic bloc will emerge. Because of the loosening of political bonds among the Six, however, British membership would pose fewer quandaries for Whitehall. In one sense, at least, there is now an opening for British leadership on the continent that has not existed since 1955.

[16] See Royal Institute of International Affairs, *Britain in Western Europe* (London, 1956), pp. 62–63.

In terms of defense, a concentration upon Europe is more logical than it has been in some years. It was possible to talk of British responsibilities overseas as a major alternative to Europe as long as those burdens were not excessively onerous. If Commonwealth tasks could be discharged without great effort while a "European" policy demanded additional exertions, a "world role" was most efficacious for Britain. If, on the other hand, overseas responsibilities absorbed a large proportion of British military resources without adding appreciably to the security of the United Kingdom, Europe was a more attractive focus. In recent years, overseas defense burdens have grown, while those in Europe have declined or remained the same. Erstwhile imperial tasks have been more than theoretical formulas, and while they have continued, the British Army of the Rhine has become a strategic reserve for extra-European conflicts. In the net, the costs and gains have augured for a strategy more narrowly focused in Europe. It was no longer true that military investment in Europe was more taxing than commitment elsewhere.

Other assumptions about British alternatives have had to be modified. The older notions were that a choice would have to be made between the United States and Europe. Submersion in a politically integrated Europe would put an end to the "special relationship" with the United States. Today the choice seems between Europe and overseas interests, with the U.S. tie a presumptive feature of either course. The relative costs of a European initiative, both political and military, have greatly declined. At the same time the grounds of British policy have shifted since the mid-1950s. In those years it was assumed that British freedom of action and an "independent role" would maximize British influence in world politics. If the continent did not unite, Britain would remain the fulcrum for the application of American power in Europe. The really fundamental decisions, lacking Western European integration, would be taken by the Anglo-American partnership. A major British commitment to Europe, then, would serve to diminish London's political capital. Britain should be the "balancer" between halves of the Atlantic alliance.

Merely to state such notions is to observe how rapidly events have outpaced theory. British "independence" is no longer British "strength." Partially because of its intermittent isolation from continental affairs, Britain has been taken less seriously by the United States than it might otherwise have been. Under Secretary Dulles, the fulcrum for U.S. foreign policy became Bonn not London. And although President Kennedy was a warm supporter of the Anglo–American alliance, there is little evidence that British views were decisive for the course of U.S. policy in Europe.[17] Britain-in-Europe would today command greater attention in Washington than Britain-in-the-world. For all of these reasons the absence of major disadvantages to a European role are matched by major advantages flowing from it. Because of intervening changes in American policy, the best way to choose the United States at the moment is to choose Europe.

A major imponderable of future British defense policy is the constraining influence if permissible expenditure. In 1953, 11.3 percent of the Gross National Product was devoted to defense; in 1965 the figure was 7.1 percent. By 1970 it is hoped, the burden will be less than 6 percent. If this planned reduction occurs, British abilities to meet major crises in Europe and overseas will be greatly reduced. Defense officials have recognized henceforth that Britain could "not undertake

[17] The Nassau Accord remains the one signal exception to this rule.

major operations of war except in cooperation with allies."
Defense estimates for 1966–67 totalled only £2,172 million, a
decrease in real expenditure from the year before.[18] Savings,
however, accrued partly through the postponement of reequipment outlays. By 1970 these would occupy a much
larger fraction of the military budget, potentially threatening
the £2,000 million ceiling (in 1964–65 prices). In the next
year or so, then, new savings in manpower costs must be
found. If the army and navy are to be pared in size, however,
the commitments which they sustain must also be reduced.
For planning purposes, it was assumed that Indonesian "confrontation" of Malaysia and Singapore would be ended by
1970, and that no new massive overseas commitments would
emerge to be handled by Britain alone in the years to come.
Reliance upon the United States would perforce accompany
any British overseas role.

The reason for such rigid defense targets is provided by the
laggard domestic economy. Balance of payments crises have
been chronic in recent years, and the growth rate has not yet
attained the desired 4 percent. Price and wage increases have
rapidly absorbed gains in productivity. The result has been a
domestic inflation, imperiling the value of the pound sterling.
If resources released from defense could be turned effectively
to the export trade, both inflation and the trade gap could be
checked. Short of such limitations on government spending,
the British economy seems destined to continue to reel from
heavy blows in the international money market.

The change in financial fortunes is in part testimony to
shifts in consuming patterns of the British public. In the late
1940s and early 1950s the electorate seemed content to bear
the burdens of empire and of spiraling defense costs. Ration-

[18] Expenditure in money terms, 1965–66, was £2,120 million.

ing, shortages of consumer durables, and inadequate leisure were characteristic of this period; essentially wartime sacrifices were prolonged into the postwar period. Korea brought forth a magnificent governmental and public response, and consumption was once again postponed. At some point, however, the British public sought a greater share of the products of a consumer economy; domestic demand began to compete with international demand for the production of British goods. To some manufacturers, the home market became a more predictable outlet for British products than foreign buyers, and exports suffered. Governmental expenditure on defense also appropriated resources that might be used by the export industries. Since it seemed impossible once again to deny the British worker the fruits of his labors, government spending had to be cut. Today there seems no prospect of devoting 10 percent of the Gross National Product to defense; the sacrifice involved would be politically unacceptable. However, much one hears of the "spirit of Dunkirk," it is unlikely to be revived.

There are important ensuing differences between American, Australian, and British industrial experience in recent years. The United States was least dependent upon foreign trade and possessed substantial unused capacity. In a military crisis, it might merely bring new resources into production, and it might do so, in general, without a grave worsening of its balance of payments. Domestic growth rates permitted growing military spending. Australia was more dependent upon international markets and had less unused capacity. Since World War II, on the other hand, it has concentrated upon domestic growth under the impetus of large-scale immigration. It may now use its substantial present and prospective productivity increases to finance rearmament. Its major export staples—primary produce—have not suffered greatly from a diversion of resources in the direction of defense. In the British case, in contrast to the others, domestic growth has had only recent priority. Britain's great power role and the need to repair a shattered industry prevented an early emphasis on productivity in the immediate postwar years. Korean rearmament further delayed such concerns, and when the military crisis eased, domestic consumption promptly took up the slack. Sheer production, for export and home consumption, delayed necessary capital expansion. Military spending, moreover, continued to draw crucial resources from the export trades. Up to the present, expansion in the British economy has been an expansion of production for consumption and an expansion of armaments; it has too infrequently been an expansion of industry for export and home consumption. Today, then, while Australia and the United States can use their growth for military purposes, the United Kingdom must use its military plant for purposes of economic growth. Each country focuses now upon what it has previously neglected.

The paradox emerges that those nations which have constricted military spending in the past, nations like West Germany, Japan, Italy, Australia, and to some degree, France, may in the near future cut a larger military figure than Britain, a power with great military savoir faire and historic achievement. Since economic strength is more than ever regarded as precedent to military strength, however, British retrenchment and economic growth may yet reveal semblances of grandeur. In the next five years, the use of British military resources will be far more important than their quantity. A dismantling of extra-European responsibilities and a new exercise of leadership in Europe may yet produce a greater security and influence with fewer resources. Even if it does not, the example of President de Gaulle proves that major power influence is not to be measured by military strength alone. In both diplomatic and military fields, Britain is now in a position to make contributions to Europe, the like of which have not been seen for more than a decade.

CHAPTER TWO

DEMOBILIZATION, DISENGAGEMENT, AND OPTIONS FOR THE FUTURE, 1946–1947

THE IMMEDIATE POSTWAR environment demanded change in British policy, but it did not clearly indicate the direction in which to proceed. Because exports were essential, the defense bill had to be cut. These determinants, however, did not in themselves decide the shape of future policy. Cuts in governmental expenditure and the pursuit of domestic deflation might have been much more thoroughgoing than in fact they were. Hugh Dalton, the first postwar Chancellor of the Exchequer, was more worried about a major recession after a transition period than he was about inflation in the interim.[1]

Thus it did not seem imperative to hold governmental and consumer spending to an absolute minimum while the export industries caught hold. It was presumed that exports would reestablish themselves eventually, particularly since the long-run threat seemed deflationary. The real problem became that of getting over the transition period. If the Japanese war had

[1] See J. C. R. Dow, *The Management of the British Economy, 1945–60* (Cambridge, 1965), p. 19.

continued for a year or two after the defeat of Germany, exports might have been brought up during the conflict itself. As it was, the end of the war and the sudden termination of lend-lease (which had in fact substituted for export earnings), necessitated another means of financing the period of readjustment. The American loan of $3,750 million was the alternative. Had Dalton been right, by 1947-49 the major problems of transition would have been overcome, and Britain would have had domestic full employment and a tolerable balance of payments equilibrium.[2] That he was wrong, however, was as much a tribute to the impingement of international economic forces on the British financial structure as to the chancellor's ineptitude.

In the circumstances British governmental expenditure was larger than it might otherwise have been. Labour's socialist and welfare measures had to be funded, and the defense estimates for 1946-47 allocated £1,667 millions to British responsibilities throughout the world. At the end of the war troops were maintained in Germany, Austria, Greece, Japan, the Far East, Southeast Asia, Palestine, the Near East, and Venezia Gulia.[3] As a percentage of population, Britain had almost twice as many men under arms in 1946 as the United States.[4] British commitments, moreover, were taken as basic reference points, not to be jettisoned until the United Nations was in a position to provide a greater security.[5] Immediately after the war then, economics and finance seemed to permit a

[2] *Ibid.*, pp. 13-20.
[3] Cmnd. 6743, *Statement Relating to Defence* (February, 1946).
[4] R. N. Rosecrance, "British Defense Strategy: 1945-1952," in R. N. Rosecrance, ed., *The Dispersion of Nuclear Weapons: Strategy and Politics* (New York, 1964), p. 69.
[5] See C. R. Attlee, *House of Commons Debates*, Vol. 434 (March 4, 1946), col. 46.

much more leisurely demobilization than took place in the American case; concrete defense responsibilities could themselves determine allocations. Yet actual threats to British security were minimal, almost nonexistent; future enemies were not then or only barely in sight. After 1947–48 when dangers loomed, the economy did not permit substantial expenditure on defense.[6] Such relationships suggest that international patterns of threat are not necessarily decisive for defense policy; in certain circumstances they may even be marginal to eventual determinations. Economic factors help to decide the shape of future threats.

There was absolutely no question at the end of the war that Britain would go ahead with the atomic bomb. During the war scientific advisers had recommended not only an experimental establishment, but also a plutonium facility of 100,000 kilowatts. The government approved the former shortly after Mr. Attlee became Prime Minister; a decision on the latter was put off until September, 1945, when it would be less likely to prejudice the joint Anglo-Canadian project at Montreal. A delay would also avoid American objections to British resumption of work on a large-scale atomic plant before the end of the war. As early as April of 1945, moreover, the British had agreed on basic designs for a low-separation gaseous diffusion plant for the production of moderately enriched U-235.[7]

After the war, decisions were quickly taken to develop nuclear research and production facilities. On October 29, 1945, Attlee revealed to Parliament the creation of a research

[6] This observation holds true at least until July, 1950.

[7] Margaret Gowing, *Britain and Atomic Energy, 1939–1945* (London, 1964), pp. 334–36.

and experimental establishment "covering all aspects of the use of atomic energy," [8] and in February, 1946, a nuclear production unit was set in motion. "The remit given to the new organization was the production of plutonium for military purposes." [9] From that point on there could be no doubt that Britain would be a nuclear power, though the pace at which she would develop weapons was uncertain. The decision to build production reactors at Windscale was made in March, 1946, and the initial steps in creating the low separation diffusion plant at Capenhurst followed in October. Before mid-1946 the Royal Air Force was planning on the basis of British nuclear weapons. To complete the plutonium process, work on the chemical separation plant at Windscale was begun at the end of 1947, and the plutonium fabrication plant was completed at Aldermaston between April, 1950, and March, 1951. The production pile at Windscale went "critical" in July, 1950, and by early 1952 military quantities of plutonium were beginning to be produced. Britain's first atomic test (involving a Pu-239 bomb) was held on October 3, 1952, in the Monte Bello islands off Australia. It was a signal success.

The final achievement of military fission should not obscure the process by which it was attained. In 1946 and 1947 there was little urgency to the nuclear program. Until the McMahon Act of August 1, 1946, it was possible though not likely that Britain might derive considerable assistance and information from the United States, thereby speeding her own production effort. The absence of a specific foe, also

[8] *House of Commons Debates*, Vol. 415 (October 29, 1945), col. 38.
[9] Sir Leonard Owen, "Nuclear Engineering in the United Kingdom —the First Ten Years," *Journal of the British Nuclear Energy Society*, Vol. 2, No. 1 (January, 1963), p. 23.

made rapid nuclear preparations less imperative. It was not until some time in 1947 that Prime Minister Attlee decided to give the program formal "priority."[10] Even then the time between the achievement of a "chain reaction" in the first experimental reactor and the explosion of a plutonium bomb was almost twice as great as in the American case.[11] To be sure, British atomic scientists were scarce, and the bomb project had to compete with the export trades for engineers and technologists.[12] Unlike the United States at the beginning of its atomic work, however, the British already possessed the essential secrets. British scientists knew a great deal about the Oak Ridge diffusion plant, and they were familiar with the Clinton, Tennessee, reactor. In fact, the Windscale production pile was simply a scaled-up version of its U.S. counterpart. They had not been permitted at Hanford, on the other hand, and therefore had less knowledge of the really massive U.S. reactors. It nevertheless seems likely that Britain could have developed the bomb more quickly than she did. The Chiefs of Staff pressed particularly for more rapid authorization and greater finance for the British gaseous diffusion plant, and even Windscale attained its scheduled production only weeks before the Monte Bello explosion.

That Britain did not proceed more rapidly with the bomb in the first postwar years is probably partial testimony to her particular motivations in acquiring it. Though the U.K. program was doubtlessly accelerated in 1949-50 as potential foes materialized, the original decisions were unrelated to any

[10] Alfred Goldberg, "The Atomic Origins of the British Nuclear Deterrent," *International Affairs*, Vol. 40, No. 3 (April, 1964), p. 420.

[11] See Rosecrance, pp. 62-63.

[12] See Sir Christopher Hinton, "British Developments in Nuclear Energy," *Nucleonics*, Vol. 12, No. 1 (January, 1954), p. 6.

specific foreign enemy. The bomb was wanted, not to defeat an opponent, but for a series of unspecified future contingencies. Britain, after all, was one of the three major victors of World War II. Not only the United States and Russia, but also smaller states, were at work on the bomb. If the United Kingdom had abjured development, she would in effect have abdicated her position of power in world politics. Equally, if not more important, as Prime Minister Attlee put it: "We had to hold up our position *vis à vis* the Americans. We couldn't allow ourselves to be wholly in their hands, and their position wasn't awfully clear always. . . . We had to look to our defence—and to our industrial future. We could not agree that only America should have atomic energy." [13]

During the war Britain had several times considered resuming her own nuclear effort but had hesitated for fear of harming the joint project in the United States. After the war, she would not be denied.[14] The scientific and military momentum behind the British nuclear investment was formidable. With one possible exception, there is no record of opposition to the British bomb among her military and scientific community in the immediate postwar period. As in the United States and France, the scientists were a major force behind the decision to proceed. Finally, there was a distinct fear of U.S. isolationism. No alliance existed between Britain and America. In two world wars Britain had had to stand alone for a prolonged—and nearly decisive—period; there was no assurance that the United States would enter a future 'fray early enough to protect basic British interests.[15] Speaking of

[13] Quoted in Francis Williams, *A Prime Minister Remembers* (London, 1961), pp. 118–19.

[14] Attlee to Truman, quoted in Williams, pp. 114–15.

[15] See Rosecrance, p. 57.

the United States, Attlee later declared: "We had to bear in mind that there was always the possibility of their withdrawing and becoming isolationist once again. The manufacture of a British atom bomb was therefore at that stage essential to our defence. . . . Although we were doing our best to make the Americans understand the realities of the European situation—the world situation—we couldn't be sure we'd succeed. In the end we did. But we couldn't take risks with British security in the meantime." [16]

If such factors augured positively for a British bomb, there were no offsetting disadvantages. Not only would potent weapons of war be derived, peaceful electric power programs would benefit. Nuclear energy might bolster Britain's dwindling coal reserves, and as Attlee pointed out: "The successful manufacture of bombs from plutonium shows that the harnessing of atomic energy as a source of power cannot be achieved without the simultaneous production of material capable of being used in a bomb. This means that the possible industrial uses of atomic energy cannot be considered separately from its military and security implications." [17]

Nuclear weapons, in addition, posed no technical or strategic difficulties. At the time there seemed no particular delivery problem linked with the nuclear bomb. The Hiroshima and Nagasaki bombs weighed 9,000 and 10,000 pounds respectively. Heavy bombers were quite capable of carrying such a load, even over substantial distances. More important, the existence of such destructive power in a single bomb load justified risking quite heavy losses in bomber strength. It was natural to assume that the bomb would reach its target. In

[16] Quoted in Williams, p. 119.
[17] *House of Commons Debates*, Vol. 415 (October 30, 1945), col. 346.

those days very complex delivery capacity was not necessary to ensure success. Guided or ballistic missiles were not required to penetrate the enemy's defenses. Hence it was not necessary to presume that the atomic bomb would involve an immense additional expense in warning, delivery, and defense systems. The bomb could be fitted to existing technology; it could, therefore, appear less expensive.

Third, and partly because of the absence of delivery problems, the bomb would not create new vulnerabilities for the nuclear state. There was no danger that an opponent would be tempted to attack British nuclear installations, hoping thereby to prevent retaliation. Thus, the possession of atomic bombs did not make for a period of enhanced vulnerability before a reliable retaliatory force could be developed. Even more significant, there was no enemy nation whose nuclear force, by virtue of British capability, would now be targeted on British forces and industrial installations. The net gain from nuclear weapons was equivalent to the gross gain. They did not make the United Kingdom more vulnerable in the short run; they made her more formidable over all.

Finally, British weapons were not redundant. There was no American nuclear umbrella at the time. While there could be no question of a real or vital divergence between Britain and the United States, it was also not certain that the United States would use its nuclear weapons for the defense of the United Kingdom. In fact, as we know, the United States had no more fabricated bombs in existence, though it was in process of building them. A British nuclear capability, in the circumstances, would not merely replicate American power; it would be a net increment in Western strength.

In short, the decision for weapons was not taken against a backdrop of attendant liabilities. In 1945–46, the achievement of a nuclear weapons capability seemed to mean a status parallel with that of the United States. Bombs did not simply duplicate American power; they conferred a special international status on their possessor. Nuclear weapons were the same thing as nuclear capacity. At the same time the bomb was not developed with the stimulus of a specific foe. It was not the intransigence of the Soviet Union which caused British efforts; it was the need for such weapons in general, against a series of future contingencies. Britain was the first nation to develop the weapon as a long-range strategic asset, unrelated to dangers posed by the overt hostility of a specific opponent.

British experience was distinct from that of other nuclear countries. First, since the future of Anglo-American relations was decidedly unclear at the time, the British decision for bombs was taken in a nonaligned environment. Alliances might not emerge to assist British security. Second, Britain was one of three great world powers; both of the others were working to capacity or had already developed the nuclear weapon. A British demurral on the bomb would have been equivalent to contracting out of Great Power status. Further, the bomb had few if any defects; it was relatively inexpensive; it was deliverable; it contributed to electric power programs. Since it was not assumed that the Soviet Union and the United States had an irrevocable lead in nuclear matters, atomic potency was a means of retaining British strategic equivalence. As one Briton later pointed out, nuclear weapons could be a "great leveler." While there was fear that atomic bombs might one day be acquired by other states, a British decision to build them was not a straightfoward contribution to the spread of nuclear weapons. Britain already knew the secrets and understood the technology; she was merely acting on the information she possessed. Her acquisition would have no important impact on the decisions of others. Finally, the nuclear club was more select than at any subsequent time. The prestige deriving from membership was unquestioned; the feat entailed in joining unchallenged. To decide in 1945–46 to make bombs required enormous scientific power, and no little political prowess and presumption. Such decisions were reserved to the major actors of the international stage. The merits of nuclear status were unequivocal; the disadvantages almost nonexistent. It was not surprising that Britain opted for bombs; it would have been remarkable if she had not done so.

Aside from the nuclear weapons program, the most important decision affecting defense which the British government had to make after the war was the choice of a major alliance partner. It was unthinkable to any British regime that the United Kingdom should resist splendidly and alone. As Sir Ian Jacob put it later: "The idea of the United Kingdom fighting a war except as a partner in a coalition has always been contrary to the whole of her policy." [18]

It remained, however, to choose among several possible allies and arenas of interest. Broadly speaking these were Commonwealth, European, and Atlantic. The least promising option was provided by the Commonwealth and dependent empire. Imperial federation, even if it could be achieved, would not be a solution to Britain's defense problems. Europe was also an undesirable major focus: European states, though crucial to British defense, were ready to submerge the auto-

[18] "The United Kingdom's Strategic Interests" in Royal Institute of International Affairs, *United Kingdom Policy: Foreign, Strategic, Economic* (London, 1950), p. 55.

nomy of the nation-state in a new economic and political amalgam. If Britain participated fully, she would have to sever or radically reform her links with the Commonwealth, and her own national policy determinations would be affected. The American option, on the other hand, did not attenuate the Commonwealth bond, dilute British sovereignty, or offer a negligible military support. As one student has put it: "No Foreign Secretary in the period ever lost sight of the fact that the defence of Europe, and hence of Britain, was inconceivable without American participation, and that it must be a fundamental objective of British policy to see that this was always forthcoming." [19] The American option was ultimately chosen, in part, because it offered imperatively needed military support and did not rule out other connections and interests.

This being so, it did not follow that the path of Anglo-American relations would always be smooth or that fundamental agreements would be concluded immediately. At the end of the war, particularly, differences over economics, Palestine, and the atom supervened. The abrupt halt to lend-lease in August, 1945, meant that Britain had to find some other means of financing her exports in the next few years. An American loan was the only solution to the problem, but the negotiations with the United States were niggling and drawn-out. "As the talks went on," Hugh Dalton revealed, the United Kingdom "retreated slowly and with bad grace and with increasing irritation from a free gift to an interest-free loan, and from this again to a loan bearing interest; from a larger to a smaller total of aid; and from the prospect of loose strings, some of which would be only general declara-

[19] See Max Beloff, *New Dimensions in Foreign Policy* (New York, 1961), pp. 16–17.

tions of intention, to the most unwilling acceptance of strings so tight that they might strangle our trade and, indeed, our whole economic life." [20] The most constraining of these was the agreement to restore convertibility within one year of the coming into force of the loan accord. And even after these unsatisfactory terms had been accepted in December, the U.S. Congress stalled and then nearly failed to ratify the accord in July, 1946. As the British had predicted at the beginning, the attempt to restore convertibility in the summer of 1947 had to be abandoned with humiliating international consequences and an accompanying domestic economic crisis. The cordiality of Anglo-American economic relations was far from unwavering.

The Palestine muddle was an equal exacerbation. After the Potsdam Conference, President Truman wished to let more Jews into Palestine, and an Anglo-American Committee of Inquiry was appointed to survey the situation and make recommendations in November, 1945. These were both diffuse and vague, and another binational committee was constituted to review the matter. A new plan emerged, providing for provincial autonomy under a strong central regime possessing powers to regulate immigration. After prior acceptance of the scheme by both Jews and Arabs, 100,000 Jewish immigrants were to be allowed into Palestine. The issue simmered through the summer of 1946, without agreement, then on October 4 Truman publicly supported the creation of a new Jewish state with control of immigration and urged the immediate admission of 100,000 Jewish migrants, thus repudiating the plan of his own negotiators. Bevin flew into a rage when he heard about the President's intentions, and

[20] Hugh Dalton, *High Tide and After: Memoirs, 1945-1960* (London, 1962), pp. 74-75.

"begged" the State Department to forbid publication of Truman's proposed statement. When this request was denied, negotiations broke down. Failing British-American agreement, London turned the issue over to the United Nations.[21]

The most vexed issue of all, however, was the question of the atom. Britain had hoped that her relations with the United States on this question would be governed after the war by the Hyde Park Agreement, signed by Prime Minister Churchill and President Roosevelt on September 19, 1944. It provided, *inter alia,* that: "Full collaboration between the United States and the British Government in developing tube alloys [the wartime code-name for the atomic project] for military and commercial purposes should continue after the defeat of Japan unless and until terminated by joint agreement."[22] In the autumn of 1945 such sentiments were revived in an accord signed by Truman, Attlee, and Mackenzie King equally stipulating full and effective cooperation in atomic energy between their three countries. Neither of these promises was ever fulfilled. In the United States a coalition of atomic "monopolists" and "international controllers" emerged to prevent further sharing of atomic results with Britain. The one group wished to keep the bomb for America, the other to share with all, but only under conditions of full international control.[23] Actually, it seems that progress was being made on the atomic Combined Policy Committee in drawing up a list of topics on which information would be exchanged when it was pointed

[21] See the account in C. R. Rose, "The Relation of Socialist Principles to British Labour Foreign Policy, 1945–1951," pp. 133–45. Unpublished dissertation, Nuffield College (Michaelmas Term), 1959.

[22] Text in Gowing, p. 477.

[23] See Raymond Dawson and Richard Rosecrance, "Theory and Reality in the Anglo-American Alliance," *World Politics* (October, 1966), p. 24.

out to Secretary of State James Byrnes that the arrangement possibly conflicted with Article 102 of the United Nations Charter. From that point on, no cooperation on atomic matters was forthcoming from Washington. Attlee decided to test American intentions by formally requesting that bombs be made available to Britain or, at minimum that full information on nuclear production be given. He pointed out to the American ambassador that, if the McMahon Bill (which would foreclose all atomic cooperation with other powers) became law in the United States, Britain would have to develop her own civil and military atomic programs.[24] But Truman remained adamant during a fruitless correspondence with the British Prime Minister, April–June, 1946. When the McMahon Bill received congressional approval, it was signed by the President on August 1.[25] The final collapse of the sharing arrangement gave ground for the charge of an American "breach of faith" with wartime agreements.[26]

Anglo-American conflicts on atomic exchange, however, did not characterize all British-American relations in this period, nor were they even summary of all contacts on the atomic issue. Even in the period of greatest discord, certain agreements were worked out. Before the impasse on exchange had been reached, British and American negotiators had tentatively concurred on a draft which would have removed the Paragraph 4 restriction on postwar British commercial exploitation of the atom specified in the Quebec Agreement of August, 1943.[27] Though this draft was abortive, the Brit-

[24] The last was somewhat disingenuous as the basic decision to proceed in both fields had already been made in the United Kingdom.

[25] See the account in Goldberg, pp. 413–14.

[26] Attlee's attitudes are well revealed in Williams, pp. 117–18.

[27] Paragraph 4 contained the following clause: "the British Government recognise that any post-war advantages of an industrial or com-

ish did reach firm accord with the United States on an approximately equal division of uranium ore in May, 1946. The new arrangement was of considerable importance both to Britain and the United States. On the one hand it reflected British generosity in that London had tied up Congo ore supplies during the war and, in the absence of American and Canadian production, effectively controlled the world sources of uranium. On the other, it showed U.S. willingness to accept a more equitable division with Britain, in that wartime agreements had allotted all ore obtained by Britain, Canada, and the United States to the American Manhattan Project. The major sacrifices, however, were clearly made by Britain; she arranged for American access to ore needed for the U.S. nuclear program, but she failed in return to exact an information exchange to benefit the British program. In one sense, at least, the Americans got the best of both possible worlds; the McMahon Act had presumably ruled out nuclear bilateralism, but while the United States insisted on unilateralism with regard to information, development, and manufacture, she benefited from bilateralism in terms of uranium ore supplies. If the British had decided to go slow on the latter, they might have forced a reconsideration of the former. Attlee pointedly reminded Truman of this when he observed: "We have not thought it necessary to abandon [our joint control of raw materials]—in my opinion, quite rightly. Why then should we abandon all further pooling of information?" [28]

There were also other areas of cooperation. Though the

---

mercial character shall be dealt with as between the United States and Great Britain on terms to be specified by the President of the United States to the Prime Minister of Great Britain." Text of the Quebec Agreement in Gowing, pp. 439–40.

[28] Quoted in Williams, pp. 116–17.

personal ties of Attlee and Truman could hardly be so close as those of Churchill and Roosevelt, the two men gradually developed a working relationship. Truman was conscious that Britain would be America's chief ally if another war came. At the time of the crisis caused by the Soviet failure to evacuate troops from Iran in March, 1946, Averell Harriman was appointed American Ambassador to the Court of St. James. The President apparently reasoned that it would be crucial to have one of his most trusted emissaries in London to develop the closest possible accord with the British government if it should come to war with the Soviet Union over Iran. And while formal military relationships between Britain and the United States did not exist, there were a number of specialized service links. At the end of 1946 it was announced that the U.S. Army Air Force and the R.A.F. had agreed to continue their wartime collaboration in staff methods, tactics, equipment, and research. On January 1, 1947, this cooperation was extended to officer exchanges for training purposes. In the same month, high-ranking U.S. Air Force officers visited their R.A.F. counterparts, and in June there were demonstration flights over Britain by nine B-29s. An information exchange between army staffs was also arranged early in 1947. By the end of that year, the British-American Combined Chiefs of Staff, left dormant at the end of the war, was approaching its former effectiveness.[29] Perhaps the most far-reaching measure of military cooperation was proposed by Field Marshal Montgomery as early as September, 1946. On a mission to the United States and Canada to discuss military standardization, Montgomery seems to have broached the idea of a much wider cooperation embracing the whole field of combined

[29] Joseph Alsop in the New York *Herald Tribune*, December 12, 1947.

action in the event of war.[30] Within the American military, his reception was warm and cordial, but his initiative was in advance of political possibilities as seen in both London and Washington. It was not until the first half of 1948 that American policy-makers were able to think in terms of a formal alliance uniting both countries.

The deductions to be drawn from the somewhat checkered career of Anglo-American relations in the first two years after the war are far from straightforward. Informally both countries thought in terms of an operative Anglo-American accord in any future military crisis. Neither conceived of fighting a major conflict without the assistance of the other. In this sense the revelation of mutual friendship preceded the revelation of hostility toward an outside state. But the consciousness of fundamental unity and potential or prospective alliance did not entail direct overtures for a specific military relationship in the immediate aftermath of the war. It was not until December, 1947, that the United Kingdom began to think of a military alliance with the United States, and even then U.S. policy-makers held back.

More important in this early period was the profusion of informal contacts and informal working arrangements. As early as July, 1946, U.S. Secretary of the Navy James Forrestal learned that individual British political and military officials wanted very close ties and informal diplomatic and military cooperation with the United States.[31] Navies, armies, and air forces consulted each other; foreign offices compared notes. In the words of one American officer at the end of

[30] Viscount Montgomery of Alamein, *Memoirs* (London, 1958), pp. 438–40.
[31] Walter Millis, ed., *The Forrestal Diaries* (New York, 1951), p. 183–85.

1947, a considerable amount of "healthy hanky-panky" was going on through a variety of Anglo-American channels. Alliance was not yet thought of, but the infrastructure on which it would rest was already being built.

Great Britain is one of the few powers of the modern age which has developed viable defense plans against unspecified antagonists. Her insular situation has permitted planning not against individual foes, but against functional threats: to maritime supremacy, to the Mediterranean-Middle East, to British home security.[32] Shortly after Field Marshal Montgomery had been appointed Chief of the Imperial General Staff in mid-1946 he prepared a paper summarizing British defense objectives which observed:

(*a*) We must plan to build up the strength of our potential allies in Europe and establish a strong western bloc, so as to protect the peoples, territories, and civilisation of the western world against any invason from the east. We ourselves must be prepared to fight on the mainland of Europe, alongside our Allies, with all that that entailed.

(*b*) We must ensure our freedom to use the major oceans and seas. In particular, we must fight for the North African coast line and thus enable our communications through the Mediterranean to be kept open.

(*c*) We must fight for the Middle East, which, with the United Kingdom and North Africa, would provide the bases for the launching of a tremendous air offensive against the territory of any aggressor from the east. The Army must maintain a Corps H.Q. in the Middle East, available to go off anywhere to handle an emergency.[33]

His Air and Naval colleagues concurred in the second two points but refused to accept the first.[34] The core of agreed

[32] *Ibid.*, p. 423.   [33] Montgomery, p. 435.   [34] *Ibid.*, p. 436.

doctrine then consisted of secure sealanes, the Middle East bastion, in addition to an understood defense of the home islands. British sea power would prevent challenges to Britain's insular position; it would also keep open the lines of trade and communication with the far-flung Commonwealth and empire. The Middle East was crucial, not only because it bestrode the route to India and the antipodes, but also because it controlled the European flank. Predominance in the Middle East and North Africa would permit, as it had done in World War II, British and allied counterthrusts to "roll-up" southern Europe and menace or defeat an invasion launched from the East.

One of the advantages of this strategy was its functional character. Planners did not have to decide who a potential enemy might be, or to indicate the specific direction in which an attack would be likely to occur. If the three "pillars" of British strategy were adequately provided for, additional precautions were unnecessary. One could afford a more "theoretical" attitude concerning possible antagonists and modes of warfare. In the nineteenth century, such precepts had largely sufficed, and they had been entertained shortly before the outbreak of World War I. Immediately after World War II, and before concrete opponents appeared on the horizon, they could also have a measure of application. The problem, however, was that "functional" notions were basically precautionary. They gave Britain enough time to prepare specific defenses against specific foes; one had little enough to do until a pillar shifted under its burden. At that point, however, it had to be bolstered. Forces had to be contingently allocated to campaigns in a given geographic area, enemies disposing specific capabilities had to be countered, and weapons of war had to be devised and held ready for employment. Functionalism had to yield to particularity.

In 1946 there seemed little need to plan against specific enemies. It did not seem that Russia would be ready to wage a contest in Europe for many years to come.[35] The only power capable of challenging the foundations of British security was the United States. The U.S. fleet was large enough to threaten British positions in the Middle East, the Mediterranean, and in the Channel itself, but no British military man conceived of the United States as a potential foe.[36] As one British admiral declared: "Never since Trafalgar has there been a time when sea security, and all that it means to our nation and empire, seemed less endangered; never has it given strategists less anxiety." [37]

The lessons of the late war also helped to reinforce functional considerations. One of the enormous disadvantages which Britain had suffered at the beginning of two world wars had been the initial commitment of several divisions of ground troops. These forces had in both cases been forced into humiliating withdrawals, culminating in the second instance in evacuation from continental Europe. Unless American support were given without stint from the beginning of a conflict, no effective defense of Western Europe could be organized.[38] This justification itself helped to account for the British emphasis upon close defense ties with the United States extending, ultimately, to military alliance. In the absence of that alliance, however, the British were hesitant to

[35] *Ibid.*, p. 456.

[36] See W. J. Crowe, Jr., "The Policy Roots of the Modern Royal Navy, 1946–1963," p. 63. Unpublished Dissertation, Princeton University, 1965.

[37] *Sunday Times*, December 1, 1946.

[38] See Denis Healey, "Britain and NATO" in Klaus Knorr, ed., *NATO and American Security* (Princeton, N.J., 1959), pp. 209–10.

give any ground force pledge to Western Europe. As late as the end of 1947 and the beginning of 1948, British joint planners were convinced "the best strategy [for defense of Europe] appears to be the air strategy." [39] This doctrine was apparently conjoined with the traditional notion that even if the continent were occupied another "Overlord" invasion could be mounted to liberate it. In any event British home security would not be fundamentally menaced until bases capable of mounting massive strikes on the home isles were seized by an enemy. Until that time Fighter Command could be expected to offer reliable defense against air attack.

The absence of obvious enemies in the first two postwar years also made possible basic revisions in defense planning. No one knew what the atomic bomb portended for future strategy. As the 1946 White Paper declared: "This is not the time to come to decisions about the eventual shape of our postwar forces. The great strides made in the realm of science and technology, including the production of atomic bombs, cannot fail to affect the make-up of our forces. Time is wanted for the full effects of these startling developments to be assessed." [40]

Essentially the same position was asserted a year later. In the absence of a concrete plan for the future, there was to be a maximum reliance upon stocks built up during World War II. It was not believed necessary to reequip the forces on a substantial scale, but rather to introduce in a very limited way jet-propelled airplanes, modern antiaircraft weapons, and armored vehicles. In the circumstances, then, the strategic conception of 1946–47 was essentially that of the "expandable nucleus." Armaments would not be designed for a specific future war with a specific future enemy. It was

[39] Montgomery, p. 500.   [40] Cmnd. 6743, p. 3.

presumed that there would be enough advance warning to ready the forces through a substantial mobilization effort before war occurred. Thus military expenditure was allowed to fall from £1,667 million in 1946 to £899 million in 1947. Military manpower was reduced from a total of over 2 million in early 1946 to approximately 1.3 million in March, 1947. That as many men were retained in the services two years after the war was to be attributed more to the residual commitments of that war than to the recognition of a particular future adversary. As one example, by the end of 1947, the British had 57,000 troops in Palestine alone.[41] Malaya and Greece were also formidable tests of British resolve and resources. These burdens could not be lightly shed. As the 1946 White Paper pointed out: "We could not abandon our responsibilities in many parts of the world. To do so would have been to throw away the fruits of victory and to betray those who had fought and died in the common cause." [42]

One factor underlying the postponement of contingency planning was the adoption of a ten-year "no-war" planning assumption in the winter of 1946. This decision was not an agreed forecast by the defense chiefs, but rather a basic presumption of their political masters. Nonetheless, its adoption meant that all services would have to postpone reequipment and maximize the usefulness of their wartime stocks. When new weapons were developed, they would have to be good for a future ten and more years away. Thus, when the specifications were issued to the British aircraft industry on January 1, 1947, for a four-engine jet bomber, that bomber (ultimately the three V-bombers) had to penetrate to its distant target and drop atomic bombs against whatever oppo-

---

[41] Millis, p. 376.   [42] Cmnd. 6743, pp. 2–3.

sition an enemy state might mount a decade hence.[43] It was not surprising, therefore, that the Air Ministry planned for a considerable development of existing jet engines to provide the thrust and range for such a role. In the meantime, Lincolns were being produced and the jet light-bomber, the Canberra, and the Venom were ordered for the near future. Fighter Command would be the first line of defense; strategic bombing of enemy cities and industrial capability had a secondary priority. Even Fighter Command, however, was not given its needs if conflict were only several years away; again the assumption of a lengthy period of peace helped to delay large-scale expenditure on new aircraft.

There was yet another reason for the postponement of radical new strategic conceptions after World War II. It was still unclear what impact the atomic bomb would have upon military strategy. In large part its effect would depend upon the stockpile and destructive power of bomb capabilities on two opposing sides and upon bomber penetration and fighter defense capacities at the outbreak of war. In 1946–47, however, it seemed totally unlikely that atomic war, waged by strategic bombers, could be decisive. Even if atomic bombs were dropped on urban populations, conceivable stockpiles would not be sufficient to end the conflict by themselves.[44] The war would in the end turn upon a massive ground campaign, not entirely unlike that which had decided World War II.[45] If ground warfare were to be ultimately decisive, there

[43] Alfred Goldberg, "The Military Origins of the British Nuclear Deterrent," *International Affairs*, Vol. 40, No. 4 (October, 1964), pp. 605–6.

[44] As the *Times* military correspondent pointed out: "For some time . . . these missiles will be enormously costly, difficult to produce, and rare." *Times*, September 26, 1947.

[45] *Times*, July 31, 1947.

seemed less reason to prepare in advance to wage it. The war itself would be determined by intrawar mobilization and training of manpower and by a wartime production effort. The United Kingdom would be more vulnerable in such a war than other states, largely because its cities and industrial complexes were geographically concentrated and densely settled. As one military observer stressed: "Few uses [of atomic bombs] are likely to be more effective than that of dropping them on this country." [46] All the greater importance had to be given, therefore, to Fighter Command and antiaircraft defense. Unless these arms could be perfected, Britain would scarcely be able to survive a drawn-out conflict.

The Army, however, would be the force eventually to win through to victory. In 1946 it was apparently decided that the postwar Army in action would have to be an amalgam of the Regular and Territorial armies. Not only would the Territorial Army house technical support units which could not be carried by the Regular Army in peacetime, it would also provide the trained reserves adequate in quantity and quality to fight modern war. The Territorial Army would be built up for this task through a succession of intakes of reservists returning from National Service. After twelve months' service with the Regular Army, conscripts would spend six years in Territorial Army reserve training. On this basis Territorial Army ranks would have received their first National Service units in January, 1950, and the size and readiness of the Territorial Army would have reached a maximum in January, 1955. Prior to that time a maximum war emergency would have required mobilization of World War II veterans (the Z class reservists). As events unrolled, however, the government decided to increase the National Service period to eighteen

[46] *Times*, September 26, 1947.

months in December, 1948, and it was not until July, 1950, that the first conscript reservists entered the Territorial Army.

Two features of these plans should be noted. First, the twelve-month National Service plan had been introduced when the Labour government faced revolt on its back benches and was based on the assumption that short-term overseas commitments would be liquidated and that no more would arise, "that there was no enemy to fight, and that there was no need for any unit of our field force to be kept immediately operational—in other words, full peacetime conditions." Second, the long-term plan was founded on the assumption that general war could be avoided for a considerable period. Initial army planning in 1946 presumed that small scale conflicts could be avoided until 1951, preparations for a major war did not need to be complete until ten years later.[47]

If this were true, immediate reequipment of ground forces could be postponed for some time; World War II stocks could suffice for an interim period.

The ground war strategy which flowed from the late war was in part a reflex response to the uncertainty of the future military environment. "Until we knew what form . . . aggression. . . . would take we had to prepare in the way we knew best and that was based on the experience of the last war, particularly in its closing stages." [48] In part it must have stemmed from the knowledge that no potential enemy yet had atomic weapons. Even when it acquired those weapons, they would be scarce and expensive, and unlikely to be deci-

[47] *Montgomery*, pp. 479, 435.
[48] Frederick Bellenger, Minister for the Army, quoted in *Times*, July 31, 1947.

sive in a near-term conflict. Again, an army strategy seemed appropriate.

The functional character of British military strategy after the war gained credence from political imponderables. No one yet knew what future Soviet policy would be. It was possible that British retrenchment and disengagement from wartime obligations and imperial responsibilities would be accompanied by Soviet cooperation or acquiescence. Early in 1946 Prime Minister Attlee believed that British withdrawal from areas in which clashes with the Russians were possible might remove the grounds for friction between East and West. There is no reason to doubt British sincerity in wishing to lay down burdens in Indonesia, Palestine, Jordan, Italy, and Japan. Even India was conceived as a potential liability, and there was a modest but unsuccessful move in some political circles to divest Britain of her Egyptian role. The North African campaigns of the war, however, were too well remembered to permit such an abdication of power, and an assessment of the effect of atomic weapons upon the Middle East bastion was yet to be made. The granting of independence to India, Pakistan, Ceylon, and Burma proceeded in tandem with notions of regional security for members of the older Commonwealth. Australia, New Zealand, and South Africa would have to make provision for their own defense; no longer could they rely completely upon the British fleet. Even the decision to cease political and military aid to Greece and Turkey in March, 1947, may have been partly influenced by the need to "put a wide glacis of desert and Arabs between ourselves and the Russians." [49] As the Americans quite

[49] See Dalton, p. 105.

rightly observed, there were other burdens Britain might have discarded besides those generating the most friction with the Russians.[50]

British friendship with the United States in the immediate aftermath of the war, moreover, should not be interpreted as hostility to the Soviet Union. In 1946 Ernest Bevin had told his Labour colleagues: "I have not pressed unduly even for an alliance with France or with the Western Powers because I have been actuated all the time in this approach by the wish not to divide Europe." [51] The British Foreign Secretary, in fact, was pursuing a "dual policy," endeavoring to hold out options in both American and Russian directions. Choice between options was implicit as early as the Marshall Plan overture and Bevin was influential, even decisive, in the Russian decision not to participate. In formal terms, however, the "dual policy" was maintained until the London Foreign Ministers meeting in November–December, 1947. At that point further attempts to cooperate with the Soviets seemed fruitless.

As long as future Soviet policy remained opaque, however, contingency war plans were less imperative. Defense policy could consist largely of phased withdrawals from immediate postwar responsibilities and a run-down of forces. Nor did Conservative leaders challenge demobilization; they argued in fact that it was not proceeding fast enough. Since force levels at the end of the war were assumed to be far larger than normal requirements, they could be allowed to dwindle, without having to establish the size of the postwar Army, Navy and Air Force. And in April, 1947, the twelve-month National Service period had been posited on condition that remaining British commitments overseas would be terminated

[50] See Millis, p. 303.   [51] Quoted in Rose, p. 111.

or sharply reduced by January, 1949.[52] Neither of these actions could have been predicated upon axioms of early military conflict with the Soviet Union. Though British political leaders were quicker to fasten on Soviet intransigence than their American colleagues, they did not lose hope for Soviet cooperation until the spring of 1947.

Even more interesting, perhaps, after Soviet obduracy had been amply proved, few deductions were drawn concerning additional military preparations. Financial factors forced retrenchment as the lineaments of Soviet hostility were being revealed. By the end of 1946, Chancellor Hugh Dalton's "cheap money" policy was running into difficulty. Investment was not overstimulated, nor was home demand encroaching upon needed export production; but the dollar position was steadily worsening. In February, 1947, dollar deficits were over $200 million. Arrangements to tie up sterling balances before the onset of convertibility were only partially worked out. Some holders of large sterling balances were expected to exercise self-restraint in transferring sterling into dollars. Others were free to do as they liked. In a situation of an international shortage of dollars, it was not surprising that worldwide holders of sterling seized upon convertibility as a means of increasing their dollar balances. Probably no policy the British government could have followed would have avoided the run on sterling in the summer of 1947. Certainly, the outflow cannot be laid to the deficit on current trade account.

What is chargeable to the government and their financial advisers is the inability to see in the months immediately preceding how devastating a course full convertibility would be. The government was also responsible for a series of

[52] Montgomery, p. 478.

blunders that compounded the dollar problem. The Chancellor's mildly inflationary policy was only checked in April, 1947, and in June an increased import program was permitted. Taxes were again increased in October, but by then the damage had already been done.

If domestic inflation and greater imports increased the international liabilities of the British government, the fuel crisis needlessly reduced necessary exports. Late in 1946 the coal supply became dangerously short, but nothing was done until February when industrial customers were cut off from electricity, and domestic power was severely restricted. "It was later estimated that the disruption of production cost £200 million in exports." The convertibility crisis continued during the summer until the American loan of the year before was completely exhausted. Convertibility was suspended on August 20, 1947, and the loan, which had been expected to last three years or more, was spent in a year and a half. From then on Sir Stafford Cripps, who succeeded to the Treasury in October, presided over a resolutely disinflationary program.[53]

The impact of the British economic crisis upon defence planning was influential, even decisive. In March, under pressure from the Chancellor of the Exchequer, it was decided that Britain could no longer sustain economic and military commitments to Greece and Turkey. In 1947 alone, the assistance would cost $250 million.[54] A U.S. assumption of these roles, however, was delayed. The initial U.S. legislative authorization was limited to military and economic aid; it did not provide for U.S. troops. And in the end 5,000 British

[53] Dow, p. 22; for an account of British economic policy and problems, 1946-47, see pp. 21-29.
[54] Millis, p. 245.

soldiers remained in Greece until after the beginning of 1948. At the time of maximum Yugoslav pressure in the summer of 1947, the British had to take the brunt themselves.[55] Even after the U.S. aid program was underway, London yielded to pressure from Washington to avoid precipitate troop withdrawals.

The reduction of the British position in Greece and Turkey was accompanied by other measures to ease the financial burden of defense. "On 30 July, 1947, a speed-up in demobilization was ordered and on 30 August, as part of dollar crisis economies, Attlee announced a further cut which would bring the [forces] down to 1,007,000 by 31 March, 1948. This was further cut in December, 1947 to 937,000 by the same date." [56]

At the same time the government was attempting to establish a defense ceiling of £600 million, involving estimates of £270 million for the Army, £160 million for the Navy, and £170 million for the R.A.F. These figures were approved by the government in October, 1947. They were, however, not the last word in Army cuts. Early in the following January, the government sought to reduce the Army share of the £600 million to £222 million, providing for a regular component of only 185,000 men.[57]

The justification for this allocation had been offered two months previously when the Minister for Defence, A. V. Alexander, indicated in Parliament that defense research would have first, the Air Force second, the Navy third, and the Army fourth priority in government allocations. The argument underlying such decisions implicitly acknowledged

[55] See Herbert Nicholas, *Britain and the United States* (London, 1963), p. 43.
[56] *Ibid.*, p. 44.   [57] Montgomery, pp. 480, 482.

that the government was not preparing for a short-range crisis. Defense research would mature into finished and produced weapons only after a lengthy lead-time. The Air Force would not be capable of dealing a telling blow to the Soviet heartland for almost a decade. Even Fighter Command was not ready to absorb a Soviet air assault. The Navy had just emerged from one of the most drastic immobilizations in its long history. In October, 1947, the home fleet had been temporarily reduced to one cruiser and four destroyers. "The defence of a world-wide Empire [was] entrusted to four aircraft carriers and fewer than a dozen cruisers." [58] Apart from the desire to save on money and manpower, the Navy slash was due to a government demand to economize on fuel, and thus prevent a repetition of the crisis of the previous winter. The Army could be slighted because its peacetime responsibilities were being reduced, and there seemed no prospect of a major conflict in the near future.

Defense planning in 1947 proceeded on an altered footing from that in 1946. In the first year after the war, no enemy had been in sight, but demobilization had proceeded relatively slowly. A variety of commitments deriving from the war required British attention and British forces. Financial stringencies were not great, and wartime taxes were reduced by 10 percent. The major financial threat envisaged in the future was deflation not inflation, and it was assumed that the U.S. loan would provide for deficits on current account until British exports met and exceeded prewar levels. Britain continued to carry the burdens of a world power. In 1947 the situation was fundamentally changed. Though Soviet enmity was not taken for granted, it was much clearer in mid-1947 than it had been the year before. There were major disagreements over

[58] *Glasgow Herald,* October 20, 1947.

Germany, the Polish elections had clearly been controlled, and the threats to Iran and to Greece and Turkey had been stated unequivocally. The Council of Foreign Ministers ended in acrimony. If there was no indication that the Soviets would make or were capable of war in the short run, Soviet military predominance was greater in 1947 than it had been in 1946. If future patterns of international threat had been wholly governing, British defense expenditures in 1947 should have been higher than in 1946.

That this was not the case should be attributed, not to faith in future Russian intentions, but to the constricting influence of finance. British financial troubles were far more evident in 1947 than they had been a year earlier. Retrenchment was imperative if the dollar drain was to be halted; domestic contraction was necessary, if imports and exports were to reach a balance. One could no longer tolerate the previous luxury of $200 million expenditure on American fruit, vegetables, and dried eggs.[59] Tax increases and import restrictions were necessary. Even the Marshall Plan, though it might eventually prove Europe's financial salvation, would be of no use in 1947 and little enough in 1948. Domestic retrenchment had to come first. The deduction that had to be drawn was that modest changes in the world political environment would not be allowed to determine British defense outlays. In the absence of actual or near crisis, financial considerations would be decisive.

The first two years of postwar British defense planning were of necessity occupied in drawing the contours of future policy. For the most part, the rundown of forces could take place without specific decisions on the size of the postwar

[59] See Dow, p. 26.

Army, Navy and Air Force. It was assumed that 1946 strengths were far above what would be needed in peacetime. Concrete responsibilities around the globe had to be served; in this context demobilization could proceed only as rapidly as disengagement. In 1946, British forces were withdrawn from Indonesia and Indo-China, and they were phasing out of British India, Burma, and Ceylon. A year later the Asian Commonwealth was inaugurated. In the Middle East, British ground forces were withdrawn from Iraq and from the Nile delta into the Suez Canal zone. "Bevin intended to move the Middle East base eventually from there to Kenya." [60] British troops left Iran, and at the end of 1947 they were shortly to lay down a draining commitment in Palestine. Greece and Turkey were prospectively turned over to the United States, though the transformation had not yet fully taken place. The Italian issue had been disposed of, though Germany and Austria lingered on. Aside from demobilization and withdrawal, only general defense planning had been done. This made general provision against future threats, but it did not denominate enemies, specific arenas of conflict, and military allies. Only in the most general sense did it establish an outline of future war, and that outline was at least initially derived from World War II. For the nonce, the atomic bomb, the gradual buildup of the Regular and Territorial armies and fighter defense sufficed. Functional policy preceded specific applications.

Only at the very end of 1947 did future options begin to become concrete. By the London Foreign Ministers' meeting, the Soviets had identified themselves, to political as well as military leaders, as the probable future foe. The United States

[60] C. M. Woodhouse, *British Foreign Policy Since the Second World War* (New York, 1962), pp. 21–22.

had previously been viewed as the major ally of the United Kingdom in a future war, but there had been no urgency to negotiate a specific and contractual form of military cooperation. A war crisis was relegated to the indefinite future. In December, 1947, however, Ernest Bevin decided to seek a military relationship with Western Europe that would eventually include the United States. He told Field Marshal Montgomery that he had informed the French "that the time had come to begin the formation of a federation or union in Western Europe, and if possible to bring the Americans into it." [61] Staff talks would be initiated with the United States after Britain had formulated her own ideas on Western European defense. The range of British military decision was already being circumscribed.

[61] Montgomery, p. 498.

CHAPTER THREE

THE YEAR OF CHOICE, 1948

IF THE FIRST TWO years after the war involved planning for unspecified future contingencies and the creation of options for the future, the year 1948 made defense policy much more concrete: enemies were formally denominated, allies directly approached, and the nature and strategy of probable military campaigns tentatively laid down. The Chiefs of Staff began to talk more realistically about Britain's contribution in the event of another European war. These considerations were given point by political arrangements that Foreign Secretary Bevin had set in train. At the end of 1947 he had begun to speculate about the need to expand the Dunkirk Treaty of 1947 (fundamentally a British reassurance to France in the event of the future development of German power) into a Western Union, including the Benelux countries and possibly others as well. Scandinavia and the Mediterranean states might also be approached. When the idea was broached to Secretary of State Marshall, the American lent his warm support and encouragement. Washington's favorable response led Bevin in turn to believe that the United States might eventually join a wider alliance. In December, 1947, however, American planners were not yet ready to accept new obligations. "They were not prepared to face up to Congress at that time on the question of a military commitment to fight in Europe." [1]

When Bevin decided to go ahead with a Western European pact, however, it was with no thought that America had said its final word on the subject. Since both a European and an Atlantic relationship were desired, the first would be secured, even if the second had to be postponed. While "third force" notions were wholly absent from the European plan, Bevin apparently did not regard the Western European nucleus as a more effective means to American participation. [2] That support would be forthcoming in America's own interest in due season. It was only slightly before Bevin's formal proposal of a European treaty arrangement in the House of Commons on January 23, 1948, that he decided on its particular form. Scandinavian and Mediterranean nations were left out, though the Foreign Secretary emphasized that a treaty including France, Britain, and Benelux was simply "an important nucleus," and went on to add: "We are now thinking of Western Europe as a unit." [3] The immediate result was the conclusion of the Brussels Treaty of March 17 between the five powers. The pact was not specifically directed against Germany as its predecessor had been; armed attacks were to be resisted from whatever quarter. There was little doubt that

[1] Viscount Montgomery of Alamein, *Memoirs* (London, 1958), p. 499.

[2] In fact, however, it was precisely that. There is little doubt that the United States was more willing to enter an alliance with a series of Western European nations than a bilateral accord with any one of them.

[3] *House of Commons Debates*, Vol. 466, col. 397.

the potential threat from the east was held uppermost in the minds of the treaty framers.

As political developments proceeded, military planning had to take account of them. In January, 1948, the British Joint Planners prepared a paper outlining three possible courses of action in defense of Europe: 1) an air strategy, 2) a continental strategy, and 3) "a semi-continental strategy, involving holding Spain and Portugal and liberating Europe by an offensive through the Pyrenees." The paper went on to reject the continental strategy, and then expressed a preference for the air stategy as against that of holding a line at the Pyrenees. Field Marshal Lord Montgomery, then C.I.G.S., denounced the plan and pointed out that Western Union could have no hope of success unless Britain were ready to resist on the continent and as far to the east as possible. The Navy and Air Chiefs, however, disagreed. "They argued that it was militarily and economically impossible to do this, and further that it was useless to discuss our own European strategy until we knew what the Americans would do." [4]

The issue was then taken to Attlee: should Britain resist on the continent or confine herself to air operations? In one sense it was unthinkable that either political or military leaders would set the stage for another Dunkirk; Britain should not be forced into hasty military retreats yet a third time. On the other hand, Montgomery had a convincing political case. If Britain were not willing to fight on European soil in the event of another war, what meaning would the Western Union have? Attlee initially espoused the air strategy and deprecated a British ground commitment in Western Europe; but after all, British troops were already in Germany; would they refuse to fight if the Russians attacked? Bevin and A. V.

[4] Montgomery, pp. 499–500.

Alexander acknowledged the point, and it was decided to consider the military implications of a continental strategy including its impact upon the shape and size of British forces. The net result seems to have been a British decision to fight with the forces available in Germany, even though these and other allied troops would be too weak to stem a Soviet offensive. As Montgomery put it: "Of course we needed American help; but unless that country was convinced that all would fight, whatever the situation, we would not get her help—nor would we deserve it." [5]

Even after adoption of a marginal continental strategy, however, it was clear that British forces there could not hold out for long. Until land forces in Europe had been built up very considerably, there was no possibility of effective resistance. As chairman of the Brussels Treaty Commanders-in-Chief Committee Montgomery recommended an immediate reinforcement of the British Army of the Rhine if war broke out. Reluctantly the British Chiefs agreed to send one infantry brigade group, but when the recommendation was forwarded to the government it was rejected in January, 1949. In effect, therefore, the British continental strategy amounted to little more than a pledge of a brief engagement in the initial stages of war. It did not involve the commitment to sustain a real campaign. After a short period, Britain would have withdrawn in expectation of an American intervention and an eventual 'liberation' of the European continent.

Western Union strategy, in the short run at least, was little more than a ratification of British notions. After the onset of the Berlin blockade it had seemed necessary to concert defense plans and command arrangements with the other Brussels Treaty powers. Agreements resulted to create committees

[5] *Ibid.*, pp. 500–1.

of foreign ministers, defense ministers, and chiefs of staff. The last was served by a permanent military committee sitting in London which effectively did the initial planning for war. American observers were invited to attend meetings of the military group and the initial Brussels plans became precursors for NATO strategy. The first Brussels plan was essentially short term in nature. It was a stop-gap designed to save as many troops as possible in a future war. "It mounted to little more than assignments to withdrawal routes, the authority to commandeer ships in British and Allied ports to be used for evacuation, and perhaps a desperate hope . . . . that Franco might let the Allied troops pass through Spain, or even stand with them in an attempt to hold at the Pyrenees." [6] This was little more than the British continental strategy writ large; all that had been gained was a fighting withdrawal.

In one respect this result was hardly surprising. Bevin's policy had been to involve the United States in the defense of Europe ever since the end of 1947. If Britain made too great a commitment, and the United States did not come to her aid, or did not do so in time, scarce British military resources would be lost. If American commitments to the continent would not proceed in tandem with those of Britain, they should at least not lag too far behind. Hence at the very signing of the Western Union, Bevin dispatched a telegram to Washington expressing hope that it would lead to a more comprehensive defense grouping. And even before, he had proposed that the five-nation pact be strengthened through arrangements for Atlantic and Mediterranean security. [7]

[6] Roger Hilsman, "NATO: The Developing Strategic Context," in Klaus Knorr, ed., *NATO and American Security* (Princeton, N.J., 1959), p. 14.

[7] Walter Millis, ed., *The Forrestal Diaries* (New York, 1951), p. 392.

Failing American agreement, on April 23 the British approach was renewed. Bevin reasoned in a top secret telegram to Washington that "the summoning of a conference by the United States to discuss defense arrangements for the North Atlantic area would be the best guarantee of peace at the present moment." He pointed out that the French would not agree to the rebuilding of Germany, except within the framework of an Atlantic security system, and "then expressed the opinion that it would be very difficult for the British or other free nations, to stand up to new acts of aggression unless there was a definitely worked out arrangement, which included the United States, for collective resistence against aggression." [8] In response to these various overtures the American administration gradually began to take steps which would permit a military association with Europe. By the end of April, 1948, the basic provisions of the "Vandenberg Resolution" had been formulated, which would put the U.S. Senate on record in favor of regional security arrangements "based on continuous and effective self-help and mutual aid." The permissive foundations of NATO had been laid.

Senate adoption of the "Vandenberg resolution" in June and the onset of the Berlin blockade, however, did not lead to an early agreement on Atlantic defense. The reason for the delay is not altogether clear. On the one hand, practical defense cooperation between Britain and the United States as a response to the Berlin situation was reaching a new peak; it was perhaps less necessary to codify that cooperation. On the other hand, the American election in November may have made it difficult for the Truman administration to undertake new and formal defense commitments at the time. This may

[8] Harry S. Truman, *Memoirs*. Vol. II: *Years of Trial and Hope* (Garden City, N.Y., 1956), pp. 244, 245.

have been the more true in that it was generally anticipated that President Truman would be defeated by Governor Thomas E. Dewey of New York. If Truman had pledged himself to a foreign "entangling alliance," he might have further complicated existing electoral difficulties; if the alliance had been concluded, his own defeat might have altered its impact and affected prospects of Senate ratification. In any event it was clear that Senate action could not take place before November.

Informal cooperation for the time being seemed a better course, and it was the one President Truman adopted. There was, moreover, no uncertainty about American military solidarity with the continent in the event of war. In June, 1948, the U.S. administration wished to reemphasize its military concern over the continuing Berlin impasse by sending two B-29 groups to Germany and two to England. Britain immediately concurred, and the first two bomber groups arrived in July to operate from three East Anglian bases. Two months later, another group was added. As Sir Winston Churchill later pointed out, this completely informal arrangement became Britain's most important defense commitment in the postwar period. The United Kingdom had in effect become "an unsinkable aircraft carrier" that might ultimately be used for the strategic bombing of Soviet Russia. The understandings governing U.S. flights from British bases were not formally worked out until October, 1951, just before Attlee left office. There were several reasons for postponement of a written accord. First, atomic bombs were not present on British soil when the first American bombers arrived. In the United States a custody battle was still going on between the Atomic Energy Commission and the services. It was not until September, 1948, that the President even agreed to use the bomb in event of war.[9] Second, the Americans were very sensitive about possible external restrictions on their decision to employ nuclear weapons. Only in January, 1948, had they succeeded in removing a British veto on separate American use of atomic weapons anywhere in the world (see below pp. 84–86), and they did not wish to introduce analogous controls in Europe. For their part, the British did not want to insist upon overly strict limitations. These might have had the impact of forcing a redeployment of the U.S. bombers, or alternatively, of hampering their effectiveness in an emergency. In line with Bevin's policy of increasingly implicating the Americans in European defense, London regarded the bombers as an asset and wanted them to remain. Thus, no formal rules were elaborated until October, 1951, at which time, Attlee reasoned, he might have to account for his stewardship to an incoming Conservative regime. The formula then agreed provided that "the use of the bases in an emergency would be a matter for joint decision by the two Governments in the light of circumstances prevailing at the time." [10] This arrangement, it should be observed, did not accord Britain an indefeasible right of veto. "Joint decision" was modified by "circumstances prevailing at the time." Every possible attempt would be made to reach an agreed decision, but if the circumstances did not permit it, action was not definitively forestalled. When Parliament was casually informed on July 28, 1948, that "The B-29s at R.A.F. stations are here to carry out long-distance flying training in Western Europe. It has not been decided how long they will stay," [11]

[9] Millis, p. 487.
[10] Statement by Prime Minister Harold Macmillan, *House of Commons Debates*, Vol. 579 (December 12, 1957), col. 1431.
[11] *House of Commons Debates*, Vol. 454, col. 123.

it was witnessing the revelation of a commitment of the first importance.

Bases were not the only evidence of *de facto* Anglo-American military cooperation. In Newport, Rhode Island, between August 20–22, the U.S. Joint Chiefs made far-reaching plans for the defense of Britain and Western Europe. The first provided for immediate Western Union defense needs and was to be urged upon America's "European allies" even though no contractual allies at that time existed. Presumably it provided for strategic and command relationships in Western Europe in which Britain would perforce have to take the leading role. The plan was followed shortly by Montgomery's appointment as Chairman of the Commanders-in-Chief Committee, Brussels Treaty. The second plan outlined U.S. action in wartime. It authorized "a Supreme Allied Commander-in-Chief (West) who should be an American" and outlined other U.S. contributions to European defense, provisions which would not be applied until December, 1950, when General Eisenhower was appointed NATO Supreme Commander.[12] Both plans clarified American military thinking in regard to European defense; both assumed that the United States and Western European states would be allies and that they would jointly resist an aggression launched from the east. In this sense both rested on the assumption that a North Atlantic alliance reflected basic American interests.

Final steps toward the treaty seem to have been taken shortly after the U.S. election. As late as November 12, Secretary of Defense Forrestal was still inquiring whether European nations would be satisfied with an implicit military relationship and "substantial military shipments" from the United States. Was it additionally necessary for America to

[12] Millis, p. 478.

"sign a pact to support the Western European powers in the event of hostilities"? The British Chiefs replied that while military aid would be better than nothing, it would still be "totally inadequate." [13] By January, 1949, however, the Brussels powers and the United States had agreed to proceed to a security treaty including not only themselves but also Norway, Denmark, Iceland, Portugal, Canada, and Italy. The Western Union nucleus had been expanded, and Ernest Bevin's fundamental goal achieved. On April 4, 1949, the North Atlantic Treaty was signed in Washington.

There was no doubt by the beginning of 1948 that the Soviet Union was the putative future foe, and that the arena of conflict would most probably be Western Europe. If the developments of 1947 had left any doubts on this score, the Czechoslovak coup in February, and the Berlin blockade in June, 1948, erased them. During the summer of 1948 Bevin continually pressed Washington for an Atlantic security arrangement in light of Britain's exposed position in the "front line" of a potential military conflict. At the same time there seems to have been little thought that war would occur in the short run.

The need for NATO was as much political as military. Meetings of Brussels Pact members with U.S. representatives during the summer of 1948 had produced the conviction that the most serious problem was "a constant danger of incidents developing from the international tension" rather than a Soviet "timetable for armed aggression." Various Russian unilateral moves had resulted "in an atmosphere of insecurity and fear among the peoples of Western Europe. Something more needed to be done to counteract the fear of the peoples

[13] *Ibid.*, p. 525.

of Europe that their countries would be overrun by the Soviet army before effective help could arrive." [14] To allay European fears, it was not necessary actually to build the forces that would defeat a Russian aggression in Europe. A political reassurance of Western peoples that the United States would participate in any new European conflict from the outset would be sufficient. Western European states could then turn to more important tasks of recovery and economic progress. In the absence of such a commitment, each new Russian move would create a war scare and foster a climate of uncertainty. As long as Soviet maneuvers and political assaults were not indications of an intention to attack the West militarily, Western nations should not pay too much attention to them. If, for example, France, Italy, the Low Countries, and Western Germany had been asked to provide the divisions needed to meet Soviet aggression on the central front, they would have lost more than the ground gained by the Marshall Plan. Rearmament would defeat the rehabilitation of European economies. The attractive feature of the North Atlantic Treaty, as then conceived, was that it supplemented, but did not detract from, the European Recovery Program.

In such a context British forces on the continent served equally as agents of domestic stabilization and defenders against external attack. The Atlantic Treaty and U.S. occupation forces in Germany offered American reassurance; Western Union and the British Army of the Rhine provided the British pledge. Questions of concrete infantry capabilities, or the need for reinforcement in the event of war, could be handled on political grounds; they might be postponed. Further, London did not want to make great military exertions on behalf of Europe unless and until the United States

[14] Truman, II, 248.

was also committed. Part of the delay in the negotiation of NATO was due to British (and continental) hesitancy to administer a rebuff to Russia until U.S. support had been guaranteed.

This assured, it was possible to devote greater thought to the less immediate future. In 1948 it began to appear that in a future war respective atomic stockpiles might themselves decide a conflict. The February White Paper observed prophetically:

The advent of weapons of mass destruction must profoundly influence both the preparations for and the conduct of war. Though it is not yet possible to assess with any accuracy what their effect on strategy will be, it can be said provisionally that their existence increases the possibilities of surprise attack, since the effort required to deliver devastating attacks with these weapons will be smaller than that which would be demanded by the use of conventional weapons, and that decisive results might even be obtained by their use alone.[15]

There were several inferences that might be drawn from such views. Some derived from American atomic weapons, others from future Soviet bombs. As to the first, if U.S. nuclear strength would itself "win the war," there was less need to develop ground formations, logistics, and air and sea support necessary to a conflict of the World War II type. U.S. bomber strength operating from Britain might defeat a Soviet ground offensive. These conclusions made it easier for the government to accept the arguments of the Air staff and challenge those of the Army. If air power would "prevail," a British air strategy was as appropriate as an American air strategy, and monies could be spent accordingly. Since the

[15] Cmnd. 7327, *Statement Relating to Defence* (February, 1948), p. 10.

United States had a considerable lead over the Russians in both atomics and air strength, the near-term future would make Britain even more secure; she had to do little enough in her own defense.

In the longer run, of course, growth of Soviet strategic bombing and corollary atomic capability also could be foreseen. Such capabilities would pose three different threats to the British Isles. In their earliest manifestations, Russian bombers might reach the Channel without atomic weapons. The Russian subsonic bomber then in production, the Tu-4, was nothing more than a Soviet edition of the wartime B-29. High explosive bombs would do considerable damage, but Fighter Command, now almost completely equipped with jet interceptors could destroy their carriers. Later on Russian conventional explosives might be delivered in jet bombers, or alternatively a limited number of atomic weapons might be dispatched in the Tu-4. In either case, Fighter Command could work a sufficient attrition to prevent massive devastation of British cities. Only still later, when jet bombers would deliver substantial quantities of atomic explosives, would fighter defenses cease to be effective. At that point British defense would either depend upon surface-to-air missiles, or, more realistically, upon British abilities to launch strategic atomic attacks on Soviet Russia. As defense became less adequate, offense would supplant it.

Eventually British jet bombers would have to be ordered, but in the interim, and particularly given assumed Soviet capabilities, the best strategy seemed to be to concentrate on Fighter Command. The Secretary of State for Air announced in the estimates that all but one of Fighter Command's interceptor squadrons had been reequipped with jet aircraft. The introduction of a jet bomber was delayed "until the new jet engines with which future types are to be equipped have been fully proved." [16]

Though it might be argued that atomic bombs had revolutionized warfare and that "decisive results might even be obtained by their use alone," a future military order was clearly meant. For the present (1948–50) it seemed wholly unlikely that the atomic bomb could determine the outcome of a conflict with the Soviet Union. The British Chiefs were quite aware that a land invasion of Europe could only be stanched by troops in the field. That they were not planning to provide those troops indicated that war did not seem likely in the short run. An air strategy, after all, was a future strategy.

A similar conclusion had been reached by American planners. The budget for the 1950 fiscal year (which had to be prepared for the President by the end of 1948) did not provide for either an air strategy or a ground strategy. Three alternative budget formulations were considered. One, of $17–$18 billion, permitted an atomic offensive launched from Britain and combined military and naval operations to hold open the Mediterranean in the event of war. A second, of $14.4 billion, sanctioned atomic strikes from Britain, but canceled the Mediterranean strategy. It confined "Army and Navy requirements to those necessary to support the Air Force mission at home and in England." [17] A third budget proposal, also of $14.4 billions, gave roughly equal shares of the defense dollar to Army, Navy and Air forces and in so doing stunted the Air Force build-up that would have been

[16] House of Commons Debates, Vol. 448 (March 4, 1948), cols. 542–43.
[17] Warner R. Schilling, "The Politics of National Defence: Fiscal 1950," in Warner R. Schilling, Paul Y. Hammond, and Glenn H. Snyder, Strategy, Politics and Defense Budgets (New York, 1962), p. 178.

necessary to carry on an air offensive from Britain. On December 9, 1948, the President accepted the last formulation and rejected the other two. The American assumption seemed to be that it was better to concentrate upon a phased development of all three services for an indeterminate future conflict than to concentrate resources for the purpose of greater short term effectiveness. The U.S. planners, like their British counterparts, did not envisage war in the next few years.

Even if the strategic air offensive had been endorsed, it was by no means certain it would be effective. Two questions were involved: the first was whether Air Force bombers would be able to penetrate to and drop atomic bombs on target; the second was whether the results of the bombing would compel a Russian surrender. In October, 1948, special studies were initiated on both topics by the U.S. Joint Chiefs, but no agreement was reached. It was unclear how many bombs would hit their target; but, even presuming 100 percent success in delivery, it was still unsure that Russia would be knocked out.[18] An air offensive would probably not be decisive, and in any event, the American government was not providing the capability to launch one.

The British Chiefs were no more sanguine on these topics than their U.S. colleagues; their decision in favor of an air strategy really reflected the postponement of war to a time when novel technology would be in hand. In the meantime, Fighter Command would successfully repulse attacks on the home islands, the British Army of the Rhine would fight a

[18] It has since been revealed that the total megatonnage in the U.S. atom stockpile at the end of 1948 was approximately the same as the amount of TNT dropped by the United States in World War II. At the time this would probably have meant less than 100 bombs. See Schilling, p. 172.

delaying action in preparation for withdrawal, and the Navy would be able to operate briefly in the Mediterranean. If the Russians seized southern Europe, however, land-based air would control the Mediterranean, denying it to British carrier forces.[19]

The Middle East would also be a crucial battle zone in a future European war. If forces could be got there quickly enough after the start of hostilities, the Middle East base might be held for a time as it could be resupplied from the Red Sea and did not depend on the Suez Canal. British forces there would be able to threaten the Russian left flank. If Western Europe were absorbed, however, Russian forces would eventually seize the Middle East over the land bridge offered by Iran and Turkey. Western resistance to a Soviet attack in 1948 could scarcely have been more than token in the initial stages. Without mobilization, the United States itself could not send more than an additional division to fight anywhere in the world. If war occurred in the immediate future it would turn on a massive ground engagement following upon an equally formidable mobilization, production, and training effort. Despite the atomic bomb the war would be similar to World War II in its closing stages.

While conventional military plans could not be neglected, both Britain and America were giving a great deal of attention to their atomic programs. The British were eager to get more information to facilitate their effort; the Americans were concerned to build an atomic stockpile and to free themselves from wartime constraints governing its use. The 1943 Quebec Agreement had provided that the two parties would not use the bomb against each other, but also "that we will not use it

[19] See Millis, p. 525.

against third parties without each other's consent." And Britain had in fact given willing assent to the use of the bomb against Japan.[20] The Existence of this agreement was not known to Senator McMahon, author of the U.S. Atomic Energy Act, nor to any but a small group of presidential advisers. When it was revealed to influential congressional leaders at the end of 1947, the reaction was immediate. Senator Vandenberg claimed the restrictions were "astounding" and "unthinkable" and that they should be removed forthwith. "Failure to revamp the agreements would have a disastrous effect on congressional consideration of the Marshall Plan." [21]

Washington was not only concerned about its right to use the bomb; raw material shortages were agitating both congressional and executive opinion. The May, 1946, accord had provided for an approximately equal division of uranium ore controlled by the joint Combined Development Agency. By 1947, U.S. weapons production was being held up because of ore shortages. From the U.S. point of view, it seemed imperative to gain a greater access to ore sources. For its own part, Britain also wished to make changes in wartime agreements, and she was interested in resuming the exchange of atomic information. In particular British negotiators were eager to remove the Quebec Agreement's Paragraph 4 restriction which limited postwar British industrial and commercial development of atomic energy. They hoped as well to glean information that would be useful in the total British program.

[20] Text in Margaret Gowing, *Britain and Atomic Energy, 1939–1945* (London, 1964), pp. 439, 370–73.

[21] See Arthur H. Vandenberg, Jr., ed., *The Private Papers of Senator Vandenberg* (Boston, 1952), p. 361.

The result was the *modus vivendi* of January 8, 1948. It ended both Paragraph 2 and Paragraph 4 restrictions in the Quebec Agreement, freeing the United States to make unfettered use of its atomic weapons and eliminating any American control of U.K. atomic programs of a commercial character. It also relieved U.S. raw material shortages by allotting Washington the entire Congo output for 1948, slightly over half the 1949 output, and an option on any 1949 production not required by Britain.

In return, the United States agreed to an information exchange covering nine specified areas. These included, initially at least, natural uranium reactors, the metallurgy of plutonium, the detection of nuclear explosions, and nuclear cross sections. At first it seemed that the information gained would be of considerable value to the British, but then the reactor item was deleted, and the United States made sure that information given under the other categories was largely innocuous. There is no doubt that the United States was the major gainer from the accord.

At this remove it may seem difficult to understand why the British made so many important concessions and got so little in return. In the first place, they hardly believed their veto on separate American use of the atomic weapon had much significance. In their eyes Robert Lovett, the Undersecretary of State, argued cogently when he pointed out that the Quebec Agreement was "obsolete." The restrictions on both British and American initiative in the atomic field had emerged in wartime when scientists of both nations were engaged in a single research and production effort. As separate national programs emerged, individual vetoes on aspects of each other's development were harder to justify.

The British also had an important stake in removing commercial restrictions on their program, particularly as they intended to pay special attention to nuclear power generation. Because of the McMahon Act, they had been unable to remove such limitations in the spring of 1946; it seemed all the more important to eliminate them early in 1948. The ore and information questions were also less vexed than they seemed on the surface. Of course, Britain hoped to get information she could put to use in her own production effort, but the McMahon Act meant that the range of really valuable data could only be very narrow. She was also quite aware of congressional interests in the matter and knew that a wide exchange could be used to embarrass the U.S. administration. As to uranium ore, the *modus vivendi* did not restrict the British atomic effort at all; she had all she needed.

The question really was whether it was in Britain's interest to make sure that there were no unnecessary delays in the American weapons program. The answer to this was clear. The British knew that the atomic bomb was the major weapon in the Western arsenal in 1948. The United States and Britain could not match the Soviets in ground troops, but America had the bomb. If Britain had held up ore allocations, she not only would have reduced America's potency, she would also have impinged upon the basis of Western strength at a time when Soviet intentions were increasingly hostile. There could be no doubt that she would grant what America asked. Given such justifications it is still wise to remember that Britain heeded only the most enlightened version of self-interest in the atomic negotiations with the United States. A narrower perspective could have legitimately required a much more forthcoming attitude from the United States. Such forbearance was to be characteristic of British policy on the atomic question.

When Sir Stafford Cripps became Chancellor of the Exchequer in October, 1947, the most urgent economic and financial need was for greater exports. Exports in turn required a retrenchment in government spending, postponement of private consumption, and new taxes. Domestic prices would then be held down to levels that would attract foreign buyers. And in fact "production rose rapidly; exports rose even more spectacularly; and the balance of payments appeared at last to be swinging into surplus." [22] The consequences for defense expenditure were obvious, and in February, 1948, a cut of more than £200 millions was announced. British troop strengths in March, 1948, were 147,000 smaller than had been projected in the 1947 defense paper.[23] In a catalogue of factors influencing future planning, the Defence Ministry mentioned first "the economic position of the country." [24]

These reductions, however, were taking place in a deteriorating international atmosphere. Czechoslovakia and Berlin seemed object lessons in Russian intent, and a Soviet miscalculation of Western resolve could not be entirely ruled out. Weaknesses in British troop strength, moreover, were not entirely numerical. Demobilization of World War II veterans had left all forces crucially dependent upon national servicemen. In March, 1949, 300,000 of the 700,000 then to be in the forces were conscripts. A sudden emergency in

[22] J. C. R. Dow, *The Management of the British Economy, 1945–60* (Cambridge, 1965), p. 38.
[23] Projected totals were 1,087,000; actual, 940,000.   [24] Cmnd. 7327.

Europe or elsewhere would have required mobilization of the Z-class reservists, and even then needed equipment was lacking.[25] On two occasions during the summer of 1948, the government was informed by the Chiefs of Staff that the state of British forces gave grounds for alarm. For financial and other reasons, however, the government temporized until autumn.[26] Then it announced that all national servicemen due for release in the last few months of 1948 would be retained for an additional period of three months; in December the government extended the national service period from twelve to eighteen months. New recruiting efforts were also decided on for the three services and the Territorial Army. Production of jet interceptors and small arms ammunition was doubled, output of antiaircraft ammunition greatly increased and production of armored vehicles accelerated. To finance this measure of rearmament, new monies were provided.

The reasons for these preparations were both practical and precautionary. It did not seem that the Russians were likely to make an attack in Europe, and there were no visible signs of aggressive troop deployments. At the same time the Malayan campaign was absorbing increasing numbers of British soldiers, and it could not be sustained on the basis of twelve months' national service. Of Britain's overseas commitments, only the British Army of the Rhine could be kept up to strength through a one-year conscription period. Regardless of the Russian threat, then, British commitments East of Suez required a longer period of service. One did not have to

[25] Montgomery, p. 486.

[26] Delicate negotiations were then in progress on an Atlantic pact in Washington. Until the United States was more firmly committed to the defence of Europe, London did not want to make possibly provocative arms increases.

believe in the threat of major war to accept the need for larger British forces.

But while a major war was not likely, it could not be entirely discounted. When and if it occurred, it would be decided by an enormous ground engagement. At the same time there would undoubtedly be air attacks on the British Isles, and to defend against these Fighter Command was crucial. Britain's jet interceptor strength was important, however, not only to protect the home population, but also to ensure the safety of U.S. bomber bases. Sir Stafford Cripps told Secretary of Defense Forrestal: "Britain is placing its main reliance on the development of fighter aircraft to insure the security of Britain. Britain must be regarded as the main base for the deployment of American power and the chief offensive against Russia must be by air." Later Prime Minister Attlee stressed that British public opinion would endorse use of the atomic bomb in another war.[27] If war occurred, an Anglo-American atomic alliance would make possible strategic air attacks on the Soviet Union. If the Soviets decided to attack, they would have to face this eventuality.

In 1948 strategy and finance interchanged roles. For the better part of the year and during peaks of international tension, finance was governing. Britain continued to plan for the remote war and to skimp on forces in being. Toward the end of the year, strategy forced increasing expenditure, not only to handle existing conflicts (as in Malaya) but also to provide against the enhanced dangers of a major conflict. If the Russians attacked, they would suffer atomic reprisal, and in this sense, Fighter Command was not only protection against a future war, it was a means of waging (though perhaps not

[27] Millis, pp. 491, 523.

deciding) a near-term battle. Though its mechanisms were not well understood at the time, deterrence of attack was becoming an established military objective.[28] The year 1948 was genuinely a year of decision for British arms. The Soviet Union was the future enemy; the United States and Europe the major allies; the war, if it occurred, would be fought in the West. Forces were being readied for a future encounter, but they were not yet strong enough to provide a reliable defense. And it remained uncertain whether strength and resolve were sufficient to deter a resolute opponent.

[28] As the Defence Paper put it: "The best deterrent is tangible evidence of our intention and ability to withstand attack." Cmd. 7327.

CHAPTER FOUR

DETERRENCE, EUROPE, AND
THE UNITED STATES, 1949–1950

IF THE YEAR 1948 was perhaps the most crucial for British postwar defense policy, it did not resolve major doctrinal questions. Russia was the putative foe; Europe was the arena of conflict; and the United States the major ally. It remained uncertain whether war was in fact inevitable, and if so, when it would be fought. At least three different notions were entertained on this score. The first held that war might be avoided and that the Russian threat was more political than military. The second claimed that war would come, but not for a considerable time. When it did, it would be decided by use of the atomic bomb. The third maintained war might occur in the next few years and would turn upon a rallied ground encounter akin to World War II in its closing stages. The advantage of all three conceptions was that heavy rearmament was not called for. Even the most proximate conflict would largely rest upon intrawar mobilization and production; one did not have to be completely prepared at the beginning. All three notions, then, permitted economic re-

construction and advance. NATO was not allowed to undermine the Marshall Plan.

Only after 1948 was it possible to begin eliminating rem-
nant strategic uncertainties. In 1949 and the first half of 1950,
it was believed that war could be avoided through a new
policy of "deterrence," a conception quite different from that
of "defense." Further, there were now ideas of what forces
and doctrines had to be applied to make deterrence effective.
Moreover, 1949 was the first year of distinctively Atlantic
strategy. President Truman was not allowed to give military
aid to Europe until a "strategic concept" for NATO had
been laid down. For the first time in the postwar period, then,
British strategy became allied strategy. From that time on
military planning could not take place in isolation.

And 1949 was a critical year in other respects. August gave
the first evidence of Russian nuclear capability. Russia had
done in four years what some experts predicted would take
twenty-five.[1] Though the significance of the Soviet detonation was not fully appreciated at the time, its impact upon
European strategy was fundamental. Prospectively, at least,
the Soviet bomb and supporting capability precluded another
sea-borne invasion of the European continent. "Overlord"
could not be successful against an air and ground atomic defense. If a ground strategy in the West were to be decisive, it
had to stop the Russians at or near the onset of war. There was
no longer time for a massive Anglo-American mobilization
after war had begun; the delays which attended the opening
of World Wars I and II could no longer be tolerated. Two
alternatives were permitted: either Western nations had to
deter a war before it started, or they had to achieve virtual

[1] The official estimate by then was a Russian atomic explosion in
1952.

war footing to be able to fight it. In either case strategy had to be revamped. In 1949 the decision was to "deter" a war which had not yet become inevitable.

In several respects the first part of 1949 marked an easing of cold war tensions. The Berlin blockade was halted, and the North Atlantic Treaty signed without provoking a new confrontation. There was measurable growth in the cohesion and resolve of Western nations. The latter part of the year, however, bore witness to the first major setbacks since mid-1948. By July, it was a foredestined conclusion that a Communist regime would rule mainland China. In September, President Truman announced the Soviet nuclear detonation to the world, and the Russians moved rapidly to tighten their control of satellite armies. This succession of events made a firm and coherent NATO position all the more important. With the U.S. Congress watching over military aid appropriations, moreover, an agreed "strategic concept" became the *sine qua non* of legislative approval. Deterrence won rapid acceptance as the major military doctrine. Foreign Secretary Bevin put it this way: "I would emphasize . . . that the real purpose of this pact is to act as a deterrent. . . . The situation which we had in 1914 and 1939 and particularly 1940 and 1941, when we had to hold the fort waiting and wondering when other nations would realize the gravity of the aggressive menace, while at the same time we were using up and exhausting our resources—that situation should not be allowed to occur again." [2]

The question remained, however, what degree of strength the Western nations would have to manifest to "deter" the Russians. At the time the ratio of immediately available Rus-

[2] *House of Commons Debates*, Vol. 464 (May 12, 1949), col. 2016.

sian to allied divisions on the central front was approximately 100 to 12. The Brussels planners, together with American advisers, had come up with a long-term requirements plan which allotted 80 to 85 divisions to the central front and stipulated 100 divisions in all.[3]

Such totals were utterly beyond Western efforts; to many they were also beyond Western requirements in late 1949 and early 1950. Deterrence, in other words, was not equal to defense. The Soviets might hesitate to attack even if Western forces in being and in reserve were not sufficient to defeat a ground invasion of Europe. U.S. Secretary of State Dean Acheson provided the necessary rationale: "We do not believe that to discourage military aggression it is necessary to create Western European defense forces which are by virtue of their size capable of successfully resisting an all-out attack. What is required is, rather, sufficient strength to make it impossible for an aggressor to achieve a quick and easy victory."[4]

In the short run at least, this meant military aid to European forces, not an increase in U.S. armed strength. General Omar Bradley testified that the $13 billion budget was adequate and made no mention of the Soviet bomb.[5] After discussions with his Western Union defense partners, Bradley also outlined the strategy and apportionment of roles for a future European war:

[3] See Roger Hilsman, "NATO: The Developing Strategic Context," in Klaus Knorr, ed., *NATO and American Security* (Princeton, N.J., 1959), p. 16.

[4] *U.S. Department of State Bulletin*, Vol. 21 (August 8, 1949), p. 193.

[5] See Paul Y. Hammond, "NSC-68: Prologue to Rearmament," in Warner R. Schilling, Paul Y. Hammond, and Glenn H. Snyder, *Strategy, Politics, and Defense Budgets* (New York, 1962), p. 304.

First, the United States will be charged with the strategic bombing. We have repeatedly recognized in this country that the first priority of the joint defense is our ability to deliver the atomic bomb.

Second, the United States Navy and the Western naval powers will conduct essential naval operations, including keeping the sea lanes clear. The Western Union and other nations will maintain their own harbor and coastal defense.

Third, we recognize that the hard core of the ground power in being will come from Europe, aided by other nations as they can mobilize.

Fourth, England, France, and the closer countries will have the bulk of the short-range attack bombardment and air defense. We, of course, will maintain the tactical air force for our own ground and naval forces, and United States defense.

Fifth, other nations, depending upon their proximity or remoteness from the possible scene of conflict, will emphasize appropriate specific missions.[6]

Two points about these plans should be underscored. The first is that the strategy outlined could not win a European war in the near future. The U.S. bombing offensive against the Soviet Union would not be decisive, leaving a substantial disparity to be made up by ground troops. But British and continental ground forces, even with U.S. military aid, could not make a "forward defense" in Europe; they were incapable even of holding the Rhine. In the longer run such plans had greater relevance, but as Bradley himself pointed out: "It may take five years, ten years, for these countries to build up their defenses to the point where they can stop an aggressor."[7]

[6] House of Representatives, Committee on Foreign Affairs, *Hearings, Mutual Defense Assistance Act of 1949,* 81st Cong., 1st Sess., p. 71.

[7] Senate, Committees on Foreign Relations and Armed Services, *Hearings, Military Assistance Program of 1949,* 81st Cong., 1st Sess., p. 108.

Since no such European force buildup was foreshadowed or in train, even the longer term prospects were far from luminous. Irrespective of time-scale, deterrence did not equal defense.

Acheson's deterrent formula then was based on the minimum assumption that the Russians did not intend to wage war in the near future. Deterrents would be linked to presumed Soviet motivations for attack. Modest incentives might be overborne by modest defenses. Only if the Soviets became more overtly expansionist or if their strength increased would it be necessary to raise additional bulwarks against aggression.

These deterrent notions are well worth noting, if only because they vary so greatly from later conceptions. There had always been a classical notion of deterrence in which deterrence and defense were synonymous: a nation would not launch a military onslaught unless it believed it was likely to win. In more recent years, reliable defenses have been harder to come by, and more emphasis has been placed on other means of dissuading offenses. Full-blown doctrines of deterrence have offered strategic retaliation in response to attack. Though an enemy's blows could not be parried, they might be returned with great force upon his homeland. His external gains would be canceled by internal losses. Acheson's formulas, however, fell into neither category. A state would be deterred from attacking if the costs of attack were merely increased; a state would be deterred even if his aggression could not be defeated or his homeland devastated.

Both classical defense and contemporary deterrence assumed that defensive and offensive power were roughly commensurate with the power of aggression. In one case an equivalent blow was delivered to an enemy's forces; in the other an appropriate retaliation was levied on his population. The punishment fitted the crime. Acheson's notions, however, implied disproportion between attack and defense. Defense merely raised the ante, it did not offer an equal riposte. Deterrence was defense on the cheap.

Another difference between conceptions was marked by the distinction between capability and intention. Classical defense and contemporary deterrence were rejoinders to an opponent's physical capability; they would blunt or reply to forces in being. Acheson's deterrence applied much more to enemy intent. One did not have to have ready the forces actually to defeat or destroy an opponent; one merely had to have forces large enough to counterbalance his presumed aggressive intentions at any point in time. If his bellocosity increased, deterrents would have to be raised proportionately.

Into this climate of strategic opinion the Russian bomb intruded. At first it seemed that the Soviet acquisition made little difference, and the strategic concepts of January, 1950, were little different from those of six months earlier. U.S. General J. Lawton Collins even argued that the Russians might not have achieved a device capable of "autonomous explosion." [8] Parliamentary and governmental opinion did not immediately adjust to the altered strategic environment.[9] At length, however, military and diplomatic planners began to assess the impact upon European security.

In the United States, a joint Defense–State study group formulated NSC-68, a document which assessed the longer range significance of Soviet atomic capability and its implica-

[8] *Le Monde*, June 7, 1950.
[9] R. E. Osgood, *NATO: The Entangling Alliance* (Chicago, 1962), p. 53.

tions for American military planning. It "estimated that within four years the Soviet Union would have enough atomic bombs and a sufficient capability of delivering them to offset substantially the deterrent capability of American nuclear weapons. In comparison it emphasized the inadequacy of the Western capability to meet limited military challenges due to a lack of conventional forces, shortcomings in the Western alliance system, and the military and economic weaknesses of western Europe." [10]

The practical conclusions of NSC-68 supported higher U.S. defense spending, though precise increases were apparently not spelled out. At the London meeting of NATO foreign ministers in May, 1950, Secretary Acheson put the argument to his alliance colleagues in terms he was to use constantly thereafter: "We have a substantial lead in air power and in atomic weapons. At the present moment, this may be the most powerful deterrent against aggression. But with the passage of time, even though we continue our advances in this field, the value of our lead diminishes. In other words, the best use we can make of our present advantage in retaliatory air power is to move ahead under this protective shield to build the balanced collective forces in Western Europe that will continue to deter aggression after our atomic advantage has been diminished." [11] Since only four years were available before the Soviets would have a major atomic capability, other deficiencies in NATO armed strength had to be made up in short order.

[10] Hammond, p. 306.

[11] Senate, Joint Committee on Foreign Relations and Armed Services, *Hearings Assignment of Ground Forces of the United States to Duty in the European Area*, 82d Cong., 1st Sess., p. 79, See also Joseph Alsop in the New York *Herald Tribune*, June 5, 1950.

The argument underlying such formulations was noteworthy. *Prima facie*, it seemed to rest on relative rather than absolute calculations. Deterrence would be procured not by achieving a capability to do a certain *absolute* level of damage to the Soviet Union; it would be found only in terms of a *relative* balance between forces. Deterrents had to exist across the board; if the Soviets had countered Western advantages in strategic striking power, then the West had to counter Soviet advantages in ground forces. Nuclear power provided a deterrent only so long as the Soviets were deficient in that respect.

Hypotheses explaining such views are several, and not wholly consistent. In the first place, it may have been believed that Western strategic power, though much larger than Soviet capabilities in the next few years, was inadequate in absolute terms. Though the Strategic Air Command could deliver telling blows on the Soviet homeland, it might not, of itself, win the war.[12] Even if war potentials and stockpiles in the Soviet Union were destroyed, the Soviet army might move across Europe, effectively trading support from the Russian economy for support from the Western European economy. The exchange might conceivably be worth the consequences risked.

The point, of course, was moot. One might have argued in rejoinder that if the Russian economy were truly destroyed, the movement of Soviet armies westward would merely be to jump from the frying pan to the fire. The impact upon European Russia might be so destructive as to question the utility of such a dangerous thrust. But even if Western nuclear power might not be great enough in 1950–51 to

[12] See the statement by General Hoyt S. Vandenberg, quoted in the New York *Times*, December 15, 1950.

levy "unacceptable damage" on the Russian target system, the future envisaged by NSC-68 was 1954. By that time, surely, the absolute damage created by an American nuclear strike would be large enough to give the Russians pause. Regardless of Soviet capabilities at that future time, the Strategic Air Command would be able to "destroy" the Soviet Union.

Another interpretation was that as Soviet nuclear strength grew, the dangers of an atomic strategy for the West increased in direct proportion, forcing it back upon a conventional response. Walter Lippmann put it like this:

> Suppose American atomic weapons are 100 and Russian are 25. Then a purely atomic war is unlikely. For while the Russians can do fearful damage with their 25, they will suffer more damage from our 100. On the other hand, we cannot consider a preventative strike because the retaliatory force of the Soviet's would be so fearful. But in fact there are also the conventional forces where the ratio of power in Russia's favor is about as 100 is to Europe's 15. If this disparity persists, then when Russia has the atomic weapons to knock out Western Europe, it can invade Western Europe with its armies. For we shall be deterred from striking with atomic bombs at the Russian cities because of the helplessness of London, Paris, Brussels, and Frankfurt in the face of Russian bombs. This I believe is the bare bones of the argument as to why the rapid increase of the defensive power in Western Europe is so important.[13]

This theory suggested that the United States and its North Atlantic allies would be willing to fight a purely conventional war for the defense of Europe. If the Soviets would be deterred from using their bomb stockpiles in a new war, so would the Americans. And indeed, some influential British planners were projecting just such a conflict.[14] The question

[13] New York *Herald Tribune*, August 15, 1950.
[14] See Maj. Gen. Sir Ian Jacob, "The United Kingdom's Strategic Interests," in Royal Institute of International Affairs, *United Kingdom*

seemed to be what the West would do if the Russians attacked in purely conventional terms. Would she escalate and bring upon European populations the deadly hail of Russian bombs?

A further theory was that two tasks were involved in charting military strategy in Europe: the first required reliable deterrence of Soviet attack; the second, presuming the efficacy of the first, required political reassurance of sensitive European populations. Even if the Russians were quite credibly deterred by the threat of retaliatory strategic bombing, the Western commitment in Europe had to be made visible for Europeans as well as Soviets to see. The greater the conventional presence of U.S., British, and other Western forces on the continent, the greater the confidence of European populations. In this sense reassurance of Europe might be a larger task than deterrence of the Soviet Union. There was finally the argument that stemmed from different tactical tasks and command responsibilities. Western Union and later NATO commanders wished to be able to deal effectively with challenges from corresponding Soviet arms. Armies agitate for the wherewithal to defeat armies; navies, navies; and air forces, air forces. Uncountered advantages in any sphere call for redressment. As the Western Union and NATO organizational structure took shape, then, it was natural to ask for additional conventional forces.

The revelation of Russian atomic potential in August, 1949, did not produce immediate strategic agreement. Tactical steps were more clearly articulated than the doctrines to justify them. Increased ground strength might be espoused from a variety of points of view. If Western planners were thinking exclusively of a Soviet menace which would emerge in 1954, they did not have to worry about deterrence in the interim. But of course the Russian capability betokened intentions as well as physical force. If Soviet forces would reach a maximum in 1954, Soviet intentions remained unclear. After the series of political setbacks to Western interests at the end of 1949, it was unsure how long the Communists would stay their hand. A war in the shorter term would catch the West unready in two senses: first, U.S. and later British strategic bombing capability might still be insufficient to decide a conflict; second, Western conventional forces were sadly lacking. In this sense, the defense furor in the spring of 1950 can be understood as a response to a heightened and more immediate danger of war.

The most persuasive explanation of the shift in strategic and tactical requirements in response to Russian nuclear strength is that given by the need to bolster deterrence. In late 1949 and early 1950 deterrence had been equivalent to preventing the enemy from winning "a quick and easy victory." This was scarcely sufficient to dissuade a Russian attack based upon calculation of probable gains and losses. In the period immediately before Korea, the Soviets could have marched to Bordeaux in a fortnight; U.S. strategic bombing would not have knocked Russia out of the war. Aside from deficiencies in bomber strength, the U.S. atomic stockpile contained only about 100 bombs.[15] In London in May, 1950, Secretary Acheson had argued that as the Soviet capability grew, Moscow might be tempted to believe that the United States would not respond atomically to a Soviet ground attack

[15] Statement by General Noel F. Parrish, University of Colorado *Conference on World Affairs* (Boulder, Colorado), April 13, 1961.

because of the damage to European populations that a Russian nuclear counterstrike would cause. Actually, the United States would not exercise such restraint. If war occurred, America would use the nuclear weapons in its arsenal to destroy the Soviet heartland. If Russian retaliation then took place upon European cities, it would be deplorable and destructive, but it would not add decisively to the already difficult European predicament. If war broke out, whatever happened and whatever weapons were used, Europe would be very badly off. What the West should do was to concentrate on preventing war. This required a strategy which would not only mete out devastation in fact, but deliver a credible riposte in theory. One had to be sure that the Soviets were not counting on American atomic restraint to reap the benefits of their ground superiority. The ground strategy outlined in May was designed to make deterrence credible to the Soviet Union and to Western nations as well.

However necessary such doctrines may have seemed at the time, they were clearly an expensive means of deterring the Russians. Implicitly the West was asked to develop "balanced deterrence," offsetting each Soviet military option in its own terms. If a substantial disequilibrium existed in any particular balance of forces, the Russians might be tempted to exploit it, relying upon Western hesitancy to bring radically different weapons to bear. Local imbalances in one range of weapons required local equilibration. Short of this, deterrence might not be maintained. These arguments were accepted despite the fact the West was not planning to confine its response to the tactics and forces used in the initial aggression. Strategic power would in fact be employed in response to a Soviet ground invasion. If, at the time at which the Soviet threat seemed most dangerous (1954) an attack occurred, it would call down a powerful and even decisive nuclear retaliation upon the Soviet homeland. The ground force buildup, foreshadowed in NSC-68 and in Acheson's presentation before the NATO foreign ministers, was therefore basically expenditure on behalf of credibility. By 1954 and without such a buildup, adequate deterrent nuclear capabilities would be in hand. Given NATO's intention to employ strategic forces in a major conflict, one is tempted to ponder whether other less expensive means might have been found of convincing the Soviets that the West was serious.

British strategy in 1949 and early 1950 reflected assumptions that were shared by many other NATO members. The White Papers of both years were predicated upon a crisis some years away. Both stressed expenditure upon production and research; both further reduced the number of men under arms. In accordance with the agreed NATO strategic concept, Britain used her production capacities to furnish jet fighter aircraft to European allies, and enhanced her own fighter-interceptor strength. The doubling of the jet fighter strength of Fighter Command was completed, and the new jet fighter-bomber, the Canberra, made its first flight in 1950. The defense crisis, briefly underscored by increased service demands at the end of 1948, was met in 1949 and 1950 by increased production, particularly for the Air Force and Navy. Full and necessary reequipment for the Army was postponed until new monies were available. It was, in retrospect, a striking feature of these years that a European crisis seemed remote. The most pressing cold war needs, in Malaya and Hongkong, were occupying greater attention, and the Army was deployed and structured to take care of them. Though the Russian atomic bomb occasioned a review of British defense thinking, it did not lead to plans for a near-term conflict. Government spokesmen continually stressed that Britain was planning military production and available reserves for readiness at some future time.[16]

These deductions were understandable, at least initially. The Berlin blockade ended in 1949, and the United States pledged its fortunes to European defense. Overall, the deterrents against an attack seemed to have grown relative to Russian expansionism. Even the Soviet bomb was not direct testimony to a desire for war with the West. The United States did not take the threat seriously enough to increase its arms budget, and at the same time Britain was facing major crises overseas. There was a real question whether Malaya could be held and whether it was desirable to reinforce Hongkong against the possibility of an aggressive move by China. These questions, as well as those posed by European defense, were made more critical by virtue of international pressure on the pound sterling. Outside members of the sterling area were running up a sizable deficit on current account, and the United States, reclining into the 1949 recession, was building up a formidable surplus. In the afterglow of the improved export position in late 1948, the Treasury had allowed a larger import bill. These trends had themselves produced speculative capital flows from the pound into dollars, and the pressure for devaluation by the end of August was virtually irresistible. Even an improvement on current account would not have offset the speculation then in train.

At some point after the war it was no doubt desirable to devalue the pound with other European currencies; the at-

[16] At the end of 1948 when compulsory service was increased to eighteen months, the reserve obligation was reduced to four years.

tractiveness of dollar holdings and the price of American exports both militated in favor of such a decision. But the delay in action and the loss of reserves which preceded devaluation cost Britain heavily. Austerity was the more necessary if reserves were to be regained and exports set upon a proper footing. Once again defense expenditure had to be cut.[17] Government retrenchment, a postponement of investment, and continued curtailment in private consumption seemed the only possible remedies. Eventually, of course, these turned the trick; a favorable balance of payments, new reserves, and a steady 4 percent growth rate had been achieved by the end of 1950. Marshall aid could be terminated.

In the interval, however, the £100 million cut in government spending had to be found mainly in the defense sector, and this necessity meant some hard choices. There was first the question whether Hongkong should continue to be garrisoned. Under pressure from Sir Stafford Cripps, it was almost abandoned in April, 1949. Its defense required the equivalent of an infantry division, over and above the Gurkha division, and large supporting British forces in Malaya. A decision was made in June, however, to maintain the British presence in both Hongkong and Malaya; the results of this course had an important impact on British strength in other areas.

At the end of the war, Britain had begun negotiations with Egypt hoping to scale down its presence in the Middle East. In those days the magic word on Bevin's lips had been "Mombasa," a conceivable East African alternative to the Suez Canal base. Because of disagreement over the future of the Sudan, these negotiations had come to naught. As late as

[17] See J. C. R. Dow, *The Management of the British Economy, 1945–60* (Cambridge, 1965), p. 46.

May, 1948, however, the British government had thought in terms of abandoning a direct defense of the Mediterranean and concentrating forces in Kenya.[18] The new conception was justified on grounds that the canal would quickly be closed in the opening stages of a new war. Forces dependent on its use would not be able to defend the Middle East or the Persian Gulf. In its fullness the new notion involved a major port, airfield, and barracks at Mombasa, and a major stores depot, 70 miles inland at MacKinnon Road.

By the beginning of 1949, however, the "Mombasa" option had been abandoned. New and expensive facilities and barracks would have to be constructed; in any event, East Africa was far distant from the areas most likely to need assistance in a major war. The greater the danger of a Russian thrust over the Middle East land bridge, the more dangerous would be British withdrawal to a second line of defense. The British position there was all the more important in that the United States was not itself planning for a major ground campaign in the Middle East. Until mid-1949, MacKinnon Road was retained as a desirable site for a major alternative base for stores. Then the Hongkong reinforcement, the extensive fortifications, and deployments to withstand a Chinese assault began to drain technical troops away from East Africa. By September construction at MacKinnon Road had all but come to a halt, and a year later the government decided to close the base. Because of Far Eastern commitments, Britain had decided to keep most of its Middle Eastern eggs in the Egyptian basket. In December, 1950, Defence Minister Shinwell told Cairo that the question of a British withdrawal of troops had "not been posed."

The Far Eastern buildup in Malaya and Hongkong also

[18] Sydney *Morning Herald*, January 13, 1949.

affected European defense posture in the event of war. As the Minister for Defence later admitted:

> I will not conceal from the House that the Forces at present available, or in sight, fall a long way short of requirements estimated even on the most conservative basis.
>
> It is not only a question of deciding on the most effective balance between men and equipment in relation to a future conflict some years hence; we have to meet present needs and these impose a special burden on the Army. This was the basis on which our inter-Service planning proceeded when we allocated the resources which early this year (1950) we decided to devote to defence. We gave the highest priority to research and development in all arms, while the Navy and the Air Force were instructed to start on a planned programme of re-equipment and the Army had to concentrate on the cold war at the price of some sacrifice in making itself ready for any future war. . . .
>
> It was the original conception that in time of peace we should be able to meet our responsibilities overseas, apart from the B.A.O.R., with Regular Forces and that behind these we should, as the years went on, build up substantial trained reserves which could be quickly mobilised in time of war. That concept, I admit, has been falsified: first of all, because the numbers of men needed overseas have been higher than we calculated, and second, because the Regular content of the forces has dropped to a much lower level than we expected.[19]

Since regular forces were insufficient to control the Far Eastern crisis, national servicemen had to be employed as well. But as a result of the eighteen-month service period, conscripts had largely to be trained on the spot. This meant that they were receiving most of their training in counter-

[19] *House of Commons Debates*, Vol. 478 (July 26, 1950), cols. 472 and 474.

insurgency operations, not infantry-armored combat as it would take place in Europe. Their Regular Army instructors, pinned down in the Far East, could scarcely make an early contribution to a conflict in the West. Given the decline in recruiting the Regular Army was expected to drop from 184,000 in early 1950 to 150,000 in 1952. Britain's two understrength divisions in Europe could only be bolstered by four divisional equivalents from other areas. In the Far East, of course, the British Army was organized differently from its counterparts in Europe and at home. In the Middle and Far East, Britain disposed "task forces" appropriate to a specific purpose; in Europe and in the home islands she was readying a modern field force with all that that entailed. The unavoidable conclusion was that Whitehall was far more worried by cold war conflicts overseas than by the threat of a war in Europe. All her preparations pointed to readiness in 1954 or afterward. Since the Soviets were not disposed to attack in any event, deterrents did not need to be specially enhanced.

These deductions were not greatly different from those of other Western nations. The United States was disturbed by the success of the Soviet bomb, but until after Korea was not prepared to make substantial increases in her own forces to meet the augumented threat. Acheson's strictures at the London NATO meetings in May were more theoretical than practical. At the Hague in April, 1950, it had been agreed "that responsibility in the early stages of a war would rest primarily with France for the provision of land forces; with the Western Union and American navies for the security of the sea communications; with Great Britain and France for tactical air forces and air defense; and with America for strategic bombing, as the atom and hydrogen bombs were regarded as the main war-winning weapons." [20]

These notions took little if any account of the impact of the Soviet bomb. Further, they stressed that Britain did not have to make extraordinary provision for an additional ground commitment in Europe. The Soviets would be deterred by the atomic weapon and its successor, the thermonuclear bomb. While the value of the Western lead in nuclear weapons might have diminished, the Hague meetings hardly stressed a conventional alternative. Nor was potential Soviet atomic interdiction of a Western air–sea invasion of Europe understood. It still seemed possible to withdraw, retrench, and then effect another "liberation" of Western Europe. Much of the training of Territorial Army units would take place after a declaration of war, and therefore after initial reverses. As one brigadier put it: "Our peace-time army is maintained only at strength and state of readiness sufficient to meet our initial commitments and, in conjunction with the other services of our Allies, take the first shock in a major conflict. For the ultimate requirements we rely on completing our training and expansion after the declaration of war, and our peace-time plans and organisation cater for this." [21]

Just as army strategy required only partial readiness, other arms were also not preparing for an early conflict. The emphasis upon Air Force and Navy construction meant that the Army had to "sacrifice in making itself ready for any

[20] Air Vice Marshal W. M. Yool, "The Structure of Defence," in *Brassey's Annual, 1951* (edited by Rear Admiral H. G. Thursfield), p. 5.

[21] C. N. Barclay, "Historical Background, General Policy and Tasks of the Army," in *Brassey's Annual, 1950* (edited by Rear Admiral H. G. Thursfield), p. 143.

future war." In accordance with Western Union and NATO plans, Britain continued to concentrate on fighter defense and on the introduction of a fighter-bomber. The Navy was modernizing its carriers and working on a new class of destroyers. In neither case was the objective readiness for an early war. Both services were planning to deal with Russian sea and air challenges at some future time; neither offered a war-winning capability against a formidable ground opponent. Fighter and fighter-bomber defenses would blunt enemy attacks on the home islands, attacks, which despite the nascent Soviet bomb capability, were not expected to be fatal. The Canberra, in prospect for later 1950, would also be useful against rocket bases which the Soviets might set up as they moved West, but again the contingency rested on a successful Russian advance. Such an event was not anticipated for several more years. In general the British concentrated upon long lead-time items, leaving the Army to make do as best it could. As the year of preparedness approached, there would be time enough to get the Army into shape.

Such emphases were most clearly underscored by British acquisition of seventy U.S. B-29s as part of the U.S. Mutual Defense Assistance Program. The function that these heavy strategic bombers would perform related to a future several years off. Until later 1952 and even after, there would be few if any British atomic bombs to fill their bomb-bays. Even after the Monte Bello test in October, U.K. atomic bombs were in short supply for several years.

The B-29s were also unrelated to the possible need for British planes to carry U.S. bombs. American production was not large at this stage, and there was no shortage of aircraft to deliver the bombs. And even if U.S. bombs had been available in great quantities, British pilots in U.S. planes did not enhance delivery capabilities; for this purpose, British aircraft would be needed.

Even more interestingly, the B-29s were not related to any NATO doctrine or requirement. In its various versions, NATO strategy had stated that "the United States will be charged with the strategic bombing." While such phrasing was probably not intended to preclude British strategic capacity, it certainly did not mandate that capacity as a near-term requirement. British acquisition of B-29s under MDAP, then, is probably largely to be explained by British needs for the period 1952–54 when U.K. bombs would begin to be available.

Bomber Command had, of course, been agitating for a major reequipment of the wartime force since 1946. And while progress was being made with V-bomber research and development, no procurement of a heavy bomber had been ordered. Fighter Command had effectively absorbed the R.A.F. production budget. Even before he became Chief of the Air Staff in January, 1950, Air Chief Marshal Sir John Slessor had argued for a modern British bomber force, fitted to distinctively British needs. A "pressing requirement may be for action against enemy submarines in harbour and in production," he contended. "Are we going to leave all that to the Americans, who, with the best will in the world . . . cannot be expected to take the same view of the anti-submarine war as we are bound to do, and would have a host of other commitments and priorities for the Bomber Force?" For future defense against rockets, Britain could not simply say to the United States: "Of course we shall rely on you entirely to defend England against V2 attack—the fighter bomber is not much use for this sort of thing and you'll have to find the heavies needed for the job." Unless Britain had a bomber striking force of its own, it would have no voice in the direction of an allied bomber offensive, "of which the effects might be of such literally vital concern to us as a nation." [22]

The B-29 or the "Washington," as it came to be known, was really the first installment on the reequipment of Bomber Command. It helped compensate for the cancellation of the S.A. 4 (an interim jet bomber) and for the production delays in the Valiant, and later the Victor and Vulcan. The financial limitations imposed by the government might partially be made up from abroad.

Aside from performance of future tasks, conventional bombers might be used in a tactical role to interdict enemy supply and communications; they would also be useful against enemy bomber bases. As longer range rockets were developed fighter bombers would yield place to the "heavies" in retaliatory raids upon opponent launching sites. In this sense bombers had a role to play in a near-term conflict. If war broke out next week, the British B-29s might be employed effectively. At the same time, the transfer of "Washingtons" from America to Britain did not add to Western strength in the short run; it did so only as British atomic production commenced. Consummation of the deal in March, 1950, was further evidence that Britain did not expect a war in the next few years.

The British atomic program also concentrated on long lead-time items. In February, 1949, and at the urging of the Chiefs of Staff, the government removed the budgetary ceiling on expenditure on the low-separation gaseous diffusion plant to be built at Capenhurst. Production from the low-separation plant permitted the building of enriched uranium reactors,

[22] *Sunday Times,* May 22, 1949.

and it also gave British scientists experience with U-235 which would be useful for alternative bomb designs. It was well understood, however, that the construction and operating costs of Capenhurst would increase as a greater purification of U-235 was achieved. The British asked themselves whether it was worth building a high-separation plant on their own or whether they could benefit from cooperation with the United States.

Thus began a series of remarkable negotiations in July, 1949; if they had succeeded, there might have been no British "independent deterrent" and no distinct British nuclear program. A real pooling of the two nuclear efforts might have been achieved. At this time the United Kingdom had already completed the first two production piles at Windscale, and begun the low enrichment cascades at Capenhurst. Britain did not propose to dismantle any of its completed facilities, but it did hope that additional expenditures might be avoided.

Between July and December, 1949, the British made the following proposals to Washington: Britain would give up the third reactor at Windscale and not construct a high-separation plant. She would send British scientists to Oak Ridge and U.S. gaseous diffusion facilities to work with the United States on production of weapons-quality U-235, thus gaining continuing access to U.S. technology in the field. Plutonium production from the two Windscale piles would be sent to the United States where it would be shaped into requisite sizes and put into the bomb envelope. A stock of completed bombs would then be sent to the United Kingdom under British custody and control, to be used, however, "in accordance with joint strategic plans."

London also asked that pure U-235 be sent to Britain where it might fuel enriched reactors and afford British scientists experience with the metal and its properties. In return, the British agreed not to produce atomic bombs at home.[23] They would continue research "into the possibility of developing new atomic weapons," but would keep the United States fully informed and not proceed to national production. The United States would agree to a full exchange of atomic weapons information. A written agreement to this effect would be negotiated for three years.

By the end of December, 1949, British and U.S. officials had all but reached agreement on the terms outlined. Some members of the British government were hesitant to put British atomic fates into the hands of the United States, particularly since Windscale would shortly produce its first quantities of plutonium. They were generally overborne, however, by considerations of time and efficacy. A single weapons project would make more and better bombs in less time, a factor of no little importance after the Soviet atomic explosion. Some members of the U.S. military did not like the idea of bombs in Britain where they would be closer to Russia; others contended that for tactical use bombs had to be nearer the theater of operations than the United States or Canada. On the American side, the British plan was supported by Secretary Acheson, Atomic Energy Commission Chairman David Lilienthal, and George Kennan, and received backing from President Truman.

When the subject was broached to influential members of the Joint Congressional Committee on Atomic Energy, however, a storm of criticism broke loose. Senators Hickenlooper and Vandenberg insisted that the proposal was tantamount to giving Britain the bomb. Despite repeated attempts by American officials to make clear that the British knew the essential

[23] See James Reston, New York *Times*, January 4, 1950.

secrets and that their own nuclear program would soon reach national fruition, the opposition did not dissipate. President Truman reluctantly concluded that to press the case might endanger the apparatus of NATO cooperation, and in January, 1950, when Klaus Fuchs was arrested, ensuing doubts about British security finally dissolved all prospects of a significant sharing of information or hardware. Not long afterward, Britain went ahead with her own national plans. The plutonium fabrication plant was built at Aldermaston between April, 1950, and March, 1951. By the latter date the high-separation diffusion plant was in train at Capenhurst. The first Windscale pile went divergent in July, 1950, and shortly afterward the British inquired whether they might use American nuclear testing facilities between July and October, 1952. The United States refused, largely on grounds of security and the prohibitions of the McMahon Act, but stated its willingness to consider new forms of cooperation. After further probing of intentions, the British concluded that the United States was not ready for additional cooperative arrangements and approached Australia. Agreement on the Monte Bello test site was reached in 1951. The first British bomb was a plutonium implosion device. In 1953 an extension of the Capenhurst gaseous diffusion facilities was ordered, and by 1954 the first production of U-235 commenced for a second generation of weapons and for the British hydrogen bomb.

At this remove it is difficult to speculate on what would have happened if the United States had accepted the British offer of December, 1949. At minimum the British bomb would have been available earlier, the costs of the high-separation and fabrication plants saved, and a full information exchange obtained. Britain would not have become a full-scale nuclear power in the sense of national possession of a complete range of production facilities, but she would have had a stock of bombs under her own control, and would have participated fully in the American nuclear (and presumably thermonuclear) effort. The U.S. program would have been a joint program. The strategic plans of both Britain and America would have been even more fully integrated, and the arguments, like those of Slessor's, for distinctively British priorities in strategic bombing would have been reflected in joint targeting arrangements. In respect of production and strategic planning there would have been no spread of nuclear weapons. And while Britain would have had a stock of bombs under her own control, these weapons were to be used "in accordance with joint strategic plans."

The international consequences of such an agreement would probably have been less significant. It was inconceivable that the United States would extend nuclear sharing rights to one allied country after another. And even if France had been admitted (itself a dubious assumption), this would simply have spurred others to national efforts. Wherever the sharing line were drawn, there would be those excluded with powerful incentives for national acquisition. Only a universal sharing scheme would have obviated these demands, and that was unthinkable. Even if the British plan had been accepted, it would have remained a monument to the Anglo-American alliance, incapable of erection elsewhere.

Despite the failure of the atomic negotiations in January, 1950, the British did not decide to withhold cooperation on ore supplies. The *modus vivendi*, negotiated in January, 1948, was to last only until the end of 1949; at that point an approximately 50–50 division of available ore would be resumed. In a temporary agreement at the end of 1949, however, the United Kingdom once again conceded to American requirements. Later, in the mid-1950s, when South African ores became available, Britain acquiesced in a shift in the basis of division from roughly 50–50 to 80–20 in favor of the United States. Again London refrained from using its powerful negotiating position to bring U.S. agreement on an information exchange. Particularly after the Soviet bomb explosion the British did not want to be responsible for weakening the basic nuclear deterrent of the West. It was also true that Britain had all the ore she needed for her own, smaller program. A balanced assessment, however, would still have to stress that London yielded with remarkably good grace to ill-founded arguments current in the U.S. Congress. In retrospect, it is difficult to understand her forbearance.

The year 1949 and the first half of 1950 witnessed a further emphasis upon war to be waged only several years hence. The Army was neglected overall, and its specific commitments were more and more defined in cold war terms: Malaya, Hongkong, and the Middle East. The stress upon naval and even more clearly upon air forces was also to reinforce deterrents against a future conflict. This did not mean that the R.A.F. and the Royal Navy would not have an important role in a near term outbreak. Bomber Command, as Sir John Slessor pointed out, would "have to be employed to a far greater extent than in 1944 on more direct and intimate support for the armies." [24] Navy destroyers and fast frigates would undertake to deal with Soviet submarines. But the Defence Estimates of 1949–50 and 1950–51 (pre-Korea)

[24] "Air Power in War," Address to Allied General Officers of Western Union, March, 1950, in Sir John Slessor, *The Great Deterrent* (London, 1957), p. 111.

did not permit a major rearmament. They called for expenditures of £759 million and £780 million respectively. Both involved increased expenditure on production and research at the cost of a smaller number of men under arms. Both provided essentially for "a long-term national defense plan" in which British preparations could be limited because of support rendered by allies. While the 1949 Estimates allowed a sizable increase over the year before, those in 1950 were bound to reflect the further retrenchment necessitated by devaluation in September, 1949.

In early 1950 Britain returned to habits of yesteryear; the defense budget should be calculated in terms of financial abilities, not international threats. Technically, the worsening international atmosphere of late 1949 could well have led to a substantial increase in defense spending. The communization of China, the Soviet atomic bomb, and a succession of cold war crises—each of these might have brought about an upward revision of defense allocations. Yet short months before the Korean crisis it was estimated that the Regular Army could be allowed to fall to 150,000 in 1952. British defense policy did little to anticipate peaks in international tension; in this respect, however, it was hardly inferior to planning in Washington. Secretary of Defense Louis Johnson was embarked on a rigorous economy drive at the time of the attack on South Korea. America could scarcely have been more poorly prepared for that war and for its ultimate consequences.

CHAPTER FIVE

DEFENSE, EUROPE, AND THE
UNITED STATES, 1950–1951

ALL BRITISH AND NATO strategy was reshaped as a result of the North Korean attack on South Korea, June 25, 1950. This was not simply because a new military doctrine was called for, but because its possible application might now be much nearer. Even the most pessimistic American planners had not believed the "year of maximum danger" would come before 1954. After Korea, a possible Soviet attack was expected as early as 1952. Equally important, the attack on Korea had undermined confidence in Western deterrent strategies. In face of American (and later British) possession of the bomb and the ability to deliver it, the Soviets would not risk an attack. The very prospect of sustaining major damage in a new war would make the Russians hesitate.

But Korea cast doubt on all this. It was not merely that aggression had taken place despite Western atomic superiority; the war was also carried on without use of nuclear bombs. If the United States could be persuaded to reply in conventional terms to Communist onslaughts, it was not impossible that the Soviets would try a conventional invasion of Western

Europe. The Korean attack, moreover, could even be viewed as prelude and preparation for the later assault. With large numbers of American troops pinned down in the Far Eastern "quagmire," Europe was all the more vulnerable. Korea might be the necessary diversion for an attack on Europe. Very little attention seems to have been paid at the time to the fact that Secretary Acheson, in extending the U.S. defense perimeter in January, 1950, to include Japan, had omitted the defense of Korea. While the Soviets might not underestimate the degree of Western commitment to Europe, they could well be misled by flat statements about Korea. In the light of events, the intention to attack the one probably had little if any bearing on incentives to attack the other.

Uncertainties about Soviet strategy of the moment, however, led Western states to the most pessimistic conclusions. If Korea did signify a more aggressive Russian posture, European defense had to be bolstered. Most obviously it seemed that the deterrents against attack had to be further increased; unless this was done, Russia might seek to absorb Europe in the next two years. Joseph and Stewart Alsop put it this way:

Last March, in the crucial Directive No. 68, the National Security Council set the time of utmost peril as 1953-54. By then the council agreed the Soviet Union would be ready for major aggression. Before then, the council therefore concluded, the defenses of the West must be urgently rebuilt. The May meeting of Atlantic pact Foreign Ministers in London, which did little else, at least accepted this timetable established by our Security Council. Then in July when the Korean aggression occurred, the State Department initiated an amendment to NSC No. 68. The time of utmost peril was now set as 1951-52 or at best 1952-53.[1]

[1] New York *Herald Tribune,* December 22, 1950.

The consequences of an earlier Russian thrust would be potentially decisive. U.S. strategic bombing strength would reach a peak in 1954 along with Soviet atomic power. Before that time, it was quite uncertain that American raids on Soviet industrial centers and war potential would end the war. A really massive assault waited upon the hydrogen bomb, which would not begin to be available until 1953. In the interim a joint ground–air strategy would be necessary to halt a Soviet attack. General Hoyt S. Vandenberg explained the short-run situation along the following lines:

Let us take, for example X country, which has overwhelming ground forces and is relatively poor in its manufacturing capacity. Let us say that the Air Force succeeds in knocking out its potential to fight a war. Now the army of this X country is at least smart enough to know that [our] air potential exists, and, as every army does, it stockpiles behind its line enough for a certain period of time. Suppose we knock out the entire supporting industry of that army. It picks up its stockpile and it moves into a country that has a better and more modern facility for producing war materials than the country we have destroyed, and that army imposes its civilization upon the overrun country. Obviously the Air Force then cannot have succeeded in its task of preventing this new country from being overrun. The overrun country becomes slave labor, and their factories and technicians become available to X country and to all intents and purposes X country at least is as well and perhaps better off than before the Air Force destroyed the potential of X country. . . . The reason we want a number of ground forces opposing this great mass of X army is to force them, before they overrun the attacked country, to expend their gasoline, their food, their ammunition, and since they are not able to have them replaced by X country, whose industry has been knocked out, retarding the advance to the point that X army runs out of these essentials before it can superimpose itself on the industry of the captured country. That is the theory of the air-ground-naval team.[2]

[2] *Ibid.*, December 15, 1950.

These notions seemed to suggest that when U.S. bomb supplies were large enough, they might be delivered on Soviet army stockpiles as well as industrial capacity; then the war could be won by air power alone. In the meantime, ground forces would be necessary to blunt a Russian offensive and force attacking armies to deplete their stocks. Without replenishment Soviet armies would be defeated as the air attrition took its toll. Thus, an early Russian attack might succeed unless there were Western forces in being and in place on the central front in Europe. Even then, however, air power advocates did not believe that a long conventional campaign need be waged. One did not have to program forces to defeat a Russian onslaught in conventional terms; one had only to offer enough resistance to make the air attack effective. Early aggression, therefore, could be deterred without a massive buildup of Western land forces.

Changes in British, American, and NATO strategy, however, were not determined solely by the need to be ready for a possible attack in 1952. There was also the problem of countering or neutralizing greater Soviet nuclear strength in 1954. In part, as NSC-68 foretold, there would be the requirement for buttressing Western nuclear credibility. The Soviets would be much more powerful then; would the United States risk employment of its nuclear capacity in response to a Russian ground attack? In addition, there was the possibility that Russia might be better able to deal with Western air power later on. As U.S. Undersecretary of the Army Tracy Voorhees argued: "We hold no insurance policy that several years from now our bombers will be able to reach primary targets with the requisite frequency, accuracy, and tolerable attrition rate in planes and nuclear weapons to justify counting on this as our sole reliance. And Russia, with an aggressor's priceless advantage of surprise,

may in several years also place herself in a position to threaten
not only Europe's, but America's physical safety." [3]

Thus the problem of growing Soviet nuclear strength was
not simply that a Western nuclear offensive could be answered by a Soviet nuclear offensive. It was that Soviet air
defenses might be more effective as time went on, canceling
or offsetting the growth of U.S. atomic power. Once again
the West was forced back on a ground force strategy in
Europe. This argument suggested that the crucial variables
had to do with the *absolute* damage the United States would
be able to do to Russia on a nuclear strike, not the *relative*
balance between U.S. and Russian nuclear power. The reason
the growth of Soviet atomic capability was most worrisome
was that it reduced the *absolute* effectiveness of American
strategic power. If this argument were valid, 1954 would not
see U.S. strength reach a preliminary peak; rather, it would
witness a measurable decline.

If true, the point answered objections to Acheson's calculations. The difficulty, however, was that it was not true.
Whatever gains the Soviets might make in air defense, they
could hardly be expected to offset the increase in U.S.
deliverable kilotonnage. The American nuclear stockpile was
now growing very rapidly, much faster than it had done in
the immediate postwar period. American ability to put the
bomb on target had increased as the B-50 superseded the B-29
and the B-47 in turn surpassed the B-50. The B-36 remained
the long-range work horse until 1955 when the B-52 entered
the lists. By 1953 the hydrogen bomb had begun to become
available. In 1954, therefore, U.S. nuclear striking power,
even given Soviet defenses, was probably several times greater

[3] New York *Times*, July 23, 1950.

than it had been in 1950. Absolute American strength had increased, not diminished; it was only the relative U.S. advantage which had declined. Once again, the problem was defined in terms of credibility. Would the West use its strategic strength, if the Russians could retaliate upon European cities and perhaps upon the United States? Even if it would do so, was the commitment sufficiently clear to the Russians? Might they believe that in a conventional conflict they would gain territory and resources and hence be tempted to commit aggression?

There is no doubt that the problem on the minds of American, British, and Western planners in the hot summer of 1950 was to increase alliance credibility and thereby reinforce deterrence. "The attack upon Korea," President Truman said, "makes it plain beyond all doubt that Communism has passed beyond the use of subversion to conquer independent nations and will now use armed invasion and war." [4] And Republican adviser John Foster Dulles claimed: "It may invalidate the assumption that the Soviet Union would not risk general war for several years to come—the time presumably required for it to develop a large stockpile of atomic weapons. It surely invalidates the assumption that we can continue still for a time to live luxuriously, without converting our economic potential into military reality." [5] And on July 6, Prime Minister Attlee wrote to Truman that Korea might hold precedents for Communist action elsewhere and asking that there be a meeting of British and American military and diplomatic representatives. He added: "My colleagues and I attach very great importance to reaching the closest possible understand-

[4] U.S. *Department of State Bulletin*, Vol. 22 (July 3, 1950), p. 5.
[5] New York *Times*, July 30, 1950.

ing with the United States Government so that we can plan in full confidence that we understand each other's approach to these weighty problems." [6]

It was clear that Western forces in Europe would have to be increased. The existing Western atomic superiority had not deterred Communist action in Korea; it was not certain that it would do so in Europe. Further, the arguments in favor of just such a buildup had been provided in May, 1950. Even without the stimulus of the Korean attack, Secretary Acheson had contended that the relative growth in Soviet atomic strength would have to be countered by a conventional rearmament. Neither the United States nor Britain seized upon the military deductions of this view until after Korea. America continued to rely on strategic bombing, and the British refused an additional troop commitment in Europe.[7] The United States in turn rejected a British proposal for an integrated military command with an American Supreme Commander. From the British perspective, commitments by London should not exceed those of the United States.

Shortly afterward, however, the Korean War provided the justification for a massive rearmament in both Britain and America. Spurred on by France and the continental states, the United States accepted the view that Soviets might test Western strength and resolve unless the divisions in place were greatly increased. This view was the more persuasive, in that the conventional character of Western resistance in Korea might mislead the Soviets about American willingness to use the atomic bomb in Europe. The force levels that were even-

[6] Quoted in Francis Williams, *A Prime Minister Remembers* (London, 1961), p. 232.
[7] New York *Times*, May 16, 1950.

tually adopted in the Medium Term plan,[8] which provided for a defense at the Rhine, and in the Long Term plan,[9] which held the prospect of defeating a Soviet ground offensive in Western Europe, were based on conventional calculations.

The reasons for this are not hard to fathom, though in retrospect they are harder to defend. In the first place, the NATO plans stemmed from Brussels pact precursors, written when atomic weapons were not available and when a European conflict was viewed in terms similar to World War II in its closing stages. Brussels functionaries could not absolutely rely on U.S. support, and they had to plan for war as it might have to be fought. Later when U.S. support was pledged, the atom stockpile was quite low and bombs were not supposed to make an appreciable difference in the outcome or in force needs. Finally, when the United States sought to remedy specific force deficiencies in its own defense posture, the Army played the largest role, particularly in regard to European strategy. Army planners were not sure that they could count on nuclear weapons being employed, since a decision to use them depended on the other services and the President. Thus, they "felt compelled to strive toward a satisfactory defense based on conventional forces until they were specifically authorized to do otherwise." [10]

European and particularly continental planners pressed in the same direction. They wanted defense not liberation. As Henri Queuille had insisted: "The next time you probably

[8] Approved at London in May, 1950.
[9] Approved at Lisbon in February, 1952.
[10] Laurence W. Martin, "The Decision to Rearm Germany," in Harold Stein, ed., *American Civil-Military Decisions* (Birmingham, Ala., 1963), p. 649.

would be liberating a corpse. . . . The real frontier of Western Europe which must be defended must be moved well beyond the actual frontiers, because once the geographic frontiers of these countries are crossed it will be too late for America to save very much. Even fifteen days after the invasion will be too late." [11] Western strategy, it was agreed at New York in September, 1950, should be a "forward strategy"; Europe would be defended as far to the east as possible. Such doctrines undoubtedly reassured European populations who might be unwilling to commit themselves to a strong defense against attack unless they could be sure that any invasion would be stopped in short order. Rearmament which failed to provide adequate defense would merely be provocative to the Russians.

At the same time, the "forward strategy" also had a military rationale. By the autumn of 1950 it had been recognized that Soviet bombs made withdrawal from and then liberation of the European continent impossible. As General Bradley explained to Congress: "Large scale amphibious operations, such as those in Sicily and Normandy, will never occur again. . . . Appraising the power of the atomic bomb, I am wondering whether we shall ever have another large-scale amphibious operation. Frankly, the atomic bomb, properly delivered, almost precludes such a possibility." [12] If U.S. and British forces were to be pushed off the continent in the opening stages of a ground war, they might never get back again. All the more reason for a strategy which prevented a successful Russian thrust in the first instance.

[11] New York *Times*, March 3, 1949.
[12] Quoted in Roger Hilsman, "NATO: The Developing Strategic Context," in Klaus Knorr, ed., *NATO and American Security* (Princeton, N.J., 1959), p. 19.

The mere formulation of the "forward strategy" and its acceptance by European leaders underscored how far NATO was from meeting minimum military requirements. At the May meetings in London, the Medium Term plan, which provided for approximately 35 to 40 divisions on the central front and for a withdrawal behind the Rhine, had been approved.[13] At the time, American strategists calculated that a defense further east would require 25 to 35 additional divisions.[14] While France alone at the outset of World War II had fielded over 100 divisions and the United States had ended the war with 89, the gap seemed practically impossible to fill. Only 12 divisions were available in different states of readiness on the central front in June, 1950. After eighteen months of frantic rearmament that total was still less than 25. The deficit of 35 to 50 could not be made up by allied efforts alone. As early as the summer of 1950, then, it had been argued that the Germans would have to make a contribution to their own defense. This was not only because other nations were unable or unwilling to provide the required forces; it was also because if the Germans were to be defended, they ought firmly to be bound to the West. Rearmament would accomplish this, though it held risks for the delicate German political equilibrium. Its external consequences, however, might be held in check by organizing German divisions in a different way and relating them closely to an integrated NATO command apparatus. By September, therefore, Truman and Acheson had decided to raise the question of German rearmament with their NATO colleagues.

The issue would clearly be vexed; the French were against any measure of German military power, and Ernest Bevin had vehemently opposed former Prime Minister Churchill's sug-

[13] New York *Times,* December 14, 1950.   [14] See Martin, p. 655.

gestion in March to incorporate German troops in a European Army. It was not until September 9 that President Truman approved the new policy; the British and French were not informed until Bevin was already enroute and French Foreign Minister Robert Schuman on the point of departure for the New York NATO meetings. After arrival both had to cable for new instructions. Bevin persuaded the Cabinet to go along with the U.S. request, initially on the ground that the French would refuse.[15] And even after British agreement had been given, it was kept secret for a time.

The French, however, were in no position to acquiesce. As Schuman pointed out, his own agreement would mean nothing; "he could not have obtained the consent of his government, and *it* could not have obtained the consent of the Deputies." [16]

Unfortunately the plan was presented by American negotiators in the form of a "single package," including: (a) American troops for Europe; (b) an integrated NATO force; (c) an American Supreme Commander; and (d) West German troops. As long, therefore, as the French refused to grant (d), the Americans held back on (a), (b), and (c), otherwise greatly desired by both French and British negotiators. The log jam was only broken when General George Marshall replaced Louis Johnson as Secretary of Defense in late September. Then the conference reached agreement on an integrated force under a U.S. commander and postponed the issue of German rearmament. "Three more months of delicate negotiations . . . were required to gain French consent to the prin-

[15] Dean Acheson, *Sketches from Life of Men I Have Known* (New York, 1961), p. 27.
[16] Martin, p. 658.

ciple of allowing Germany to raise an armed force. During this interval France produced the Pleven Plan for a European Army in a European Defense Community. A meeting of the North Atlantic Council at Brussels in December finally proclaimed unanimous agreement that 'German participation would strengthen the defence of Europe' and 'on the part which Germany should play.' " [17]

The denouement of conventional force planning in NATO was reached at Lisbon in February, 1952, when the Long Term plan finally received Council approval. For the entire year, 1951, no agreement on force levels had been worked out. The demands of the military far exceeded the resources of finance ministers. The Lisbon goals were possible only because of American aid, offshore procurement in Europe, and resolute measures of European rearmament and financial austerity. For 1952 the objectives were 50 divisions, 4,000 aircraft, and 704 major combat vessels; for 1953, 75 divisions and 6,500 aircraft; and for 1954, 96 divisions and 9,000 aircraft "with about 35 to 40 divisions to be ready for combat at all times (including 25 to 30 on the central front) and the rest to be capable of mobilization within a month." [18] By the end of 1952 Britain was expected to have 4 divisions in place in Germany, with immediate reinforcement of at least 1 division from the central reserve at home, and presumably 4 to 5 from the Territorial Army available by D-day plus 30. She would be responsible for 10 of the 50 divisions that would almost immediately be needed on the central front. And somewhat surprisingly, after enormous rearmament efforts the 1952 goals

[17] *Ibid.*, pp. 658–59.
[18] R. E. Osgood, *NATO: The Entangling Alliance* (Chicago, 1962), p. 87.

were approximately met. By 1953 there were about 25 ready and 25 reserve divisions (in various states of readiness) allocated for duty on the central front. Though the objectives for later years could not be met without 12 German divisions, these were expected to follow when the European Defense Community treaty was ratified.

The strategy reflected in the Lisbon agreements was a conventional World War II strategy. It did not take into account the impact of U.S. strategic bombing, or of tactical atomic bombing on ground troops and stockpiles. Charles J. V. Murphy summed the situation in the following words:

It is a strange commentary on the disjointed state of our national strategy that the NATO defense plans have so far given little or no effect to the interrelationship of the atomic counteroffensive with the probable course of the ground struggle. For all practical purposes those two aspects of our general strategy might be concerned with two wholly unrelated situations. Various anomalies account for this—among them the quasi-sovereign status of the Strategic Air Command; the fact that ground strategists tend to regard tactical and strategic air as separate arms, although their functions merge; the U.S. law that forbids the discussion of atomic capabilities even with allies.

[Supreme Commander, General Matthew B.] Ridgway and his American staff planners know, of course, how many atomic weapons have been allocated for support of the ground battle, and the effect these weapons are likely to produce. But his principal European commanders, like General Alphonse Juin, in command of ground forces on the crucial central front, and Field Marshal Viscount Montgomery, Deputy Supreme Commander, are left in ignorance. Unless this somewhat ludicrous isolation is ended, it is inevitable that the NATO strategy, laid down by the infantry generals, will continue to remain a predominantly World War II strategy.[19]

[19] "A New Strategy for NATO," *Fortune* (January, 1953), p. 166.

General Omar Bradley, Chairman of the U.S. Joint Chiefs in the last years of the Truman administration had tried to cut Lisbon requirements to the bone, in hopes of winning the co-operation of finance ministers. In the end, however, as he pointed out, he could make few reductions, "for any plebe at West Point would be able to prove me wrong." Since "plebes at West Point" knew little about the impact of the atomic bomb on ground strategy, Bradley's admission underlined again the conventional nature of NATO force calculations. But even the Lisbon goals (and they were scaled down after 1952) did not truly achieve the objective of a "forward strategy" mandated at New York in September, 1950. The best the planners could come up with "was a plan for a counter-attack from the Rhine line at the southern and possibly north-ern flanks of what was assumed would be the Soviet thrust. . . . One of the ironies in NATO is that only since the deci-sion to base NATO strategy on nuclear weapons have the al-lies had any real hope of carrying our 'forward strategy' in its political sense of a stand at or near the Iron Curtain." [20]

In light of subsequent events NATO plans to 1952 were quite unrealistic. They dealt only with the prospect of con-ventional warfare, while in fact the West was planning on nuclear warfare. The figures laid down were those required to stanch a Soviet advance utilizing conventional infantry and air support. These greatly exceeded the numbers needed to resist the Soviets on the ground while the strategic air offen-sive began to take effect. The arms buildup involved in the Lisbon objectives was also far in excess of that which could be politically sustained by European economies. Hugh Gaitskell, Chancellor of the Exchequer, recognized this earlier than

[20] Hilsman, pp. 19, 28.

most, though he was to cleave to the massive rearmament plan until the very end of the Labour government. In September, 1951, he told the NATO Council that: "The prospect we face is one of prolonged tension rather than immediately threatening Russian aggression. Armed peace may well become the 'normalcy' of the next decade, to which we have to settle down as best we can. Rearmament cannot be pursued in a spirit of emergency, as in actual war. We shall need armed strength tomorrow, and the day after tomorrow, just as much as today. We must, therefore, be careful not to let today's effort disrupt the basic economic strength on which tomorrow's effort depends." [21] In many respects, the decisive turning point for subsequent British defense policy was the conventional rearmament approved at the Lisbon Conference of February, 1952.

Just as NATO strategy and force goals were reshaped by Korea, so British strategy and forces were also drastically altered. In July Defence Minister Shinwell gave a new analysis of the Russian threat: Russia was spending 13 percent of its national income on arms and had in being 175 active divisions, one third of them mechanized. Armored divisions comprised 25,000 tanks. The Soviet Union had 2.8 million men under arms and would double this number on mobilization. The Russian arsenal included 19,000 military aircraft, including jet aircraft of the latest designs, both bombers and fighters. Russia also possessed an extensive submarine fleet. British forces, on the other hand, were deficient. "I will not conceal from the House that the forces at present available, or in sight, fall a long way short of requirements estimated even on the most

[21] *Johannesburg Star*, December 10, 1951.

conservative basis." [22] British complements to meet these needs consisted of a reservoir of previously trained men and World War II equipment.

National servicemen were then passing into the reserve at the rate of 14,000 a month. A reserve army of 400,000 would be attained before July, 1952, if one included Territorial Army volunteers and regulars. The Z (and G) class reservists from the last war totalled four million men. Army equipment was inadequate; there was a large war reserve stockpile, but only limited supplies of the newest weapons. "We have to be careful not to be stampeded into any premature re-equipment with old styles of weapon which would be out of date on any modern battlefield. That is in many ways the crux of the present re-equipment problem."

The United Kingdom had sufficient stocks of small arms, mortars, field guns, and artillery with ammunition. It needed to improve the position in antiaircraft guns and predictors, antitank weapons, and specialized vehicles. There were 6,000 tanks kept in reserve from the last war, but the new Centurion was now coming into service. "In the case of the Navy, apart from minesweeping craft, we have most of the ships we need, but the modernization of those ships with the latest antisubmarine equipment, firing control systems, and means of mine detection and clearance is not as far advanced as could be wished." The reconditioning of tanks was being given high priority, and the Navy had been instructed to speed up the modernization of its ships, particularly for antisubmarine work. It had also been allowed some acceleration in new construction. The R.A.F. would press on with the development of its radar chain. In the light of the enhanced danger, an ad-

22 *House of Commons Debates*, Vol. 478 (July 26, 1950), col. 472.

ditional £100 million would be spent on production, research, and works during 1950–51. "But this is no more than a small part of the cost which would be involved fully to equip our forces to fight. Much larger sums would be required in order to put our Forces in a condition of readiness. Plainly [the Defence Minister said], we can do no more from our own resources than make a beginning on such a programme." [23]

However, on the same day as the debate took place, the new programme was unquestionably put out of date. The United States Government was aware as no European government had need to be, of its army struggling to prevent itself being entirely routed, and desperately calling for reinforcements of men and equipment. It decided to make real use of the North Atlantic Treaty.

On the day of the defence debate in the House of Commons, the Government, in common with the other countries of N.A.T.O. was approached to see what defence effort it was prepared to undertake "to help establish and maintain the communal strength at an adequate level," a level adequate, that is, to meet the new danger in Europe and Asia. A reply was urgently requested within ten days.

On 4 August the British reply was ready. The British Government concluded that it was physically possible to undertake a programme involving expenditure of no less than £3,400 million in three years. Fulfilling this programme would depend on the amount of assistance forthcoming from the United States. Compared to what had been discussed and accepted in July, it meant additional expenditure of some £1,100 million in the coming three years.[24]

Labour's £3,400 million program had been formulated in response to American urging. If realized, the program involved expenditures of 10 percent of the national income per

[23] *Ibid.*, cols. 478–79.
[24] Joan Mitchell, *Crisis in Britain: 1951* (London, 1963), pp. 32–33.

year.[25] At the same time it was clear that London was counting on substantial American assistance. U.S. Ambassador Lewis Douglas had apparently given British officials the impression that American aid would take care of any balance of payments difficulties the British might face. Thus when the announcement was made in Parliament, the government could say of the £3,400 million program: "How far it would be possible to attain that level would depend on the amount of assistance forthcoming from the United States." [26]

On September 12 Prime Minister Attlee outlined further increases even though the amount of aid to be received from the United States was still unknown. Increases in service pay had now brought the three-year total to £3,600 million. In

[25] Aside from the United States, whose post-Korean expenditure exceeded 17 percent of the national income, British defense spending was higher than that of any other Western country. Before Korea, moreover, Britain spent a greater proportion of her national income on defense than the United States. Pre-Korean figures were:

Country	Percentage of National Income Devoted to Defense (1950)
United Kingdom	7.4
Netherlands	6.1
United States	5.9
Turkey	5.8
France	5.0
Italy	3.8
Sweden	3.7
Canada	3.0
Switzerland	2.7
Belgium	2.5
Norway	2.5
Denmark	1.9

(Source: Peter Lyne in the *Christian Science Monitor*, August 2, 1950.)

[26] *House of Commons Debates*, Vol. 478 (September 12, 1950), col. 959.

the Navy, efforts would be concentrated on modernization and new construction, particularly of antisubmarine frigates, mine sweepers, and motor torpedo boats. The government also proposed to increase the strategic reserve to include a complete infantry division, an armoured division, and an infantry brigade. Additional divisions would be stationed in Germany and the 2 divisions already there brought up to strength. The 4 divisions stationed around the world would also be raised to full strength. By the end of 1951 Britain should have the equivalent of 12 Territorial Army divisions. These would be ready to take the field after a short period of training following mobilization. The nation would then have something like 10 Regular and 12 Territorial divisions. To maintain these, the conscription period was lengthened from eighteen months to two years. Steps were also to be taken to increase the effectiveness of Anti-Aircraft Command. In the R.A.F., Fighter Command would be further strengthened through additional production of jet fighters. Production of the Canberra bomber, "which would be of very great importance in any campaign in Western Europe," would also be accelerated. Finally, Attlee pointed out that Britain was reaching the limit of what it might do unaided. "Before we can decide the exact extent of our effort we must know what assistance will be forthcoming from the United States of America. . . . I cannot report final conclusions because the talks are still going on." [27]

British force increases in response to American pressure were not surprising. Bevin had staked his foreign policy on assuring the military presence of the United States in Europe. Now the Americans were heavily engaged in a Far Eastern

[27] *Ibid.*, col. 965.

venture that might draw their attentions and perhaps their troops from Europe. If the Western nations wanted those soldiers to remain, they had to offer *bona fides* of their own intent, and this meant a major increase in forces. "Given its assumptions, the Labour Government felt compelled to attempt a programme that would show America that Britain was making great sacrifices for defence, not only to strengthen Britain's own forces, but, more importantly, to assure doubting elements in the United States that its trans-Atlantic allies deserved large-scale American assistance in developing an effective NATO shield." Labour ministers were also uncertain how far the Korean conflict would go. Some believed that World War III could well result, and that only a maximum rearmament would suffice. "You can always do anything, if you want to badly enough," one official explained. "Look at what we spent in the war." [28]

Both £3,400 million and £3,600 million programs were agreed to without clear indications of American aid. The British were apparently given to expect £500 million over a three-year period, but the United States nowhere made a formal pledge. Indeed, as the year wore on, it became increasingly apparent that aid to Britain would only be determined as part of a comprehensive North Atlantic plan, and that would not be worked out until some time in the spring of 1951. Thus when Britain was asked to double her efforts at the Brussels meeting of NATO foreign ministers in December, the Treasury had little enough to go on. At that time, of course, the Korean struggle was going very badly indeed; the Chinese intervention looked as if it might push U.N. forces

[28] Richard Rose, "The Relation of Socialist Principles to British Labour Foreign Policy, 1945–1951," pp. 334–35. Unpublished Dissertation, Nuffield College (Michaelmas term), 1959.

from the Korean peninsula. Again, Britain was not tempted to stint. When the final installment of the rearmament program came in January, it had attained a total of £4,700 million for the years 1951–54. It was still unclear what if any aid the United States would give, and it was not known what impact such a mammoth program would have on the British economy. Officials almost seemed ready to spend more than they could afford.

In retrospect it was certain that such a rearmament effort, which might have attained 14 percent of the Gross National Product, would disrupt the British economy. Sir Stafford Cripps's deflationary tactics had worked quite well until the end of the year. Gold and dollars were being steadily accumulated, and exports were rising rapidly. Marshall Plan aid could be ended in December. At the same time unemployment was low; metals-using industries were largely geared for export; and consumption had been allowed to absorb an important remainder. Any major rearmament would raise the price of raw materials, transfer resources from export to defense, reverse the balance of payments, and generate inflationary pressure. The consequences would not be overt until military spending had gone into full swing, but they could be foreseen. Even more important politically, some of the defense bill would have to come from consumption. When Attlee resolved on the £4,700 million total, then, he was imperiling, no doubt consciously, his electoral fortunes. In this sense, as events were to show, he explicitly risked those consequences which had deterred Stanley Baldwin in 1935; he put defense ahead of politics and paid the price for doing so.

The magnitude of rearmament was remarkable in other respects. First, it was largely a reversal of postwar precedents.

In previous cases when finance was lacking, defense suffered. In 1947 and again in 1949 defense was cut despite the ominous international situation. And even in 1948 the government's defense increases occurred after the period of maximum danger. Postwar defense papers stressed the need to maintain a vigorous economy as the main bulwark to military posture. Compared to the United States, of course, Britain's military spending was far-sighted and prudent, but it fluctuated mainly with trends in the economic cycle.

Second, there is little evidence that Britain believed that the circumstances completely justified a massive rearmament designed to make possible a conventional defense of Western Europe. Increases were no doubt necessary, and the major conflict would more likely come in Europe than in the Far East. But the British were not certain that it was around the next corner, and even if it was, it was unsure that formidable strength on the ground was the total answer. It seemed more likely that the Soviets would take note of Western capabilities to wage both conventional and nuclear war, and would chart their course accordingly. In this sense, the British were willing to spend a great deal in defense of military principles which they did not fully share. That they did so was a signal tribute to the power of the Anglo-American alliance. Britain spent what she had to do to make the alliance secure.

The final revised program provided for a call-up of reservists. Army units recalled 235,000 Z Class veterans for 15-day service; the R.A.F. asked 10,000 officers and men to report for 15-day summer training; and the Navy recalled 6,600 officers and men for 18 months of duty. In effect the plan was to train for mobilization. Men were asked to serve with units they would actually join in the event of war. The government also continued the practice of retaining Regulars after the expiry of the Color service up to a maximum of eighteen months. As Prime Minister Attlee acknowledged:

The general purpose of all these plans is to make more effective the Regular Forces now in being, and to ensure that mobilization, if it became necessary, could be carried out more rapidly and smoothly than would otherwise be possible. . . .

I now turn to production. As regards equipment, the Forces have for the last five years lived largely on their stocks; and there is now urgent need of an increased production programme concentrated mainly on increasing their fighting strength. . . . . The completion of the programme in full and in time is dependent upon an adequate supply of materials, components, and machine tools. In particular, our plans for expanding capacity depend entirely upon the early provision of machine tools, many of which can only be obtained from abroad.

If our plan is fully achieved, expenditure on production for the Services in 1951–52 will be more than double the rate for the current year; and by 1953–54 it should be more than four times as great. By then we should have quadrupled our annual output of tanks and combat aircraft. We shall introduce new types of equipment as rapidly as possible. New types of fighter aircraft will come into service in larger numbers. Production of the twin-engined Canberra bomber will be increased, and the first order is being placed for a four-engined jet bomber.

On the economic consequences of this programme the Prime Minister said:

In meeting this situation the Government have one clear aim before them; to see that we carry as much of the load as possible ourselves, now, and refrain from mortgaging the future by running into debt abroad or reducing the investment on which our industrial efficiency depends. This will be a task of great difficulty because the industries which will have to carry most of the increased defence orders, the engineering and metal-using industries, are the very ones on which we have relied to make the biggest contribution to exports and to industrial equipment. . . .

As I have said on a number of occasions—and, indeed, as has been said by President Truman—a sound and robust economy is an essential condition for the preservation of free institutions. It is also an essential support for military strength; and, in preparing this programme, the Government have weighed very carefully its probable effect on the social and economic standards of life in this country. I make no attempt to deny that it must affect our standard of living: we shall all have to make some sacrifices in the face of rising prices and shortages of consumer goods. But, though the burden will be heavy, it is not more than we can bear.[29]

There were a number of novel features of the new defense plan. For the first time in the post-World War II period, military production was given its head; reequipment for the short run was preferred to long run preparations. Again, for the first time, the state of readiness of the Army was of paramount concern. It was not slighted in favor of other services or simply relegated to cold war tasks. Britain was getting ready to put ten divisions into Europe in case of war. The relationship with the United States also assumed a different form. Previously, British commitments and forces had occupied a far larger share of the nation's resources than those of American colleagues. Until Korea, there is no doubt that Britain shouldered the major burden of cold war; her leadership was itself responsible for involvement of the United States in the affairs of Europe and the world. Britain made initial commitments, and later the United States underwrote them. Korea was the first case in which American commitments and readiness to rearm exceeded those of her European allies. It was the major American initiative in the postwar

[29] Cmnd. 8146, Statement Made by the Prime Minister in the House of Commons, *Defence Programme* (January 29, 1951), pp. 5-7.

period. In one sense Korea was the vindication of Ernest Bevin's policy. Bevin had striven to involve the United States in the defense of Europe; he had hesitated to make new British commitments until he knew the probable American response. Now, for the first time, Europe was responding. It was all the more important not to let the U.S. effort fail. If Europe had not rallied to American support, the United States might not only have deserted Europe for the Far East; she might have embraced the "Fortress America" concept, now so vigorously propounded by former President Hoover. The stakes for Britain were very high indeed. Her response was commensurate to them.

If the Korean invasion carried British-American defense cooperation to a new peak, it also set the stage for disagreements to follow. It is a commonplace of Anglo–American relations that agreement in Europe has often been accompanied by disagreement in the Far East. At the end of 1949 Britain recognized the Communist regime in China while the United States held back. After the Korean attack, the United States "neutralized" Formosa, thereby barring mainland action to eradicate the Nationalist regime. On November 30, 1950, President Truman, at a press conference, refused to rule out use of the atom bomb in Korea. On the same day Attlee proposed that he visit Washington, and U.S. agreement was forthcoming in thirty minutes time. When the British leader arrived for talks, beginning December 4, he was resolved that the West should not become overcommitted in Asia. The primary menace was in Europe, and if the United States propelled itself into a war with China, the Soviets would have an open invitation to march westward. Further, Attlee was not convinced that China was simply a handmaiden of Russia.

Even if negotiations with the Russians on outstanding issues might come to naught, they might still succeed with the Chinese. Washington, on the other hand, was trying to salvage something from the wreckage of the Korean operation. Chinese troops were forcing U.N. forces onto three beachheads. General Bradley reported pessimistically that it was not sure that they could remain there; a U.S. withdrawal might follow. If this occurred, Secretary Acheson asked, should the West simply swallow its pride and cast about for new prestige elsewhere, or should it make it more difficult for the Communists to govern China?

As the talks proceeded and under British pressure, it became clear that America was willing to negotiate with the Chinese, but only about the narrow issue of Korea. If negotiations failed and the United States was forced out, then she might carry on "limited war" against China. This presumably meant an economic blockade and other harrassment possibly including the use of Chinese Nationalist forces. Attlee responded that "we should concentrate our limited forces on our primary areas of defense, cut our losses in Korea if we were forced out, and avoid any long-range policy of 'limited war' which would merely aggravate the Chinese into staying in the Soviet camp without really being an effective weapon against her."

Was "limited war" really a possible policy for the United States? Mr. Attlee asked. If the United States adopted it, and it did not succeed, would there not be a demand from the American people for all-out war? Would the Russians, with their alarmingly large fleet of submarines, not adopt a policy of "limited war" in retaliation? [30] In the end no agreement on

30 James Reston in the New York *Times*, December 10, 1950.

these points was reached. The United Nations were not thrown out of Korea, hence Acheson's alternative did not have to be contemplated. But differences were marked nonetheless. Britain regarded Asia as a diversionary theater, designed to distract attention from Europe. The United States regarded Asia as an arena of autonomous threat; if aggression were not penalized in the one case, it could not effectively be met in the other.

On the issue of the atomic bomb there was accord in substance if not in theory. The United States would not agree to formal consultation on the use of the weapon, but in effect that is what was privately conceded. At one point in the negotiations President Truman tentatively agreed that the bomb would not be used in Korea without British consent, but such a concession would have restored certain of the restraints of the wartime Quebec Agreement. In the end it was decided that discussion and consultation adequately met British concern. The final communiqué was even more guarded: "The President stated that it was his hope that world conditions would never call for the use of the atomic bomb. The President told the Prime Minister that it was also his desire to keep the Prime Minister at all times informed of developments which might bring about a change in the situation." [31]

The Far East was not the only focus for disagreement among Western nations. Integrationist moves in Western Europe also increasingly divided the British Foreign Minister from his continental counterparts, and to a more limited degree, from the United States. The Schuman Plan had been a subject of heated discussion between Bevin and Acheson at

[31] Harry S. Truman, *Memoirs*. Vol. II; *Years of Trial and Hope* Garden City, N.Y., 1956), p. 413.

the London NATO meetings in May, 1950. Later, when the Pleven Plan for a European army under a European Defense Community was broached by the French in October, the British also demurred. As Bevin explained to Parliament:

His Majesty's Government do not favour this proposal. To begin with, we fear that it will only delay the building up of Europe's defences. . . . We take the view that the proposal for a European Army is also too limited in scope. We cherish our special ties with our old European friends, but, in our view, Europe is not enough; it is not big enough, it is not strong enough, and it is not able to stand by itself. European unity is no longer possible within Europe alone, but only within the broader Atlantic community. It is this great conception of an Atlantic community that we want to build up. . . . We have set our hopes on this conception. We want it to develop far beyond its immediate purpose of defence into a lasting association of like-minded nations.[32]

Such British hesitations brought into the open doubts about British policy that had been harbored by continentals since the Brussels pact. Britain had been hesitant to make a firm troop commitment to Europe or to pledge reinforcement in the event of war. It was known that Field Marshal Montgomery had tried unsuccessfully to persuade his own government to contribute more to ground strength in Europe. Each rebuff increased continental suspicions. When the Schuman Plan was unveiled, Bevin first regarded it as a transparent attempt to undermine British markets on the continent. The E.D.C. plan was equally undesirable in that it was an exclusive European arrangement; even if the British joined, it would still leave the United States outside. Of course, the British did not propose to join, but only to "associate" themselves with

[32] *House of Commons Debates*, Vol. 481 (November 29, 1950), col. 1173.

it, as they had done with the Coal and Steel Community. Thus began a series of policy stands against linkage with Europe which hampered London ever afterwards.

The reasons for refusing were good enough in terms of British historical sovereignty and independence. They were less convincing when related to influence in Washington. Bevin's notion had been that Britain should not go farther into Europe than the United States. If she did, and the United States drew back, London would be left with a plate of indigestible commitments. Since Europe would drain British strength and also limit freedom of action, it was not an attractive alternative. As Europe became more united, however, the continental option went from weakness to strength. Association with Europe would at this point add to Britain's economic and military power. The question remained whether "integration" would also circumscribe British initiative. The evidence, so far as it is furnished by French policy under General de Gaulle, is negative. In this sense the British were far more "logical" than the French. Reading integrative institutions as practical federation, Whitehall declined to participate. And yet by the late 1950s the British might have had a position of unparalleled influence in both Brussels and Washington. They might have had the strength of one and the ear of the other. One wonders now how different the postwar shape of European policy might have been had Britain heeded continental entreaties in 1950. The difficulty with British policy in 1967 is not that London lacks physical power to influence Europe; it is that her influence is now greatly mistrusted, on grounds provided over more than a decade.

The impact of Korea upon British as well as NATO strategy was fundamental. Before Korea, only one type of major war seemed possible. The war could not be called "conventional," but it would still be a large-scale ground encounter, in which strategic bombing would hasten, but not itself bring, victory. As long as nuclear bombs were not decisive, the Army and Navy had a rational part to play. The Army would hold the enemy at bay on land; the Navy would be able to operate against the threat to sea communications and insure the necessary flow of supplies and goods. The British Navy, in particular, had been convinced by the Bikini tests that naval vessels on the high seas could be well insulated from atomic blasts by techniques of dispersal, armor, and washing-down. They would be less affected by atomic strategies, it was believed, than other service arms. After the Soviet bomb in August, 1949, it had dawned that amphibious operations were short-lived. A rallied ground conflict might still endure for months, but if land armies were forced to evacuate from coast lines, they could never get back to defeat their foe. Consequently both Navy and Army plans had to be advanced in readiness. Military operations had to be completely sustained from the outset; no large targets could be presented. The war would probably be shorter than first contemplated.

Then Korea occurred. In one respect the coordinated buildup of atomic and then thermonuclear arms which followed made nonsense of a World War II strategy. The Lisbon goals were patently absurd; they merely superimposed conventional upon atomic requirements. A dual and inconsistent strategy was still involved. In this sense notions of "massive retaliation" were understandable reactions to excesses in the opposite direction. But if so, what role for the Army and Navy? Both looked less necessary. Tactical combat would no doubt occur in a new war. It might take time for strategic attrition to terminate enemy resistance. But military and naval forces were useful for this time only. Arms that were once central had become peripheral. For a time it was argued that carrier forces might still launch attacks on shore targets in atomic war; but various exercises showed these to be ineffective and costly. For a time after the advent of the thermonuclear bomb, the Royal Navy was unsure of its mission.[33] The British Army was equally affected theoretically, but in practice the development of the tactical atomic weapon rapidly solved the problem. Resupply by sea-borne forces might not be realistic in a thermonuclear war. But the war was likely to commence with a ground thrust which had to be resisted in its own terms. While strategic bombing forced capitulation of the enemy homeland; tactical atomic weapons would defeat the enemy army. One did not have to believe in a long war to see a role for the Army.

In some ways the Royal Navy and the American Army argued similar cases in response to the thermonuclear revolution. In the United States, the Army stated the case for limited war forces, partially because it had no strategic role. In Britain, the Navy, dilating upon the Korean experience, argued for conventional capabilities. In both instances the case was partly a function of the inability to deliver a strategic punch. But the important point was that Korea represented the watershed between mixed and individually defined strategies. Until Korea, there was no distinction between nuclear and conventional war. And NATO rearmament, at least to Lisbon, amalgamated the two. But at some point, the excesses of each would provoke the other. The excess of conventionality led to a thermonuclear strategy; the excess of nuclearity

[33] See W. J. Crowe, Jr., "The Policy Roots of the Modern Royal Navy, 1946–1953," p. 154. Unpublished dissertation, Princeton University, 1965.

led to a conventional strategy. The Korean conflict and its aftermath stimulated them both.

Korea was important for one other reason. From 1948 on the United States had primacy in strategic bombing. The U.S. Navy was larger than the British. But until the Korean period there was a sense in which British quality offset American quantity. The British aircraft industry was one of the most sophisticated in the world; the Admiralty was responsible for a series of naval innovations; the British Army remained the world's leading cold war force. It was possible to entertain the view that when British weapons were produced they would be the equal of any in the world. By 1953, however, American weapons in being were nearly equivalent to those Britain would attain three to five years later. British weapons were in some cases outmoded World War II types, in others they were first marks of postwar production. Shortly afterward it was no longer possible to make the claim that British military quality was the standard of the world.

CHAPTER SIX

STRATEGIC INNOVATION
AND REVERSAL, 1952–1953

THE LABOUR GOVERNMENT's expenditure on defense during its last year of office reversed typical policy priorities. Since 1945 a sound economy had, with the single exception of the autumn budget of 1948, been placed ahead of defense needs. A worsening of the international atmosphere in 1947 and 1949 had not brought an increased defense program; convertiblity in the first case, and devaluation in the second, had precluded readjustments. Military threats had been attended to only in financially permissible degree. The Labour three-year rearmament plan, adopted at American urging, was of a different order. That it would cause balance of payments problems could easily be foreseen; that it would be difficult, even impossible, to carry out without American aid was also understood. Labour had moved slowly on the path of re-armament. An initial £100 million was sanctioned in July, 1950. In August, the £3,400 million program was announced, but only if the United States gave aid in the amount of approximately £500 million. In September the ante was raised to £3,600 million, on the assumption of a substantial but as yet unknown quantity of American aid. In January, however, the £4,700 million program was laid down without prior assumptions. Some aid would be forthcoming from the United States, but no one knew how much it would be. The government's economic bill would be hard to pay.

Labour had barely won the election of March, 1950, gaining a margin of only ten seats, and a working majority which was still smaller. It was all but certain that the government would have to go to the country soon again, and that it would be judged on its new defense proposals. These produced increasing acrimony, and a number of prominent left-wing government members, including Aneurin Bevan and Harold Wilson, resigned from the cabinet in April, 1951. The formal issue had to do with charges for certain health services to help finance the rearmament plan; informally, Hugh Gaitskell's succession to the Treasury after the resignation of Sir Stafford Cripps had irritated Bevan, who coveted the post.

There could be no doubt, however, as Attlee himself admitted, that defense spending would cause a restriction of consumption. Imports would be centered on raw materials for defense production. Metals-using and engineering industries would produce for defense and export. British standards of living were bound to fall. Bevan was unquestionably right when he told Attlee: "[The budget] is wrong because it is based upon a scale of military expenditure in the coming year, which is physically unattainable, without grave extravagance in its spending." [1]

Harold Wilson pointed to raw material shortages which would prevent the full production program from being car-

[1] Quoted in Francis Williams, *A Prime Minister Remembers* (London, 1961), p. 247.

ried out. U.S. financial ability to mobilize worldwide sources of raw materials was in particular a problem. "The United States, if they go on with their plan of superimposing a tremendous rearmament program upon a growing level of production, without any restriction in civilian consumption, will get into their economy a very large proportion of the raw materials required by this and other countries." The consequences would be that Britain would pay an increasingly high price for raw materials imports and suffer a corresponding reverse in the balance of payments. As Wilson correctly argued: "The overseas problem clearly arises from two factors: our exports have not risen to the levels that we had hoped; and our imports, largely due to fantastic world prices, have risen far above the estimates made a few months ago." [2]

By mid-1951 the government was in financial and political straits. "In September, the sterling area dollar deficit in the third quarter was put at $500 million. By October the estimate had risen to $64. million. In the month of October —as was known later—the drain accelerated again, and was $320 million in that month alone. The United Kingdom position worsened as spectacularly. The last public occasion on which Mr. Gaitskell reviewed the situation as Chancellor of the Exchequer was to be his speech at the Mansion House dinner on October 3. It then appeared that the balance of payments deficit, in place of £100 million which had originally been assumed for 1952, was going to be £450 million or £500 million." [3] Instead of the £244 million surplus in 1950, there was a £521 deficit in 1951; dollar reserves, moreover,

---

[2] Quoted in Joan Mitchell, *Crisis in Britain 1951* (London, 1963), pp. 222, 221.

[3] J. C. R. Dow, *The Management of the British Economy, 1945–60* (Cambridge, 1965), p. 62.

fell by about $1,000 million.[4] Even before these setbacks were known, the government had resolved on important tax increases to finance the rearmament bill. These were certain to be raised to unpopular. The tax rate was 9s. 6d., only 6d. less than it had been during World War II.

It is of course possible to argue that Labour's rearmament was a flexible program, capable of adjustment to reduced levels of raw materials and machine tools. If it could not be achieved, it could always be scaled down. Attlee himself approached the £4,700 million figure in an experimental spirit. But the fact remained that Labour's actual expenditure did cause a financial crisis and did work hardship on the British electorate. As one observer remarked: "In spite of . . . heavy buffetings, in the short time left to it, the Labour Government did not waver in its commitments to place military considerations first. Before the Government was defeated at the general election on October 25th, there was no effort made within the Treasury or the Cabinet to calculate a defence programme based upon lower spending."[5] In a real sense the government's courage on defense helped to ensure its own demise.

When the Conservatives attained office it was already clear that the three-year plan would have to be prolonged. Given raw material shortages, defense production could not attain desired levels. As Mr. Churchill's first White Paper explained:

Since the programme was started the economic position has seriously deteriorated and severe measures have had to be taken in the civil sector of the economy. About 8 per cent of defence

[4] See William P. Snyder, *The Politics of British Defence Policy, 1945–1962* (London, 1964), pp. 211–12.

[5] Richard Rose, "The Relation of Socialist Principles to British Labour Foreign Policy, 1945–1951," pp. 362–63. Unpublished dissertation, Nuffield College (Michaelmas term), 1959.

production consists of products of the metal-using industries which are responsible for about two-fifths of our exports. In the light of this and . . . other factors . . . it has been necessary to adjust the defence programme. This adjustment will have the effect of reducing the immediate burden which the programme will place on the metal-using industries. It also means that the programme must take more than three years to achieve.[6]

To reestablish the United Kingdom's external position, imports and government spending had to be cut and the interest rate increased. Under the first year of the Labour program £1,250 million to £1,300 million was to be spent on defense; because of delays in production, however, only £1,131 million was actually disbursed. For 1952–53 Labour had programed £1,500 million, exclusive of civil defense (which had been expected to cost another £100 million). In contrast the Tories resolved on £1,462 million which was reduced to £1,377 million by American aid. In the final year of the program, Labour had allocated £1,800 million, but the Conservatives budgeted a net total of £1,496 million. Net expenditure over the three-year period actually totalled about £4,000 million as compared with the target of £4,700 million. U.S. aid of £244 million, however, raised the gross rearmament program to nearly £4,250 million. This was a considerable short-fall, but the final amount reflected a smaller quantity of U.S. aid than had been hoped for in 1950. And the British economy, by 1953, had moved once again into the black. To accomplish this fortunate and surprising reversal, the government had cut defense production at the end of 1952.

Further investigation showed that, even with this spreading forward, the old load which the defence production programme

6 Cmnd. 8475, *Statement on Defence,* 1952, p. 9.

would place upon industry was greater than was compatible with the increase in engineering exports to which it is necessary to look for a major contribution to the solution of the balance of payments problem. With the decline in export demand in recent months a large contribution from the engineering industries has become increasingly important and export demand is high in those sectors of the engineering industry on which the defence programme bears most heavily. It also appeared that if the programme were maintained in full during 1953–54, heavy expenditure would be incurred in some parts of the programme on the production of equipment which was not of the most advanced types. The Government therefore decided that in the interests of true economy as well as of the vitally needed increase in exports, any substantial rise above the high level of expenditure on defence production in 1952–53 was not possible.[7]

Once again, economic factors were determining military ones.

Financial pressures, however, were not the only influence shaping defense strategy. The NATO buildup resolved at Lisbon in February, 1952, had caused a good deal of rethinking in British defense circles. If the British commitment by the end of 1952 was 9 to 10 Regular and reserve divisions, by 1954 it was set at 9 Regular divisions with an equal number to be obtained from the reserve by D-day plus 30.[8] At the maximum ground force peak of 1953, however, Prime Minister Churchill pointed out that the British Army would not exceed 22 divisions.[9] Given British commitments overseas, which required the presence of 6 to 7 Regular divisions in 1952, it was scarcely likely that Europe could be permitted to

[7] Cmnd. 8768, *Statement on Defence, 1953*, p. 4.
[8] See Charles J. V. Murphy, "A New Strategy for NATO," *Fortune* (January, 1953), p. 83.
[9] 10 to 11 Regular and 12 Reserve divisions.

absorb all but 1 to 2 divisions of the active Army.[10] The Lisbon goals, moreover, were drawn up on the basis of a conventional ground force strategy, and without consideration of the impact of the Western atomic offensive on Soviet forces and industrial potential. When in Washington in January, 1952, Mr. Churchill had been given "a highly privileged briefing at the Pentagon concerning the role of an air counteroffensive by the U.S. Strategic Air Command in the event of another general war. . . . Churchill was profoundly impressed. He returned to London convinced that the West possessed, in the combination of atomic weapons and air power, a military resource that, so long as it was steadily developed and perfected, assured the Atlantic coalition the balance of military power in the critical years immediately ahead." [11]

Such thinking, even in inchoate form, directly challenged Acheson's precepts of 1949, 1950, and 1951. Previously it had been argued that as Soviet atomic power approximated that of the Western alliance the value of the latter's lead would diminish. Churchill was perhaps the first Western statesman to recognize that the major factor governing the utility of an atomic strategy was not the *relative* balance between Soviet and Western strength, but rather the *absolute* magnitude of Western power. As one observer put it: "Strategists who are closely concerned with this problem do not believe that SAC's deterrent value will be materially affected as the Soviet stockpile of atomic weapons increases. Numbers by themselves are ceasing to be the critical military index. The controlling factor is the ability of an air force to deliver the

[10] See Hanson Baldwin in the New York *Times*, December 21, 1952.
[11] Murphy, p. 80.

contents of the atomic stockpile before the defense has taken a prohibitive toll. Here, again the evidence tilts the scale decisively in SAC's favor."

If the West was in fact planning to use "all the weapons at its disposal" in response to a Soviet attack in Europe, NATO force goals should be calculated with the atomic counteroffensive in mind. This provided not only for strategic attacks upon the centers of Soviet power, but also for tactical atomic strikes on invading armies. As the first destroyed industrial targets and Soviet bomber bases, the second would wipe out logistics and supply lines and hit troop concentrations. Inevitably the invasion of Western Europe would grind to a halt; "the American atomic advantage should assure us the power, if a general war should come to 'neutralize' effectively and quickly Soviet power for further sustained large-scale military action." [12]

Ground forces, then, would be necessary only to hold the enemy at bay while the strategic air attack worked its effect. At the end of 1950 it was possible to argue that strategic power merely supplemented ground forces; at the end of 1952, it was becoming clear that ground strength merely supplemented strategic attack. In nucleus the British had potent a rejoinder to then existing NATO strategy. They seized upon it even before Americans.

The most influential British defense paper of the postwar period was undoubtedly the global strategy paper of 1952. It was prepared by the service Chiefs, Sir John Slessor, Sir William Slim, and Sir Rhoderick McGrigor, under the supervision of Sir Ian Jacob, then Churchill's military assistant. The paper did not emerge through the usual efforts of joint planners, and early drafts prepared by the chiefs themselves

[12] Ibid., p. 85.

had been discarded in an attempt to formulate fully consistent principles governing military policy in the nuclear epoch. To reach basic agreement the Chiefs retired to a country retreat for about two weeks, and then, undisturbed, they prepared a report for the Cabinet. The paper which they wrote was divided into three sections: the first dealing with nuclear war and deterrence, the second with NATO, and the third with cold war obligations.

In the first part the authors stressed that European countries could not match American economic progress. Their strategy had to husband resources in a way unknown in the United States. The nuclear strength of the United States was already very great; in a war the Strategic Air Command would be able to destroy the Soviet Union as an industrial power. U.S. strength was not only a basic deterrent to war; it also represented an important "war-winning" capability. But the objective should not be to fight a war, but rather to prevent it from occurring. The most powerful deterrent would be Soviet cognizance that aggression would bring "instantaneous and overwhelming atomic air attack. It was especially imperative for the Allies to make clear the intention to use the atomic bomb immediately. To carry out this policy the Allies would have to give priority to the air striking forces and to maintain the quantitative superiority of those forces." [13]

British strategic forces could make an important contribution to the American effort. In the first place, though America's deterrent was formidable and would grow even more so, it might not cover all targets that would be militarily relevant to America's allies. The U.S. stockpile was not as large then as

[13] Alfred Goldberg, "The British Nuclear Program," p. 3. Mimeographed paper, March, 1966.

it might have been. British forces might hit enemy submarine pens and air bases, targets which would not present a direct threat to the United States itself. A British deterrent was designed, if it ever had to be used, to render war more tolerable to both the United Kingdom and the United States. There was no thought then, as occurred after Suez, that the American alliance might not be reliable, or that British vital interests might one day be sacrificed. U.K. strategic targeting would be helpful in that the atomic offensive, though devastating and successful, might not end all military operations. As one American observer pointed out: "The combat and operational attrition of a sustained offensive is certain to bring about a rapid waning of our striking power. Even under the 143-wing program the Strategic Air Command's total supply of atomic-weapon carriers will be numbered in the low thousands. World War II experiences, tested by recent exhaustive exercises in the new techniques of penetration, suggest that the initial offensive might see the Strategic Air Command reduced in a matter of months, perhaps weeks, to a fraction of its original strength—too small to sustain the attack." [14] At that point a period of "broken-backed" war would follow. As British defense planners argued, "If, by some miscalculation in Communist policy or by deliberate design, a global war were to be forced upon us, it must be assumed that atomic weapons would be employed by both sides. In this event it seems likely that such a war would begin with a period of intense atomic attacks lasting a relatively short time but inflicting great destruction and damage. If no decisive result were reached in this opening phase, hostilities would decline in intensity, though perhaps less so at sea than elsewhere, and a period of

[14] Murphy, p. 85.

'broken-backed' warfare would follow, during which the opposing sides would seek to recover their strength, carrying on the struggle in the meantime as best they might." [15] The more targets hit in the initial phase, the more tolerable would be the threat to British sea communications in the second phase.

British strategic bombing capacity, however, would be useful in other respects. It would undoubtedly increase British influence in the cold war and in the conduct of a future major conflict. "Although it was likely that in the event of war the United States would make atomic bombs available to the Royal Air Force, it would be wiser for the United Kingdom to have its own stock of atomic bombs. Accordingly, the Chiefs recommended pressing on with atomic bomb development. They foresaw a large increase in output of fissionable materials within a few years that would permit acquisition of substantial resources for atomic warfare." [16] In basic conception, at least, the Chiefs anticipated a British hydrogen bomb, though the decision to build it was apparently not made by Churchill until later in the year.

The second section dealt with NATO. The Conservative government had been shocked by the size of the Lisbon goals, though it had assented to them. Something had to be done to make them manageable. The tactical nuclear weapon, which had already been revealed, but formed no part of NATO thinking, provided a partial answer. If such bombs were used against invading group troops, they would have deadly effect. There would then be less need for a Western military Behemoth; troops strengths could be considerably reduced. A proper British contribution in such circumstances

[15] Cmnd. 9075, *Statement on Defence, 1954*, p. 5.
[16] Goldberg, p. 4.

might be as small as 50,000 men.[17] If NATO strategy had not been changed in December, 1954, to sanction planning for the use of the tactical atomic weapon, British doctrines would have been greatly out of harmony with other NATO thinking.

In addition, the global strategy paper revolutionized British Army conceptions. Since the end of the war, ground operations in Europe had been conceived in terms of mobilization of the Territorial Army. Despite the mobilization preparations of 1951, however, it seemed impossible to assemble and train the Territorial Army for European operations within the NATO-mandated period of thirty days. In any event, it seemed unlikely that a reserve force of the nature of the Territorial Army would be technically equipped to participate in the highly mobile and necessarily precise operations of tactical atomic war. By the time the Territorial Army would be ready to fight, moreover, the air war might well have told the tale. "Broken-backed warfare" might well continue at sea; it was harder to imagine on land. This did not mean that the Territorial Army would embrace its old role of antiaircraft defense. Antiaircraft and even fighter defense against atomic attack was becoming of doubtful efficacy. Rather, the Territorial Army would be used in home and civil defense duties.

The final section referred to Britain's cold war tasks. While it was admitted that current obligations had to be met, it was stressed that these might be considerably reduced over time. Retrenchment was the more permissible in that certain commitments were predicated on the old World War II strategy. The Middle East base in the canal zone scarcely accorded with the new conceptions. Its strategic *raison d'être* had been

[17] This contrasted with the more than 300,000 British soldiers that were required for 1954 under the Lisbon plans.

a rallied ground encounter in Europe. The Middle East bastion would then guard the Eastern Mediterranean approaches, and it would ultimately afford an avenue for counterattack on Europe's southern flank. The Suez base did little to protect the oil supplies; these were too far off; and the canal would in any event be unusable in an atomic war. The global strategy paper, then, provided a theoretical rationale for a reconsideration of major cold war commitments. Those that were founded on outmoded conceptions might have to be scaled down or abandoned.

When the Chiefs finished their memorandum, Churchill acknowledged that it was "a state paper of the greatest importance, but that does not mean that I concur in all of it." [18] Subsequently, however, he joined the Cabinet in approving it in virtually the same form in which it had been submitted. The consequences of the global strategy paper were significant for British doctrines and postures, and they had no little impact on the United States. The paper made certain that Britain would proceed with its separate atomic development and crown its effort with the hydrogen bomb. It also guaranteed the reequipping of Bomber Command.

The decision to proceed with separate British atomic development was of some importance. Within the Labour government there had always been partisans of reliance on the United States in strategic and nuclear matters. The 1949 atomic negotiations had reflected their influence, and although Labour had brought the country to the threshold of nuclear capability, they had not actually taken the vital decisions. With the beginnings of plutonium production at Wind-

[18] Goldberg, p. 3.

scale and the functioning of separation and fabrication plants, the Conservatives still had to decide to test a bomb. This Churchill did early in 1952. The hydrogen bomb, lineal successor to its fission forbears, would be dependent upon substantial production of U-235. The high-separation diffusion plant had been finally approved in March, 1951, but additional production was evidently required, and an extension of Capenhurst facilities was approved in 1953. Of course, the British could not be sure until after the Monte Bello test that they could actually make the H-bomb. And as a matter of fact, as one highly placed observer commented: "in our work after 1952, we followed several ideas that turned out to be quite wrong. It was not until 1954 that we were well on the way to the H-bomb." The basic decision to try to build the hydrogen bomb, however was taken by the Conservative government in 1952.[19]

A decision to proceed with separate British atomic and thermonuclear development also entailed construction of a bomber force. Again, Labour had laid the necessary groundwork for a decision to produce, but it had not actually ordered the V-bombers in quantity. Despite Attlee's statement in January, 1951, that "the first order is being placed for a four-engined jet bomber," the decision involved prototypes for testing and modification, not a procurement order. Indeed, the Undersecretary of State for Air, Mr. Aidan Crawley, pointed out: "The fact is that in one very large sphere—that of strategic bombing—we have planned that, for

[19] By 1951 American scientists knew they would be able to make the H-bomb. This understanding had been communicated to Britain along with information on atomic weapons effects and weapon test detection devices in 1951.

the present, the Americans should undertake almost the whole of it." [20] In face of all the pressure the Air Staff could bring to bear for a major reequipment of Bomber Command, the Labour government stood firm until the very end. Even the £4,700 million plan had not involved a bomber reequipment.

The decision, taken by Churchill at the urging of Sir John Slessor and the Air Staff, was a fundamental departure in several respects. First, NATO strategy did not allot a strategic bombing role to Britain. It did not preclude such a role, but allied leverage was undoubtedly exercised on behalf of NATO ground force and tactical air preparedness. Second, it was not certain that Britain would be able to devise the complicated sortie and targeting arrangements necessary to hit Soviet installations in a phased assault. Here the United States was unexpectedly of assistance. General John P. McConnell, later U.S. Air Force Chief of Staff, explained the procedure to Mr. Churchill and gave him confidence that the Air Staff would be able to solve all the problems. Third, a major bomber reequipment would cost a great deal; it would detract from Labour's planned rearmament; and it would go forward despite the then burgeoning economic and financial crisis. The last difficulty, however, was mitigated by the fact that expenditure would take place over time; most of the reequipment in fact would fall outside Labour's three-year program. Still the expenses were not insignificant, and some of them would be incurred in creating production lines for the new weapons. Overall the Conservative government planned to spend about £270 million on the V-bomber force. This would allow production of 215 planes at a cost of approximately £1.25 million per plane. Parliament was led to believe

[20] *House of Commons Debates,* Vol. 491 (August 1, 1951), col. 1523.

that their cost was between £300,000 and £400,000 but these estimates were not very accurate calculations of the cost of the Valiant alone.[21] As the Valiants, Vulcans, and Victors were successively given "super priority" in 1952 and 1953, they impinged upon other rearmament production. Production of the Canberra, a fighter bomber perfectly fitted to tactical interdiction tasks in Europe was cut by one-third in December, 1952.[22] The Canberra was actually to bulk larger in British strategic calculations than had initially been conceived. By 1954, it had been admitted that the Canberra could carry a small atomic bomb, and though its range did not permit strategic use against the Soviet Union except on one-way missions, the Air Staff relied upon it as an interim strategic bomber. The last B-29 was returned to the United States in 1954, but the first Valiant squadron was not activated until a year later. Perforce, the Canberra was the temporary replacement for the Washington.

The decision to reequip Bomber Command, then, represented a substantial alteration in British defense policy. It was not required by NATO plans; it detracted from other rearmament production; it would eventually duplicate nuclear strength possessed by the United States. As the hydrogen era dawned it would no longer be necessary to find forces for "broken-backed" war. The unleashing of thermonuclear power would put an end to the rational waging of war. It would no longer be possible to contend that U.S. nuclear strength displayed weaknesses which might be made up by Bomber Command. At that point, the argument for a British

[21] See the *Times*, February 18, 1953.
[22] Alfred Goldberg, "The Military Origins of the British Nuclear Deterrent," *International Affairs*, Vol. 40, No. 40 (October, 1964), p. 616.

deterrent would reduce to influence upon U.S. policy. Only after Suez was it maintained that America might not be a wholly reliable ally.

The global strategy paper, moreover, made no attempt to assess the long-run costs of a separate British strategic force. From 1948 onward Britain had divided its forces between Western and cold war commitments. Cold war costs, particularly after 1949, were a very important fraction of British military expenditure. Malaya and Hongkong were succeeded by Kenya and Cyprus, and the Middle East was draining responsibility. In addition to these were the costs of the NATO force buildup and also of the British brigade in Korea. The global strategy paper had dealt with deterrent, NATO and cold war commitments, but it had nowhere shown that a British deterrent (with reequipment and obsolescence costs) could be afforded over and above NATO and cold war forces. Of course, the basic thrust of the paper inclined to reductions in the latter two spheres, but it did not specify how and in what degree they could take place. In short, the basic paper recommending a separate British deterrent did not estimate its costs relative to other obligations over time. Britain simply presumed she could afford them.

As a response to the NATO force goals agreed at Lisbon, the British global strategy paper was a document of great analytical and historical importance. It was the first full-dress critique of NATO strategy; it was the first attempt rationally to combine conventional and nuclear elements in a strategy of deterrence of the Soviet Union. Nor did the paper indulge the later excesses of "massive retaliation." Ground forces would still be needed in Europe, even in nuclear war. Cold war commitments had to be met; for these nuclear deterrence would not suffice. As Sir John Slessor phrased the argument: "We in the West must be prepared to maintain sufficient conventional forces to deal with what are and should be, limited commitments like Korea and Indo-China by limited methods, without having recourse to the dreadful arbitrament of atomic air power." [23]

But if Western vital interests were seriously threatened, as they would be by an attack upon Europe, nuclear retaliation should follow. These doctrines in fact were already an intrinsic part of Western plans; the United States would reply to a Soviet ground assault with strategic air attacks. But theory had yet to take account of practice. Western doctrine had yet to combine strategic and tactical elements. All that the West had done, as Slessor pointed out, was to superimpose an atomic strategy on a pre-atomic one. No changes had been made in force objectives as a result. It has often been argued that Dullesian "massive retaliation" erred in overemphasizing the strategic nuclear element in deterrence; it is equally correct that Lisbon overemphasized the conventional element in deterrence; the British global strategy paper of 1952 was unique in that it succumbed to neither.

As a result of the "new assessment" of Britain's defense role, the conclusions could now be partially communicated to the outside world. At the end of July Churchill gave the first intimations to Parliament and Slessor took off for Washington. Unfortunately the impact of his visit was lessened by British defense cuts. The American Chiefs believed that the proposal "was simply a rationalization of a British intent to renege on their NATO forces commitment." And Slessor had indeed contended that "the NATO force goal of about 96 divisions . . . would place too great a strain on the fragile

[23] Sir John Slessor, *Strategy for the West* (London, 1954), p. 155.

European economies. He urged a strategy of deterrence rest-
ing chiefly on American and British air-nuclear capabilities.
Citing the apparent ebbing of the immediate danger of full-
scale war, he argued for a reduction in the ground force goals
of NATO." [24]

The calculus of deterrence, however, was not merely
economic. The Air Staff had begun to question fighter attrition rates of enemy bombers carrying nuclear bombs. Indeed,
even if past attrition rates could be obtained, they were
immediately out-dated by the nuclear weapon. As the hydrogen bomb emerged, reliable defense against attack became a
chimera. It was the more necessary, therefore, to develop a
deterrent strategy to prevent war from occurring. The American Chiefs, particularly Generals Omar Bradley and J. Lawton Collins, contended that NATO forces might possibly be
cut later; for the moment however, the Lisbon goals had to be
accepted. Tactical atomic weapons for use by ground troops
were still some years away, and until they were obtained,
"any reduction in the planned NATO ground forces would
be an invitation to invasion." [25] This argument was persuasive if the entire responsibility for defeating a Soviet ground
attack rested upon tactical forces in Europe. But if American
strategic bombing were also taken into account, the need for
the full Lisbon build-up was less pressing.

The American planners were also undoubtedly very sensitive about any reversal of NATO goals in 1952. After a series
of setbacks during 1951, NATO had only just reached
agreement on military targets for the next three years. For-

[24] Glenn H. Snyder, "The 'New Look' of 1953," in Warner R.
Schilling, Paul Y. Hammond, and Glenn H. Snyder, *Strategy, Politics, and Defense Budgets* (New York, 1962), pp. 389, 388.
[25] "Defence and Strategy," *Fortune* (December, 1953), p. 82.

ward momentum had finally been attained; a reversal, or even a marked check at that stage, could have affected NATO cohesion and resolve. The American Chiefs were unlikely to acknowledge such a fundamental change in strategy without clearing it with NATO SACEUR, at the time General Mathew B. Ridgway. Political issues were also in the balance. Continental countries were extremely eager for a strong ground force contingent in Europe and for a firm American and British involvement. If Lisbon had been abandoned, moreover, the rationale for German rearmament would probably have gone with it. This would have affected all the political arrangements for the European Defense Community and for German military integration in NATO. It seemed safer not to rock the boat.

Some of these contentions were unquestionably valid. A lowering of force targets would certainly have disrupted NATO political equilibrium. At the same time, none of the European countries believed those goals could in fact be attained. It was inevitable that they would be scaled down in practice. The question of German rearmament would have to be faced eventually, and the Eisenhower administration succeeded in confronting it, while at the same time developing a radically different strategy. It was simply a fact that the Army generals were in command of doctrine during the Truman administration. Afterwards, a growing eclecticism prevailed. In terms of the logic of the argument, the global strategy paper could just as well have been embraced by the United States in 1952 as in 1953.

The global strategy paper represented an important innovation in military thought. It anticipated changes in American strategy and helped to bring them about. It also provided the basis for a fundamental change in NATO doctrine and force postures. But it did not solve all problems. In certain respects the paper initiated a tendency in British thinking, carried to its apogee in the defense White Papers of 1957 and 1958, to rely upon nuclear weapons as a substitute for ground forces. Such an emphasis was rational wherever Western interests were vital, and it was also essential to recognize that Western strategies in Europe were dual and inconsistent. If one was really planning to wage nuclear war, there could be little sense in developing force goals based on conventional war. Korea, on the other hand, had clearly shown that conventional war was possible. Its very occurrence made many military planners desire to preclude its repetition. Korea was the "wrong war, in the wrong place, at the wrong time." Strategic deterrence should have prevented it, but it did not. Different declaratory policy, buttressed by strategic power, however, would manage to do so in the future. Since Britain was endeavoring to find an economical military doctrine, it was plausible to stint on ground forces wherever possible. In Europe, this might be done; unlimited war would be waged over Europe because unlimited Western interests were involved. But limited war would then apply to situations of limited commitment. The problem of the global strategy paper was that it did not differentiate clearly enough between these two conditions, and it even displayed a mild tendency to amalgamate them. Through some mysterious incantation, cold war commitments might be substantially exorcized. It became all too easy to view overseas burdens in terms of their decisiveness in all out war. Thus the Middle East bastion might be slighted because it would have marginal influence on the course of a nuclear war in Europe. But if a limited conflict were involved, the defense of the Middle East might be of very great importance.

The inclusion of the notion of "broken-backed" war illustrated the difficulty. Ground forces and navies, but particularly navies, would continue intermittent hostilities even after stockpiles of atomic bombs had been reciprocally exhausted. Conventional conflict would be an extension of unconventional conflict. But because there was no real doctrine of limited war in the global strategy paper, a service which did not find a role for itself in the nuclear–"broken-backed" amalgam, had no *raison d'être*. Thus, the Navy and Sir Rhoderick McGrigor insisted on a phase of warfare not entirely unlike World War II, and the Navy would not have accepted the paper without its insertion. Slessor and Slim, by contrast, were willing to talk of "broken-backed war," but it was in their minds a short-lived conception; and it would be decisively outmoded by the foreseeable advent of the hydrogen bomb. They also deprecated the Royal Navy's contribution in the early stages of an all-out war. "The British Chiefs had strongly dissented . . . from the American view that fast carrier forces could contribute materially to the ground battle. They rated carriers as 'a luxury.' " [26] As the fundamentals of thermonuclear warfare became more widely known, the Navy became even more diffident about its purposes:

Many naval officers often wondered, if the truth be known, whether their airmen colleagues were not right and whether the Admiralty's views were really reconcilable with reality. . . . They played on, however, out of loyalty to their own Service and also because of an instinct which they could not support with

[26] *Ibid.*, p. 82.

sound logic that armies and navies were not out-dated but were still essential for the security and well being of the country.[27]

Partly as a result, the Navy began to develop a new doctrine of limited war. In Korea British carriers had played a significant and successful role. The Suez operation was another tactical success for carrier-based aircraft. It was also becoming more clear that overpowering recourse to strategic air attack might not always be in a nation's interest. One naval advocate declared: "The world has apparently become accustomed to the idea of 'total war' and to assume too readily that World War III, if it ever comes upon us, must necessarily also be waged as a total war—that is to say, a war in which on Foch's principle, nothing matters but the winning of it. . . . The Service Staffs, if the world is to survive at all, must discard the ideas of Foch, and shape their strategy and their day-to-day conduct of any warlike operations that may be forced upon them, with the political aim ever unceasingly in mind." [28]

The doctrine was novel in that nations had not self consciously resolved before to limit the use of forces and weapons already in being. The greater the limitation the longer would be the conventional phrase, and the less "brokenbacked" its character. The Navy could also appeal to the practical utility of its forces, regardless of overarching doctrine. The global strategy paper might inveigh against cold war com-

[27] Vice Admiral P. W. Gretton, "Maritime Strategy," ch. 3, p. 6. Unpublished manuscript, quoted in W. J. Crowe Jr., "The Policy Roots of the Modern Royal Navy, 1946-1963," p. 154. Unpublished dissertation, Princeton University, 1965.

[28] Rear Admiral H. G. Thursfield, "Defence Policy in the Melting Pot," in H. G. Thursfield, ed., *Brassey's Annual 1955*, p. 4.

mitments, but they could not in practice be eliminated. The argument of the paper on this score was transparent: in so far as cold war positions were material to an ultimate hot war role their retention was subject to the test of thermonuclear viability. If they could not survive or participate in an all-out struggle, they were of little use. But most cold war obligations were of different nature. They conduced to political stability in a given region; they bolstered trade and the sterling area; they assured access to vital raw materials, needed in peacetime. Singapore, Malaya, Kenya, and the Middle East were not simply instrumental to a hot-war objective; they were desiderata in themselves.

In this context both navies and armies still had a significant role to play. And even Prime Minister Churchill refrained from drawing the logical conclusion implicit in the strategy paper. British NATO forces were not cut to 50,000 men. Cold war commitments, with the exception of the Suez Canal base, were not phased out; and a substitute for Suez had to be erected in Cyprus. For political reasons the Conservatives hesitated to press their logic on NATO confreres. The most important point was to keep American forces in Europe and build continental confidence in a "forward defense" which seemed to be the *sine qua non* of NATO political cohesion. As one military expert pointed out:

Once the American commitment had become a fact, with the appointment of General Eisenhower and the dispatch of more American formations to Germany, the new British government was satisfied so long as it could ensure the continuation of this commitment, framing its policy inside NATO to achieve this political end rather than to implement a purely military strategy. Churchill himself had always believed that Western Europe's immunity depended on the American atomic umbrella. More than the Labour leaders, he saw NATO as a political instrument for the defense of Europe if the deterrent failed.

On the other hand, he recognized that America would not keep troops in Europe unless some attempt was made to find a strategic role for them in war, and unless America's European allies showed themselves ready to cooperate in fulfilling this role. Thus when the RAF argued that NATO should formally admit that Western Europe's security depended upon the deterrent of air-atomic retaliation, and should trim its ground forces accordingly, Churchill rejected its advice for political reasons, and continued to support the concept of forward defense. Moreover, the Continental governments knew their peoples would not support NATO unless they could be persuaded that its aim was to defend them from occupation by the Red Army.[29]

Thus paradoxically, the condition for a nuclear strategy became a partially conventional strategy. U.S. strategic power could only be guaranteed if America were committed to Europe through the physical presence of ground troops. In order to justify the presence of American ground forces, NATO doctrine had to offer a theoretical rationale for their use. In this sense, conventional forces were not only precedent to nuclear forces; conventional doctrines were precedent to nuclear doctrines. In rejecting the logical implications of the global strategy paper, Churchill had to challenge its doctrines as well.

What emerged in the final synthesis was only a slight modification of Labour's three-year plan. The Navy continued to fend against the underwater menace, with major expenditure on antisubmarine frigates and minesweepers. The *Eagle* and the *Ark Royal* were completed during 1952–54 to

[29] Denis Healey, "Britain and NATO," in Klaus Knorr, ed., *NATO and American Security* (Princeton, N.J., 1959), p. 214.

provide a major antisubmarine warfare capability, and the "Daring-class" destroyers also served as carrier-escorts and were equipped with the most modern capabilities against the underwater threat. Minesweeping had great priority in the naval rearmament because the United States had let its own capacity lapse after 1945 and was not planning to remedy the defect through new construction. The new British carriers, however, put to sea without adequate aircraft. The *Sea Hawk* and the *Sea Venom*, interim jet aircraft, were rushed into production for purposes of day and all-weather fighter interception. The *Wyvern*, a strike aircraft, had been on the drawing boards since 1945, but was not put into production until the Korean War. To deal with the Soviet cruiser menace, the Navy was given approval to proceed with a new strike aircraft which could carry a tactical atomic bomb.[30] To bridge the gap between existent models and the new planes, the *Attacker* was acquired from the United States to replace the *Sea Fury* until the *Sea Hawk* was available in quantity. The Douglas *Skyraider* was also obtained. The deficiencies in naval air strength provoked an American observer to remark: "The British aircraft now in use are inferior in many respects to the United States carrier-based planes. . . . The chief disadvantage of the aircraft the British now use is their inferior range. Moreover, they now have no night or all-weather fighters aboard their carriers." [31] Despite these defects, expenditure on conventional naval armament continued at a high level. Practical procurement did not necessarily follow the precepts of the global strategy paper.

In the Army the situation was much the same. By 1953, the active army had reached 11⅓ divisions, of which 10⅓ were

---

[30] See Crowe, p. 127.
[31] Hanson Baldwin in the New York *Times*, September 29, 1952.

overseas—four in Germany, 2½ in the Middle East, 2 in Malaya, and the rest in Hongkong, Austria, Trieste, and elsewhere. As the Secretary of State for War acknowledged:

At present an Army of 11⅓ divisions is the biggest army . . . which we can create with the present manpower which we have. But the fact remains that with our overseas commitments as they are at present, an Army of the equivalent of 11⅓ divisions is just too small for the job. . . . eighty per cent of our fighting units are overseas and the Army is unduly stretched and strained in meeting our overseas commitments. . . . our Imperial and strategic garrisons . . . have been reduced to the minimum. In the Mediterranean and elsewhere . . . I do not think that there is any more scope for reduction. Lastly, our commitments take the form of those set aside for NATO. I have heard it suggested . . . that we should withdraw our forces from Europe. I believe that would be the most disastrous policy we could adopt. Quite apart from the effect on the unity of the West and NATO as a whole, . . . from the point of view of self interest . . . the defence of this country is inexplicably connected with the defence of Western Europe.[32]

The Army was also proceeding on a conventional tack. In the event of an all-out war, however, the Army had a clearer function than the Navy. If the conflict arose over Europe, there would be a massive ground conflict in the initial stages. This would require Western forces in place, utilizing tactical atomic weapons in support of infantry and armour. Air support and high mobility would be major characteristics of the land battle. Strategic bombing would eventually decide the contest, but ground strength would have its place. The notion of "broken-backed" warfare was less essential to the Army than to the Navy.

In the result, the global strategy paper was not really

[32] *House of Commons Debates*, Vol. 512 (March 9, 1953), col. 846.

carried out. Neither Anti-Aircraft nor Fighter Command seemed to have a crucial mission in face of overpowering strategic strikes upon populations and industrial capacities, yet neither was canceled in 1952–53. Cold war forces were supposed to be increasingly outmoded, and yet these occupied increasing British attention and resources from 1953–57. Kenya, Malaya, and the Middle East were of great importance, regardless of their defensibility in thermonuclear war. The Air Force continued with fighter-interceptor and night and all-weather reequipment along lines foreshadowed in the Labour rearmament program. The Navy went on dealing with the menace of the submarine and mine and studied the problem of countering Soviet cruiser strength. The Army maintained its European ground force commitments, though they failed to reach the Lisbon totals projected for 1954. In one sense, therefore, the global strategy paper, instead of producing cuts in conventional forces to reemphasize the "great deterrent" actually sanctioned a strategic rearmament alongside conventional rearmament. Slessor had argued that NATO strategy superimposed a conventional upon an atomic strategy; in its final impact, however, the global strategy paper superimposed a nuclear strategy upon a conventional strategy. Since 1952 there has been an underlying tension between British doctrine and British practice. Doctrinal tendencies have emphasized strategic air power, reliance upon nuclear weapons, and a smaller army. Practice has paid less heed to strategic air strength, but has frequently demanded battalions, air lift, and conventional naval forces. These disjunctions still have not been remedied.

In some ways it is surprising that the global strategy found its origin among the British military chiefs. The theory which it expounded had greater application outside of Britain and the empire than it did within. NATO doctrine had radically embraced conventional force postures, without calculation of the impact of strategic bombing. The British paper might have become the basis for a revolution in NATO strategy. The United States had also espoused a "balanced deterrent" strategy. A conventional buildup would be required as Soviet nuclear strength grew. The merit of the British paper was that it focused major attention on the *absolute* damage which American striking power could do, not upon the *relative* balance between American and Soviet forces. And, in 1953 and 1954, President Eisenhower and Secretary of State John Foster Dulles publicly endorsed many of the notions which had underlain British strategic revaluation. Even more important, the United States had the capabilities to carry out the strategic offensive which the British military had endorsed; aside from Korea, there were few cold war commitments which America had to underwrite with military force. The British on the other hand had neither the resources for a major strategic deterrent force, nor were they without cold war involvements. At precisely the time when Prime Minister Churchill decided to reequip Bomber Command, conventional requirements were beginning to increase. The British had a marvelous new doctrine for other people; but they applied it to themselves.

The practical failures of the new notions, however, were testimony to the government's sense of political proportion. European strategy could not be revamped overnight, and in any event a justification had to be found for U.S. ground troops. Challenges overseas could not be neglected. It was also important to avoid giving further offense to European allies. The refusal of both Labour and Conservative governments to join the Coal and Steel Community and the European Defense Community had already alienated European opinion. A deterrent strategy based upon "air-atomic retaliation" and involving wholesale reductions in ground forces might poison the European atmosphere and call British reliability into question. Britain might not carry out NATO strategy to the letter, but neither could she deviate from it in marked degree.

By the 1953 defense paper, the government could observe "the risk of war has receded in past months." [33] The reason in Prime Minister Churchill's view was the growing power of the Western strategic deterrent. Korea had subsided into political wrangling and dilatory conflict; the NATO buildup had made substantial strides; the Soviets had refrained from any new aggression. It seemed reasonable to extend the danger period for a possible attack to 1954 and even beyond. If Western deterrent strength continued to grow apace, moreover, the situation could become even more stable. "It may be that by a process of sublime irony we have reached a stage in this story where safety will be the sturdy child of terror and survival the twin brother of annihiliation."

[33] Cmnd. 8768, *Statement on Defense, 1953*, p. 3.

CHAPTER SEVEN

DETERRENCE, DEFENSE, AND OVERSEAS INTERESTS: ATTEMPTS AT A MULTIPLE CAPABILITY, 1954–1955

THE INTERNATIONAL technological environment was continually shifting. In 1950–52 there had been no doubt of American willingness to use strategic nuclear power in response to a Soviet aggression in Europe. The consequences of such employment if it ever became necessary, however, would be disastrous for Europeans on both sides of the Iron Curtain. Even if the Soviets could not reach the United States with a powerful striking force, they could certainly devastate Europe. American nuclear escalation in response to a Soviet ground attack, then, would provoke attacks upon European urban populations. Part of the reason for the excessive Lisbon force goals had been a desire to make clear to the Russians that the West would be capable of resisting a Soviet onslaught in conventional terms. The allies would not have to extend the war and cause additional devastation to offer a reliable defense.

At the same time, neither Europe nor the United States was planning solely on the basis of conventional resistance. Increasingly after 1951 Britain looked upon her NATO commitments as a guarantee of the U.S. position in Europe; the United States would stay so long as her allies contributed to Western defense. And the U.S. ground force posture itself reinsured the U.S. strategic deterrent. If Europe was invaded, American ground forces would be engaged, and this would bring American strategic retaliation. If the United States had no forces there, the British reasoned, Washington's willingness to fight to the death over Europe would be less clear. Developments of 1950–52, however, raised for the first time the issue of a conventional war in Europe; they also raised the question whether strategic escalation in the event of war would be in Europe's own interest. Acheson allayed these concerns by asserting that primary emphasis should be placed on deterrence of war; if Europe actually had to be defended, she would face catastrophe whether that defense was conventional or nuclear.

By 1954–55, the Soviets had developed a nuclear force which could destroy an important fraction of American industrial capacity. In this sense the deductions European states drew at the beginning of the Korean War were now relevant to the continental United States. If the United States opted for thermonuclear war in response to a ground attack in Europe, American citizens would also suffer grievously. Further, there was an additional complication for the United States. Europe's only choice was between two strategic amphitheaters: she could be the arena for conventional war, or she could be the arena for nuclear war. The remembrance of World War II was sufficient to ensure that a conventional defense would not be greatly preferred to a nuclear defense. For the United States, however, the commitment to a nuclear strategy represented the difference between American populations being involved in war or their freedom from attack. A conventional strategy in Europe, if it could remain conventional, would avert strategic bombing of the United States.

In one sense, therefore, the British global strategy paper and the American "New Look" that succeeded it were partially outdated shortly after inception. The American decision as expounded by Secretary of State Dulles to place "more reliance on deterrent power, and less dependency on local defensive power" was rational only so long as deterrence worked. If it did not work, American as well as European populations would immediately be threatened. It was all very well to say that "A potential aggressor must know that he cannot always prescribe battle conditions that suit him. . . . . The way to deter aggression is for the free community to be willing and able to respond vigorously at places and with means of its own choosing." The question remained whether the "free community" would be willing to respond in a manner which would imperil its own survival.

"So long as our policy concepts were unclear," Dulles continued, the military leaders could not be "selective" in building military power. That is, as long as the enemy was allowed to pick the time, place, and method of warfare, we had to be prepared to fight in many different places and with a variety of old and new weapons. But now a "basic decision" had been made in the National Security Council "to depend primarily upon a great capacity to retaliate, instantly, by means and at places of our choosing." This permitted the Joint Chiefs of Staff to "shape our military establishment to fit what is our policy, instead of having to try to be ready to meet the enemy's many choices. That permits a selection of military means, instead of a multiplication of means. As a result, it is now possible to get, and share, more basic security at less cost." [1]

[1] Glenn H. Snyder, "The 'New Look' of 1953," in Warner R. Schilling, Paul Y. Hammond, and Glenn H. Snyder, *Strategy, Politics, and Defense Budgets* (New York, 1962), p. 464.

"Massive retaliation" was a credible military notion so long as nations were willing to make such a threat and carry it out if their bluff was called. And in one important respect, "massive retaliation" had always been at the core of both British and American doctrine: as conceived in 1950–52, another major war in Europe would certainly have involved strategic nuclear bombing of the Soviet heartland. It remained uncertain, however, whether a strategy of escalation would be equally appropriate as symmetrical nuclear capabilities were attained on both sides.

NATO strategy until the end of 1954 was inconsistent because it presumed strategic bombing, but made its force calculations in conventional terms. The inconsistency, however, could be remedied in two ways: one was to retain the premise of strategic bombing and phase down ground troops; the other was to abandon the premise of strategic bombing and develop a fully effective conventional defense. Both the global strategy paper and the "New Look" were rational if the first course were adopted; neither was rational if the second alternative were chosen. A decision between policies turned upon the risks the West was willing to run. If ground forces could be skimped or abolished while nuclear deterrence prevented aggression, the first choice would bring the greatest benefit at the least cost. If, on the other hand, aggression occurred despite overarching deterrent forces, their use would exact the greatest cost of all. The probability of Soviet attack in face of Western deterrence was then the relevant quantity. If the Soviets were tempted to test Western intentions, "massive retaliation" was suicidal; if they were unwilling to take such chances, "massive retaliation" was the most economical doctrine.

By 1954–55 an approaching era of "nuclear plenty" meant that Soviet abilities to inflict damage on the United States were increasing rapidly. At the same time, political tensions between the Soviets and the West had been somewhat reduced. The Korean War had been replaced by an armistice; the Indo-China crisis had been overcome; the Austrian State Treaty and the "summit" conference had followed in 1955. A Soviet ground attack seemed far less likely in the new international atmosphere. Accordingly one could believe that the chance of a Soviet thrust was negligible enough that even the potential costs of nuclear escalation could be risked. A strategy of nuclear response could be developed by both the United States and Britain.

There was, however, one major difference between American and British strategy in the period after 1954. The British had not made a fetish of nuclear retaliation; they recognized that cold war commitments would have to be met in conventional terms. They did not, on the whole, believe that conflicts like Korea could be prevented by thermonuclear postulations. Thus British doctrine admitted the need for some conventional forces in NATO and for cold war forces overseas. Precept, however, exceeded practice. In 1954 and 1955 British defense papers in a context of economic imbalance placed ever growing reliance upon the deterrent. Neglecting the more rounded presentation of the global strategy paper, the 1954 defense statement observed:

As the deterrent continues to grow, it should have an increasing effect upon the cold war by making less likely such adventures on the part of the Communist world as their aggression in Korea. This should be of benefit to us by enabling us to reduce the great dispersal of effort which the existing international tension has imposed on us.

The shift toward deterrence was more fully explained in the following terms:

With all these considerations in mind, the Government have concluded that a gradual change should be brought about in the direction and balance of our defence effort. Still greater emphasis will have to be placed on the Royal Air Force because of the need to build up a strategic bomber force and because of the importance of guided missiles in air defence. For reasons explained in later sections of this paper, this emphasis will take time to reveal itself in increased allocations of funds to the Air Ministry. Defence research and development will continue to have high priority, and expenditure on it will increase, though this will be kept within bounds by concentration on projects of the highest importance. Expenditure on the Army will tend to decline, though the extent of the decline will to a large extent depend upon the commitments which the Army, as an instrument of Government policy, has to meet. Subject to these commitments and to our obligations to our allies, it will be our aim gradually to reduce the total size of the Army and to reconstitute the strategic reserve at home, the lack of which is at present a serious, though unavoidable, defect in our defence readiness. The necessity for the proper defence of our sea communications makes it unlikely that expenditure on the Royal Navy can be reduced much below its present level. As a general principle, because of the less immediate danger of a global war and because of the Government's appreciation of the probable nature of such a war, rather less emphasis will be placed on the accumulation of reserves of warlike stores and equipment for a prolonged period of hostilities.[2]

The 1955 White Paper carried this emphasis even further:

The discharge of our many overseas commitments in cold war conditions must continue to absorb a large share of the resources which we can make available for defence. For the rest we must, in our allocation of resources, assign even higher priority to the primary deterrent, that is to say to the production of nuclear weapons and the means of their delivery. Other elements of our

[2] Cmnd. 9075, *Statement on Defence, 1954*, p. 5, 6.

defence effort must be adjusted to conform to these priorities and we must, in particular, eliminate those parts of our forces which have become or are becoming obsolete in modern conditions. We must have regard also to the kind of war in prospect; and here the governing factor is the critical importance of the initial phase. We cannot, however, be sure that the initial phase will be decisive; certainly all our efforts must be directed to securing that it is not decisive against us. Some provisions, though on a lower priority, must therefore be made for continuing operations after the initial phase, particularly at sea.[3]

There were, of course, good financial grounds for cuts in conventional defense expenditure. The government was trying to restore convertibility, and the recession of 1953 had given way to the boom of 1955, causing a reversal in the balance of payments. In the latter year, Sir Anthony Eden, the new Prime Minister, decided that reductions would have to be made in service manpower. He explained later: "A shortage of manpower was one of the principal elements at the time in the country's inflationary pattern. The only contribution which could immediately be made by the Service departments was to speed the reduction in the armed forces to swell the ranks of civilian labour. This we did." Over the longer-term defense reductions also seemed necessary. The Minister of Defence told Eden in July, 1955, that "unless existing programmes were revised, the cost of defence would rise during the next four years from £1,527 million in 1955 to £1,929 million in 1959." The British economy, Eden believed, "could not be expected to stand this mounting strain." [4]

Defense expenditure had to be held to some relatively con-

[3] Cmnd. 9391, *Statement on Defence, 1955*, p. 9.
[4] Sir Anthony Eden, *Full Circle* (London, 1960), pp. 315, 370.

stant figure over a period of time.[5] The Prime Minister and the Minister for Defence, Selwyn Lloyd, decided to make cuts across the board. "In the Royal Navy, [they] reduced the plans for the active and reserve fleets, scaled down the capacity of some overseas bases and cut expenditure on war reserve. In the Army, the strength but not the fighting power of units was reduced, also the size of the strategic reserve. In the Royal Air Force, a small reduction was ordered in the medium bomber force and larger ones in Fighter and Coastal Commands." [6]

The arguments for these cutbacks were twofold. First, as the "broken-backed" phase was no longer expected to influence greatly the outcome of war, reserve forces in all three services were less necessary. Almost inevitably the conflict would be decided by forces in being and those that could be mobilized immediately. The Territorial Army would have little influence on a conflict in Europe. A large but unready reserve of pilots and aircraft could be dispensed with. If the struggle was short, they would not affect it; if it was long, new planes could be built and pilots trained. The Navy did not have to plan on a large reserve fleet which would gradually be brought to establishment after the onset of hostilities. At the same time, not only reserve, but also front-line forces were cut. Bomber and Fighter Commands were reduced, the latter because it was increasingly doubtful that fighters were the answer to enemy strategic bombing, the former because even a major deterrent force did not have to be large. When

[5] In other words, the percentage of Gross National Product spent on defense had to decline. These plans were in fact carried out, with the 1956 defense estimates held to £1,535 million.

[6] Eden, p. 370.

Bomber Command was equipped with the hydrogen bomb, fewer bombers might present an equal challenge to an aggressor. Thus it was possible to reduce the V-bomber total from 215 to about 180.

In certain respects the 1955 defense cutbacks were among the most balanced of the period before Suez. All services had to suffer; there was no singling out of limited or cold war forces for reduction while pressing on with the nuclear deterrent. Briefly at least, the strictures of the global strategy paper in favor of a reasonable balance of forces were heeded. Later, however, the bomb was to take precedence. Forces in NATO could be radically phased down. As Eden wrote to Eisenhower: "It is on the thermonuclear bomb and atomic weapons that we now rely, not only to deter aggression, but to deal with aggression if it should be launched. A 'shield' of conventional forces is still required; but it is no longer our principal military protection. Need it be capable of fighting a major land battle?" [7]

As applied to NATO and on the assumption of rapid escalation of any conflict in Europe, this doctrine was unexceptionable. As applied to cold war battlefields, however, it was less realistic. Actually, between 1955 and 1960 the Prime Minister and his colleagues planned to reduce British forces from 800,000 to 445,000, on grounds of greater "reliance upon the nuclear deterrent." Such shifts, moreover, were to occur in the face of increased responsibilities. Though Korea had been pacified, the Malayan guerrilla struggle continued; the Mau Mau situation in Kenya had worsened; and Cyprus was about to erupt. Commenting upon the state of Army manpower, the Secretary of State for War noted: "The strength of the

[7] *Ibid.*, pp. 372–73.

Army will inevitably fall from now onwards. The fall in 1954-55 will be some 13,000 men. At the same time world-wide commitments have increased." [8] At the very time when cold war burdens were becoming heavier, British ability to discharge them was diminishing.

In one respect at least, such trends were violations of the global strategy of 1952. The paper had stressed greater reliance upon the deterrent, but it had not reasoned that such conflicts could be disposed of in atomic terms. Cold war, NATO, and deterrent strategies were to be handled individually. And while atomic weapons might reduce the second commitment, they would not remove the first. Only if cold war bastions were merely tributary to the waging of all-out war could they be discarded with a saving in service man-power. In this way the plans of 1954-55 exceeded the mandates of previous strategy.

In the U.S. case the policy of nuclear retaliation was carried much further at the doctrinal level. Speaking of atomic weapons, President Eisenhower stated: "Where these things are used on strictly military targets and for strictly military purposes, I see no reason why they shouldn't be used just exactly as you would use a bullet or anything else"; and Secretary Dulles argued: if "the United States became engaged in a major military activity anywhere in the world, those weapons would come into use because, as I say, they are becoming more and more conventional and replacing what used to be called conventional weapons." [9]

Yet the American administration never drew the logical

---

[8] Cmnd. 9072, *Memorandum of the Secretary of State for War Relating to the Army Estimates, 1954-55.*

[9] Quoted in Samuel P. Huntington, *The Common Defense* (New York, 1961), p. 80.

conclusions of its own arguments. The plan advanced by Admiral Arthur Radford in 1956 to cut 800,000 men from the military forces, including 450,000 from the Army, would have carried out the doctrine of massive retaliation to the letter. Only token forces would have been maintained in Europe; other cold war commitments would have been pared. American strategic power would have been raised to a new pinnacle of importance. Yet, the Radford plan was never put into effect, and the cuts in service manpower which finally emerged were insignificant in comparison. The United States talked of massive retaliation at the theoretical level, but refrained from manning its forces accordingly. The British saw explicit needs for NATO and cold war forces in addition to strategic capacity, but increasingly service manpower was reduced. The British had the more balanced doctrine, but failed to implement it; the Americans had an inferior doctrine, but neglected it in practice.

In several respects the postwar apogee of British defense policy was reached in 1954–55. Global deterrent forces were coming into the British arsenal; despite cold war conflicts in Malaya, Kenya and Cyprus, British responsibilities were being effectively discharged. There was no evidence that a reduced list of commitments might not be fulfilled with the resources available. Though doctrines of nuclear deterrence inevitably impinged upon cold and limited war forces, Britain did not discard them. She moved increasingly toward a nuclear strategy and economized conventional forces where she might, but still did not place all of her eggs in the strategic basket. A multiple capability was disposed, and though the strains in that capability were latent, they were not yet apparent. In political terms as well, Britain was at the zenith of her power.

All of her military ventures, with the possible exception of retention of the Suez base, were successful. The atomic bomb had been developed independently; the hydrogen bomb was well on the way; procurement of advanced weapons systems was slow but steady. Although the Swift was a failure, the Hunter provided more than adequate compensation, and the V-bombers were all destined to be operational within reasonable time-spans. Because of judicious anticipation of colonial problems, the devolution of empire was orderly, and Britain parted from her erstwhile territories on good terms.

In terms of international diplomacy, in Europe and overseas, Britain maximized her influence. Though Whitehall's refusal to countenance participation in the Schuman Plan and the European Defense Community had undoubtedly lost friends on the continent, no irrevocable conclusions had been drawn. It was still uncertain whether Britain might not play a much larger role in European affairs than she had done in the past. Further, London was still the essential balancer between Washington and Europe. In order to commit the United States it was also necessary to commit the United Kingdom. The United States would have less interest in Europe, if Britain were outside it. And continental countries had grown used to regarding Britain as a major factor in their own affairs. If the United States might not be fully relied on, it was all the more important to have a firm British commitment to continental defense.

Despite the measures of European integration, moreover, Europe was still irresolute and weak. The proposal for a European political community had been defeated in 1953; it was not certain the plan for a European Army would be ratified by the French parliament. As long as the continent remained disunited British help was the more necessary. The conditions for British support in addition, were adequately fulfilled. Whitehall could participate in the contractual relations of sovereign states. Agreements with the Coal and Steel Community, with E.D.C., and with the successor Western European Union scarcely abridged British freedom of action. The situation was appropriate for the exercise of British political initiative.

There was a simultaneous faltering of American diplomacy. Secretary Dulles did not always inspire European confidence. He was determined to force a French ratification of E.D.C. even if it became necessary to retract U.S. interests in the bargain. He told the British Foreign Secretary at the end of 1953 that the West was "approaching a parting of the ways with regard to American policy. If things went wrong, the United States might swing over to a policy of Western hemispheric defence, with emphasis on the Far East. This might not be immediately apparent, but once the trend had started, it would be hard to stop. Already there was mounting pressure for such a change." [10] The United States rigidly supported an integrationist solution for Europe and viewed looser arrangements with impatience. At the time of the London and Paris Agreements in 1954, Dulles was unsure that the American Congress would accept anything but a federal solution to the problem of German rearmament. As a result, British initiatives were the more necessary.

Such attitudes were reinforced by America's growing involvement in the Far East. The Korean armistice had not produced stability in East and Southeast Asia, and Americans began to view the outcome of the French struggle in Indo-China with alarm. If Communist expansion were not stopped in Southeast Asia, it would eventually engulf other countries.

[10] Eden, pp. 57–58.

The British were less convinced. A Communist take-over in Indo-China did not have to mean insurrection in all countries of the region, to say nothing of outside states. Nor was it clear how the Vietminh victory was to be prevented. Air strikes would not do it, even massive attacks by U.S. B-29s. And if ground forces were to be engaged, they would have to be sent on a vast scale. The United States, however, did not foresee such a commitment. In a letter to Prime Minister Churchill, President Eisenhower stressed that he did not "envisage the need of any appreciable ground forces on your or our part."[11] Anthony Eden was quite right in commenting later: "Militarily I did not believe that the limited measures contemplated by the United States could achieve substantial results; no military aid could be effective unless it included ground troops. Sir Winston summed up the position by saying that what we were being asked to do was to assist in misleading Congress into approving a military operation, which would be in itself ineffective, and might well bring the world to the verge of a major war. We agreed that we must therefore decline to give any undertaking of military assistance to the French in Indo-China."[12] Accordingly the British placed their hopes in the Geneva conference, believing that no new Western military exertions would decide Indo-Chinese fate. In the end they proved to be right; agreement was reached on Indo-China, and a temporary respite from conflict earned by Southeast Asia. Dulles fulminated at the result, but was unwilling to do anything about it. The world witnessed a triumph for British diplomacy.

The European impasse over E.D.C. called for other British

[11] Dwight D. Eisenhower, *Mandate for Change, 1953–1956* (New York, 1963), p. 347.
[12] Eden, p. 105.

measures. Dulles sought an alternative supranational arrangement after the French rejected the European Army. Eden
recognized that new measures of military integration would
not be accepted by the French and that unless a more open-
ended scheme could be devised, the German divisions required under Lisbon plans would not be obtained. It was testimony to British fidelity to alliance purposes that she proposed new guarantees to allow German rearmament even
though she did not agree that a massive conventional force
was necessary on the central front.

By 1954, of course, Germany's subservient position was as
important as German military weakness, and it was imperative
to bring Bonn into direct participation in NATO, ending the
occupation regime. German membership in the Atlantic Pact
was made possible by the reformulation of the Brussels
Treaty of 1948. Italy and West Germany were added, and
Bonn was required to pledge that she would not manufacture
atomic, bacteriological, or chemical weapons. Maximums
were set for ground forces in Europe for the participating
states including Britain, thus effectively limiting West Germany to the twelve divisions allocated under NATO plans.
While Dulles had apparently been willing to go ahead with
new military arrangements without France, Eden induced her
to participate, first, by limiting German armaments, and second, by pledging new measures of British support. Subject to
majority vote in the reconstituted Brussels Treaty Council
(now called Western European Union) Britain was to maintain "on the mainland of Europe, including Germany, the
effective strength of the United Kingdom forces which are
now assigned to the Supreme Allied Commander, Europe,
that is to say four divisions and the Second Tactical Air Force

or such other forces as the Supreme Allied Commander, Europe, regards as having equivalent fighting capacity." [13]

This commitment was subject only to the possible need to withdraw forces "in the event of an acute overseas emergency" or "too great a strain on the external finances of the United Kingdom." The British undertaking was to last for the duration of the Brussels Pact, or until 1998. In contrast Secretary Dulles told the Senate Foreign Relations Committee that the Paris accords added nothing to U.S. obligations and that America was required to keep troops in Europe, "as long as it is judged in the best interests of the United States and no longer." Once again a diplomatic victory had been won by the Foreign Office while the United States abstained or temporized. On May 6, 1955, the new Western European Union came into force with French participation and support.

In several respects it was surprising that Britain made such a revolutionary pledge to European defense. The maxims of the global strategy paper might have suggested a reduction in British NATO forces over time, and in any event Britain was now moving into a phase of increasing reliance on the deterrent. She was, moreover, extremely eager to put an end to conscription and this would in turn require a substantial reduction of overseas commitments. It was apparently believed, however, that "the commitment of 80,000 men to NATO could be sustained in the face of immediate plans for military manpower reduction." [14] Greater reliance on the deterrent would economize forces overseas, and an air-lifted strategic

[13] Quoted in Royal Institute of International Affairs, *Britain in Western Europe* (London, 1956), p. 62.

[14] William P. Snyder, *The Politics of British Defence Policy, 1945-1962* (London, 1964), p. 19.

reserve would permit rapid deployment to overseas areas from bases in the home islands. Strategic air-lift then became the key to Britain's chronic manpower problem. The United States, however, in the throes of a similar attempt to reduce ground troops, did not make an equivalent pledge. The final outcomes of both policies were perhaps instructive. In the end the United States did not cut its land forces by very much, but refused to make a commitment that its force postures would easily have permitted. The British made the commitment, and then got themselves into difficulty by abolishing conscription. Britain limited her subsequent freedom of action on behalf of the alliance; the United States refused to do so.

The events of 1954–55 confirmed the prescience of British diplomacy. Since the end of 1950 there had been a divergence between Britain and America over policy in the Far East. The United Kingdom, while maintaining her cold war commitments in Malaya and Hongkong, did not wish to become tied up in a major Asian war, conventional or nuclear, with Communist powers. She was not convinced that Western interests in Asia were paramount; nor was she sure that Western interests there could be easily defended. If one country fell prey to subversion, it did not necessarily mean that adjacent nations would do so as well. Britain was also worried lest American concentration upon Asia undermine its primary position in Europe. Thus it became crucial to find some kind of settlement in Asia which would prevent wholesale American involvement and to prevent a reverse in Europe that might lead to a redefinition of American interests. With the W.E.U. on the one hand, and the Geneva conference on the other, both objectives were achieved. Britain came to be regarded as an indispensable linch-pin joining the continent to the new world. British influence in European councils has probably never been higher than it was in the spring of 1955. If the movement for European unity had not started up again, and if Suez had not occurred, Britain might have remained the prime mover in European affairs. The failure of American diplomacy certainly offered no proximate alternative.

Portents of later disequilibrium, however, were already beginning to emerge in 1954. If the American obsession was the Far East, the British preoccupation was the Middle East. And while Britain deprecated American involvement in Asia, the United States failed to appreciate the British stake in the Eastern Mediterranean and the Persian Gulf. In the period up to 1956 each country sought to involve the other in its sphere of major interest. Eden bemoaned American hesitancy over the Baghdad Pact and criticized American pressure over the Suez base negotiations. Dulles lamented the British failure to agree to "united action" over Indo-China. Neither was prepared to concede that a close alliance required each country to support the other's basic interests. If they had done so, America, for good or ill, would certainly have intervened in Indo-China in April, 1954, and the Suez operation would have been successful in November, 1956. But both diplomatists wished to conciliate different members of the neutralist camp. Dulles wanted to win over Middle Eastern countries so that he might have a reliable southern bulwark against Soviet expansion. Eden wanted to win over Asian neutralists so that the Commonwealth might be an even more effective political entity. In the end, of course, each failed in his objective. Dulles did not gain political support in the Middle East; Eden lost it in the Far East. The divergence in the Anglo-American alliance was essentially responsible for the respective national failures of each.

The British position in the Middle East had first come under attack during the last months of the Labour government. The nationalization of the Anglo-Iranian Oil Company had forced the Cabinet to decide whether it would use force to settle the issue. A socialist government would in any event have had difficulty acting to oppose nationalization of foreign assets, and it was decided to seek a solution through negotiation. When the Conservatives gained power in October, 1951, they concluded that British "authority throughout the Middle East had been violently shaken," [15] and resolved on measures to restore the position. The Labour government had set basic policy for the area; they closed down the Anglo-Iranian Oil Company until Prime Minister Mossadegh agreed to negotiate on compensation, and dispatched two brigades to Egypt to cope with disturbances against the Suez base. Until the very end Labour had hoped to create a Middle East Defense Organization, consisting initially of France, Turkey, Britain, and the United States, but with eventual membership by other countries of the region. In the aftermath of the oil nationalization, Egypt and Syria refused to join, and the project died at birth. Greece and Turkey were admitted to NATO in 1952 to make up part of the deficiency.

The British position in the Middle East had its tragic aspects. Originally it provided an indispensable link with India at a time when Indian bases and the Indian army were bastions of imperial strength. After 1947 Indian independence removed this justification, but World War II had provided another. Control of the Eastern Mediterranean would eventually mean control of North Africa, and that in turn would make possible a mortal assault on the European flank of any invader.

[15] Eden, p. 198.

Despite this, the British were tempted to center their efforts elsewhere, nearer the oil sheikdoms of the Persian Gulf and toward the southern approaches to the Suez Canal. When the cold war burgeoned, however, any southerly withdrawal might have been interpreted by Moscow as an invitation to thrust across the Middle East "land bridge." A major base in Kenya would be of little use in stemming such an assault and Whitehall was persuaded to delay its plans for transfer of the Suez base. By 1952 the basic *raison d'être* of the Suez position was accepted to be its utility in the event of ground war with the Soviet Union. This justification fitted nicely with NATO plans which were then calling for conventional strength to halt a Soviet invasion of Europe.

At some point, however, the argument of the global strategy paper would have as much impact in the Middle East as in Europe. If conventional strategies were not the basic factor in a defense of Europe, they might also be less relevant to the defense of the Middle East. In a nuclear war the canal would immediately be blocked; strategic bombing would occupy the most vital phase of the war; a "broken-backed" struggle would either be drawn out and disorganized, or brief and indecisive. In either event, planning for classical military operations on the scale of the Eastern campaigns of World War II was simply anachronistic.

Egyptian policy also militated to convince Britain that Suez would be a liability in war, and that its defense required resources which were excessive in terms of probable benefits. Dependent upon Egyptian labor, the base could not reach its full operational capacity without local support. The base occupied a vast area, as large as that of Wales; it was enormously vulnerable to harrassment of all types. The base and its 70,000 British troops provided one of the most formidable obstacles to army recruiting. Conditions were so deplorable that potential Regulars were dissuaded from joining the forces. Also the very scale of the British investment there in manpower and material made it almost impossible to abolish conscription. Suez would demand so many troops that national service would have to be continued.

Even in a major conventional war the Suez base would have its disadvantages. It seemed unlikely that the canal could be kept open under such conditions, but even if it could, land-based air power would still be able to control passage through narrow Mediterranean waters. The resupply of the base would have to take place 'round the cape. Britain might "require a base in that part of the world," but in 1954 the purposes that it would serve were incompletely thought out. In a context of uncertainty, "smaller bases, redeployment and dispersal would serve our purpose better." [16]

When agreement on the evacuation of the Suez base was reached in October, 1954, Britain made most of the concessions. No agreement on a successor Middle East Defense Organization was reached; certainly Egypt would not participate in such a grouping. The R.A.F. could overfly Egypt and had landing rights at the base. British and Egyptian technicians would seek to keep the base in working order. If any non-Arab state attacked one of the eight Arab nations, Britain could move back into the base and raise it to wartime footing. Freedom of navigation through the canal was to remain unimpaired. There was no agreement on air defense of Egypt, and British withdrawal was to be complete within twenty months' time. Defending the agreement, Prime Minister Churchill emphasized the impact of the thermonuclear weapon upon the military viability of Suez. So great a target

[16] *Ibid.*, p. 260.

could not escape unscathed and hence was obsolete. But the military alternative was Cyprus, an even more concentrated and vulnerable target. Suez would not be useful in thermonuclear war, but neither would most of the other bases the British maintained throughout the world.

The withdrawal from Suez, completed by July, 1956, concluded a chapter in British military history. Despite Egyptian pressure, the agreement reached accorded with basic doctrines of the global strategy paper. Overseas bastions whose usefulness was determined by their influence upon all-out war should be reduced or phased out as the thermonuclear revolution proceeded. The British position in Egypt since World War II had been viewed as crucial to success in another major war. But the vision of that war had been of a rallied ground encounter—on the central front and on the flanks. The Middle East was the strong point from which, ultimately, the southern flank might be attacked. But the basic fact was that the Middle East's importance was not simply to be measured by its impact upon a massive campaign in Europe or its utility in atomic combat. The Middle East was not simply a means to an end; it was an end in itself. It had oil; it controlled important communications links in peacetime; it was a region in which a firm hand was necessary to ensure political stability. In cold or limited war, it would be of great importance; if in hot war it would be a negligible factor.

The Suez evacuation, under great pressure to be sure, was one of the first manifestations of excessive reliance upon the nuclear deterrent and the paring of conventional commitments and capabilities that commenced with the new strategic assessments of 1952. In certain respects, the withdrawal from the Suez base held greater tragic symbolism than the defeat at Suez two years later. In 1954 Britain was at the apogee of its power, militarily and diplomatically. Its influence in world politics was at a peak. There was no need to prove its prowess by asserting an "independent course" or developing an "independent deterrent." The world knew that Britain had "independence" and that its policies were as likely to succeed, perhaps were even more likely to succeed than those of the United States of America.

Despite the global strategy paper, and the increasing emphasis upon deterrent power which followed, no irrevocable choices had yet been made. The V-bombers were being procured, but as 1955 demonstrated, their numbers could easily be decreased. Missiles and the hydrogen bomb were being developed, but it still was uncertain how far the government would proceed and how many would be built. In 1954 it was still not too late to place greater stress on conventional forces; with Britain's great prestige, moreover, such emphases would not have diminished its political position. We are now aware how many future countries may be tempted to rely on "token" capabilities while still achieving membership in "the nuclear club."

Britain, moreover, was in a position to make a formidable contribution to the doctrinal debate. Rear Admiral Sir Anthony Buzzard authored notions of "graduated deterrence" as early as 1955 which developed the range of alternatives between a thermonuclear holocaust and total inaction. Limited war flowed directly from these conceptions, and it was sustained by the Royal Navy as well as American strategic analysts. Even more important perhaps, cold war conflicts were a British speciality. Limited war referred to concrete abstention from modes of warfare which, while efficacious locally, might provoke escalation and strategic retaliation. Korea was in this sense an example of limited war.

Most of British involvements overseas, however, were not limited war, but cold war commitments. In Malaya, Kenya, and Cyprus there were no temptations to geographic escalation or the use of nuclear weapons. The forces actually used, classical though they were, were those most appropriate for the conflict at hand. Nuclear weapons would not decide an insurgent conflict and they would gravely penalize local inhabitants. Britain might therefore have made an important addition to the strategic argument: there were some conflicts that should not be fought by nuclear means, even if escalation posed no danger. It was not simply a matter of saying that nuclear weapons woud deter all forms of aggression and then acting as if they would, after the precepts of the American Air Force.

The withdrawal from the Suez base in 1954 was as symbolic as reentry in 1956. The first reflected the triumph of thermonuclear strategy over concrete geographic interests; the second reflected the triumph of geographic interests over the nuclear deterrent. If 1954 was correct, 1956 should not have occurred, and *vice versa*. But the problem of the Suez invasion, as distinct from the Suez withdrawal, was that it challenged all British purposes in world affairs. In 1954 strategic flexibility was still available; the deterrent was important, but still not decisive. British prestige would still have tolerated basic readjustments in defense. By 1956, it was already too late to make significant changes. Both parties wanted to end conscription; conventional retraction was the only means of doing so. Further the political–international context in which the Suez operation occurred made it impossible to deduce straightforward doctrinal lessons.

One would have thought the failure to mount a conventional military response and to carry it out in short order would have placed a premium upon classical preparedness in the future. The delays, the retraining, the weakness of the British base structure in the Mediterranean—all of these demanded conventional redressment. But the political failure which emerged simultaneously was so great that Britain had to spend all its time rebuilding prestige and asserting its independence. This could only be done by further enhancing the nuclear deterrent and proclaiming its separate ability to inflict unacceptable damage on the Soviet Union. Thus the changes in British defense emphases which might easily have been made in 1954 in conditions of unrivaled success could not possibly be made in 1956 in conditions of unmitigated failure. In many ways this lightning reversal in British political and international fortunes was one of the most tragic outcomes of postwar international relations. To this day, Suez broods over British purposes and prestige in world affairs.

The years 1954–55 also witnessed important changes in service planning and doctrine. The Army had originally worried that strategic nuclear warfare might supplant ground combat. But such fears were eventually overcome, particularly as applied to a conflict in Europe. It might take time before nuclear weapons would have their effect on the Soviet homeland; in the meantime allied armies had to resist the ground advance.

The development of tactical atomic weapons for land warfare also influenced doctrinal perspectives. They meant, first, that ground forces would have an important place in nuclear war. Land power would afford the shield as air power became the sword. One then had to know whether battlefield nuclear weapons would advantage attack or defense. It was believed that the Western stockpile of such weapons was far larger than the Soviet, and it was also argued, though somewhat later, that the side which used tactical bombs first would have considerable advantage. An enemy using conventional offensive tactics would have to concentrate his forces; these would then be vulnerable to atomic counterattack by the defense.

For the time being, however, neither the Soviets nor the West would have an adequate supply of nuclear bombs for land war; atomic weapons would still be too expensive to hazard on a wide range of tactical targets; as a result infantry and armor tactics could still bear some resemblance to those of World War II. Dispersion, mobility and firepower were the key notions. The new infantry battlefield would occupy a vast area; since fixed-line formations could not be risked, defense of specific positions would be much more difficult.

At the same time it seemed clear that Western resort to nuclear weapons represented the difference between a forward and rearward defense in Europe. Since atomic weapons would permit an economy of manpower, it was possible to carry out Lisbon objectives without achieving Lisbon force goals. Thus in December, 1954, when the NATO Council agreed to plan on the basis of using tactical nuclear weapons to halt a Soviet attack, it actually removed the necessity for attaining prior, non-nuclear, force targets. This was a crucial decision for the British, for however quickly they fulfilled the 1952 NATO program, they were unable to attain the force goals set for 1954. In face of other commitments they could not add to their four divisions in Europe; nor, doctrinally, did they see the need to do so. Eden had been quite correct when he told Eisenhower: "A 'shield' of conventional forces is still required; but it is no longer our principal military protection." The NATO decision of December, 1954, then, represented a significant attempt to harmonize British and alliance doctrine. Had it not occurred, British planning and forces would have been increasingly out of step with their continental and American colleagues.

As early as 1955, moreover, British planners were beginning to recognize that war in Europe might not be total. Until that year the British had viewed the stakes in Europe as all-determining. Limitation was out of the question because nothing short of an unlimited war could occur over Europe: American strategic retaliation would be necessary to stop the Soviet Union. Lisbon plans, predicated on conventional defense, were neither realistic nor were they necessary. Tactical nuclear war, however, could be limited nuclear war. Since neither the United States nor the Soviet Union, the latter increasingly in possession of a capability to cripple the United States, would wish to extend the war and involve its own population, something less than "massive retaliation" might be a desirable strategy for both sides. Here British doctrines of "graduated deterrence," relying upon limited nuclear responses, opened an alternative. These notions were quite important for they gave the British Army a role in limited war, and showed that Korea might not be regression to more primitive forms of warfare. This completed the Army's adjustment to thermonuclear conditions. It had always been much less affected by new modes of warfare than the Navy. The cold war would go on in conditions of tolerable peace, requiring Army garrisons overseas, whatever the mandates of the thermonuclear age. If a third world war occurred, the Army would be shield in Europe; it would be vital at least until strategic bombing worked its effect. Now the Army had found a role in limited war as well. Tactical atomic war against a major antagonist might still not lead to full-scale reprisal on home populations.

Despite the Army's consciousness of its own tasks, however, it still had to contend with its political masters. They were insisting upon reductions in manpower to fight inflation. At the same time, the London and Paris agreements committed Britain to maintain four divisions and a tactical air force in NATO subject to majority vote in the Council of Western European Union. How could such major commitments be held constant while forces were reduced? Particularly when other involvements were increasing? A solution was anticipated as a result of developments in the air-lifted strategic reserve and the strategic nuclear force. "Both new programs were expected to reduce manpower needs in the overseas areas. The air-lifted reserve would hopefully allow rapid deployments from the U.K. and thus balance smaller forces at overseas bases." [17] The strategic nuclear force would have increasing efficacy in preventing the outbreak of conflicts like Korea. The new strategic reserve was first announced in the 1954 defense paper: "It will be our aim gradually to reduce the total size of the Army and to reconstitute the strategic reserve at home, the lack of which is at present, a serious, though unavoidable, defect in our defence readiness." [18] Strategic air-lift, however, was not immediately made available to implement the new concept. And by the time a considerable air-lift capacity had been developed in 1960 and after, Britain had difficulty securing overflight rights from a series of countries. The presumptions on which it had proved possible to cut ground forces turned out not to be valid after all.

The Royal Navy, unlike the other services, went through a period of searching self-doubt. In the immediate aftermath of Korea, the Navy was unsure of its bearings. A doctrine of

[17] Snyder, p. 19.   [18] Cmnd. 9075, p. 6.

limited war, patterned on Korea, had yet to be developed; and the hydrogen bomb was undermining the Navy's role in all-out war. Desperately Navy theorists clung to "broken-backed war," but they did it without real conviction. By 1955, however, new doctrines were in gestation. In Britain, the Royal Navy was the first service to appreciate the problem of strategic vulnerability. This was in part because the Navy had always worried that the nuclear and thermonuclear epochs had made naval forces obsolete. After the Bikini tests, the Navy was much reassured. The atomic bomb might be countered by armor, dispersal, and decontamination techniques; the hydrogen bomb, on the other hand, completely altered these calculations. Ships would simply not be able to stand up to a thermonuclear blast; the accuracy of delivery of hydrogen bombs also mattered much less. Land-based air power would be able to blow aircraft carriers out of the water. The Navy found a chink in the armor of the R.A.F., however, when it pointed out that fixed-site bases would also be vulnerable to a preemptive strike by the opponent. Admiral Torlesse put the case in the following words:

> The effective range of bomber aircraft at their present stage of development being limited, it is necessary in order to reach potential enemy bases and sources of supply to have advanced bases from which to operate them; hence the presence in this country and on the continent of Europe of an American heavy bomber force whose permanent bases are in the U.S.A.
>
> Unfortunately, it is a corollary that these advanced bases are all within practicable range of a potential enemy's heavy bombers. Quite possibly some are even within range of ballistic rockets from sites now available to him. . . . Unless, therefore, one is prepared to face the odium of striking first, the possession of such advanced bases, however well equipped and kept at readiness, affords little real security. It will not even serve as a deterrent,

for an enemy will know that if he cares to strike first he has at least a very good chance of putting a large proportion of them out of action at once and the remainder quickly afterwards, and he may decide that the risk is an acceptable one. . . . And although the increasing range of the modern bomber and the perfection of the technique of flight refuelling is tending to decrease dependence on advanced bases, this cuts both ways, and there can be little doubt that the advent of inter-continental air and ballistic rocket warfare will in time bring bases anywhere in the U.S.A. within practicable range of attack. The warning is clear for all to see: now that nuclear weapons are becoming relatively plentiful, the fixed air base has become a liability, vulnerable to destruction by a single hit beyond hope of quick repair, and easy to find and hit.[19]

This argument obscured the point that NATO strategy presumed that the West would in fact have the first nuclear strike, though it would act only in response to a massive ground invasion of Western Europe. It was correct in its assessment of the dangers inherent in that presumption: the Soviets, recognizing that nuclear escalation would almost certainly result, might resolve upon a strategic nuclear attack on both Europe and the United States simultaneously. Strategic vulnerability of Western forces would then be a matter of critical importance. Neither fixed-site nor floating bases could survive accurate thermonuclear attack, but aircraft carriers at least could be moved around. Long-range missiles could not eliminate them. In theory this argument should have permitted the Royal Navy to lay claim to a strategic role equivalent or superior to that of the R.A.F. The U.S. Navy had long encouraged the British to think in such terms, and it had insisted on a major nuclear role of its own. The Supreme

[19] Rear-Admiral A. D. Torlesse, "The Role of the Aircraft Carrier," *Brassey's Annual, 1955* (edited by H. G. Thursfield), pp. 75–76.

Commander, Atlantic, had refused to confine himself only to protection of sea lanes; the American Navy was supposed to have a potent strike capability, not only at sea, but on shore. A carrier of the Forrestal class operated bombers with 1,500 nautical mile radii capable of carrying heavy nuclear weapons.

The Royal Navy might espouse such designs in theory, but in practice they were unattainable. The Navy did not get the atomic bomb until 1959, and its striking capability was based for years on the *Wyvern*, an aircraft designed to carry conventional bombs and torpedoes only a little farther and faster than its predecessors.[20] Its range and bomb-carrying capacity meant that it could not be a decisive factor in the ground battle, or launch effective strategic strikes behind enemy lines. It was not until the *Buccaneer* became available in 1964 that the Navy possessed any semblance of an effective strike capability. Naval doctrines, therefore, were not matched by naval capabilities.

Relatively greater success was won in the limited war field. Of all the British services the Navy was quickest to seize upon the lessons of Korea. Its carrier forces had performed admirably in supporting ground forces and in tactical interdiction work. Further, the Korean war had shown that carrier aircraft might operate effectively against shore targets. The Navy was not convinced that all future wars would be total. There would be brushfire conflicts and civil unrest as well as more substantial limited wars. "And in limited conflicts of the Korean type [the Royal Navy could] provide quickly, by reason of its mobility, powerful assistance to the land bat-

[20] See W. J. Crowe Jr., "The Policy Roots of the Modern Royal Navy, 1946–1963," pp. 131–32. Unpublished dissertation, Princeton University, 1965.

tle." [21] In all forms of limited aggression the Navy could offer a determined resistance and greatly assist land operations. Limited war doctrines were now of much more importance to the Navy. As one writer has observed:

> Slowly but surely under the pressures of technological advance, tight funds, and inter-Service competition the Fleet's strategical foundation was being shored up and widened. The first references to the Navy's limited war importance had crept on to the scene. At no time did the Navy's official statements go into great detail, nor did they indicate that this might possibly become the fundamental justification for the Fleet. The Country's attention was still riveted on fusion weapons, and the Admiralty still considered general war its primary concern. It was manifest, however, that the Navy's leaders no longer considered the Fleet's general war functions sufficient in themselves to keep the Navy firmly in the defense picture.[22]

Though it was not recognized at the time, moreover, naval support for limited operations might be much more effective than an air-lifted strategic reserve. Fighters and air transport were dependent upon foreign bases to a greater extent than the ships of the Navy. They were also constantly confronted with the need to get permission to overfly other countries, permission which might be suspended or canceled at short notice. Again, the great mobility of the Navy had significant attractions.

It was perhaps inevitable that the Army and Navy should have developed eclectic doctrines in response to Korea and the thermonuclear revolution. They were not and had no prospects of becoming global deterrent forces. The Navy's strictures about the vulnerability of fixed bases did not really redound to her benefit because she had neither the bomb nor

[21] Cmnd. 9391, p. 10.   [22] Crowe, pp. 154–55.

an aircraft capable of delivering it at long distance through enemy fighter defenses. The R.A.F., on the other hand, was charged with the strategic deterrent, and desired to extend its ambit in all directions. In this way the government could claim that strategic nuclear capacity might obviate future Koreas. The risk of escalation of any substantial conflict was such that even limited war could not be allowed to begin. Reliance on the deterrent was furthered by thermonuclear weapons. During the atomic epoch a successful strategic bombing campaign still depended upon large numbers of atomic bombs falling on or near their primary targets. Success depended upon attrition rates, accuracy of delivery, and numbers of bombs. Superpowers were best situated to conduct such campaigns because they could produce requisite quantities of bombs and delivery vehicles to have the desired effect; a smaller power, however, could not be certain of doing so. With the thermonuclear bomb, accuracies, bomb loads, and delivery vehicles were much less important. Prime Minister Churchill put it this way:

Let me put it simply. After a certain point has been passed, it may be said; "The worse things get, the better." The broad effect of the latest developments is to spread almost indefinitely, and at least to a vast extent, the area of mortal danger. This should certainly increase the deterrent upon Soviet Russia by putting her enormous spaces and scattered population on an equality, or near-equality of vulnerability with our small, densely populated island and with Western Europe. I cannot regard this development as adding to our dangers. We have reached the maximum already. On the contrary, to this form of attack continents are vulnerable as well as islands. Hitherto, crowded countries . . . have had this outstanding vulnerability to carry. But the hydrogen bomb, with its vast range of destruction and the even wider area of contamination, would be effective also against nations whose population hitherto has been so widely dispersed over large land areas as to make them feel that they were not in any danger at all. They too become highly vulnerable. Here again we see the value of deterrents, immune against surprise and well understood by all persons on both sides—I repeat "on both sides"—who have the power to control events.[23]

Britain was not only no more vulnerable than larger states, she also had the ability to build a strategic bombing force to carry the hydrogen bomb. These bombs would be so devastating that even though she could make far fewer than the United States, she could still pose an independent threat to the Soviet Union. The effect of the advent of the thermonuclear weapon was so profound in the R.A.F. that it precipitated a debate between Bomber and Fighter Commands. If hydrogen bombs enormously enhanced the stature of the first, they diminished the position of the second. Fighters could no longer protect Britain against attack; even if a few enemy bombers got through it would be decisive for Britain. Thus a campaign was mounted to abolish Fighter Command or to restrict it to functions of an "air police." This did not reach a head until 1957, but stemmed from the facts of the hydrogen age and the precepts of the global strategy papers.

Defense in the years immediately before Suez saw Britain at its height. The nuclear deterrent, now to be fashioned with hydrogen weapons, was well on the way. Overseas burdens were pressing, but they were nowhere unbearable. The notion of a strategic reserve, to be carried by air, seemed to make possible both the forty-three–year commitment to the Western European Union and also Malaya, Kenya, and Cy-

[23] *House of Commons Debates,* Vol. 537 (March 1, 1955), col. 1898.

prus. The withdrawal from the Suez base promised to free forces for obligations elsewhere, permit a reduction in the size of the Army, and stimulate recruiting. Costs of the nuclear deterrent were not yet prohibitive; the V-bombers were to be operational several years before their usefulness could possibly be questioned. In political and military terms, British courses in world affairs were not much less ambitious than those of the United States. Of course, everything was done on a smaller canvas. British military expenditure was greatly less than America's, and her forces were proportionately smaller. But she developed the same kind of forces, for the same kind of wars, against the same antagonists. She was preparing for both all-out and limited war, while carrying a number of onerous cold war commitments that had no parallel in American defense responsibilities. And in 1955, it looked as if she just might manage them. Certainly her political efficacy in international diplomacy provided no indication of future difficulty.

Indeed, in 1955 Britain seemed to have the best of both worlds. She had a firm alliance with the United States and strong support in Europe on the one hand, and a wide latitude of diplomatic independence on the other. The Royal Navy and the R.A.F. could well plan to integrate their efforts with corresponding American services in the event of war while the Foreign Office was taking an independent line. In addition to the diplomatic triumphs on the German problem and Indo-China, Britain afforded the major impetus to the Geneva summit conference of 1955. The United States, though it did not entirely like the prospect, was increasingly forced to recognize Britain as an independent political and military force in world politics.

The atomic issue evidenced this new attitude. After years

of jejune negotiations, in 1951 Britain was given information concerning atomic weapons effects and also on bomb explosion detection devices. In 1954, new data on "the outside of the bomb," regarding size, weight, and shape was provided in addition to information on ballistics effects. The former was particularly important because the United Kingdom had few enough bombs at the time, and in the event of war would have carried American bombs in British bomb-bays. Prime Minister Churchill perfectly reasonably wanted to know whether they would fit. The 1954 agreements also covered external data on bombs to be used aboard aircraft carriers.

At about the same time Britain and America developed a closer understanding on uranium ore supplies. Britain wanted to economize its own uses of ore so as to leave more for the American military program, and in its nuclear electric plants laid down in 1953-54, it paid particular attention to the conservation of fuels. In 1955 negotiations began on what has been one of the most fruitful but least talked about areas of Anglo-American nuclear cooperation. Britain was at the time planning a large number of civilian power plants which would also produce bomb-quality plutonium as a by-product. The United States, on the other hand, had concentrated upon gaseous diffusion facilities and had actually made bombs more cheaply of U-235 than of Pu-239. For the tactical atomic weapons that the United States planned to deploy in Europe, however, Pu-239 was preferable. At the same time British production of fissionable U-235 was still very low, and the Capenhurst facilities were much smaller than Oak Ridge. Since U-235 was an integral component of a hydrogen bomb effort, Britain was eager to increase its supplies of this vital material. Accordingly, agreement was finally reached on a plutonium-Uranium-235 exchange, Britain furnishing the plutonium and the United States the U-235. In 1966 the exchange still continued.

Many of the objectives of postwar British defense policy had been achieved by 1955. Europe had been stabilized; Britain was prospectively expecting to attain a substantial nuclear deterrent capability; the drains of conventional forces were still within British competence to handle; a viable, long-term agreement had been worked out with the United States. Once again, Britain was an independent and vital power in world affairs. From this perspective it is almost impossible to conceive the fall in British fortunes which took place with the Suez invasion of 1956.

CHAPTER EIGHT

THE BRITISH DETERRENT, 1956–1957

Suez represented a watershed in British strategic thought at once because it changed so much and yet changed so little. The military doctrines announced in the Sandys White Paper of 1957 were only extensions of those that had been enunciated earlier. In 1956 Sir Anthony Eden had asked officials and service chiefs to prepare a paper on the future of Britain in world affairs. "This paper considered our objectives in the light of the transformation of the world brought about by the existence of the hydrogen bomb. It also recognized that since the war the United Kingdom had attempted too much in too many spheres of defence, which had contributed to the economic crisis which every administration had suffered since 1954." Reappraisal was necessary if only because the period of American aid was ending, and Britain's external economic position had still not been fully reestablished. "We have to find means of increasing by £400 million a year the credit side of our balance of payments." [1]

[1] Sir Anthony Eden, *Full Circle* (London, 1960), p. 371.

A major concern was to reduce spending on forces for a major war. A third world war would not be a massive struggle, continuing over many months and perhaps years; it would be a brief and decisive encounter. The ground war and "broken-backed" aspects of the struggle could now be minimized, with a consequent saving in costs. This suggested in turn that NATO strategy might be transformed, with a far greater role assigned to nuclear deterrent forces. Eden wrote Eisenhower:

> The political need to maintain the solidarity of the European countries is as strong as ever. For this purpose, even if for no other, it would still be important that some United States and British forces should remain on the ground in Europe under N.A.T.O. command.
>
> The military purposes for which those forces are now required are, however, different from those on which the military policy of N.A.T.O. was first framed. It was originally designed to meet the threat of a Soviet land invasion, and its pattern was established before the advent of the nuclear weapon. Today, the situation is changing. It is on the thermo-nuclear bomb and atomic weapons that we now rely, not only to deter aggression, but to deal with aggression if it should be launched. A 'shield' of conventional forces is still required; but is no longer our principal military protection. Need it be capable of fighting a major land battle? Its primary military function seems now to be to deal with any local infiltration, to prevent external intimidation and to enable aggression to be identified as such. It may be that it should also be capable of imposing some delay on the progress of a Soviet land invasion until the full impact is felt of the thermo-nuclear retaliation which would be launched against the Soviet Union.[2]

By 1956 it had already been accepted that the Territorial Army could not play an important role in a land battle in

[2] Ibid., pp. 372-73.

Europe. Only two Territorial divisions were to be sent in re-inforcement after the outbreak of war. Duncan Sandys, the first Minister of Defence under Prime Minister Harold Mac-millan, simply extended this argument: since it would take three months to get the Territorials ready for a European encounter, the pace of nuclear war nullified their usefulness. And if the post-Suez paper abolished National Service and aimed to reduce British forces to 375,000 by 1962, Eden had made plans to achieve a 445,000-man force by April, 1960, and had already accepted the end of conscription.[3] Though public announcements had not been made to these effects, the pre-Suez government had been as committed to them as their successors. The words of John Strachey in the 1955 defense debate had been taken to heart as much by Eden as by Mac-millan:

The development of our nuclear weapons can put this country in the position of the bee. The bee has a sting, but if it uses that sting it dies. It is quite certain . . . that the bee will never use the sting except in the ultimate necessity. On the other hand . . . the possession of the sting by the bee deters us if we are minded to maltreat it in any way. That, no more and no less, is what the development of a nuclear programme can do for any other country today. The astonishing fact is that having accepted those facts, the [1955] White Paper goes on . . . to sketch out just the same old programme of the division of very much the same total sum in very much the same way between the three Services. That is surely the most extraordinary non sequitor. . . . What we are getting is the old, dull conventional arms programme and superimposed upon that the attempt to create a nuclear programme and the means of delivering it. The con-sequences are that the Government are trying to get something

[3] See Laurence Martin, "The Market for Strategic Ideas in Britain: The Sandys Era," *American Political Science Review*, Vol. 56, No. 1 (March, 1962), p. 27.

of everything and are succeeding in getting enough of nothing;
. . . trying to be strong everywhere and succeeding in being
weak everywhere.[4]

Nor was it true that the rupture of the Anglo-American
alliance at Suez conveyed utterly novel lessons about the
dangers of relying on the United States. Even before, Eden
had laid it down as a mandate that Britain should not become
dependent on the United States "for supplies of atomic
weapons, warheads, or fissile material."[5] Sir John Slessor
commented that the Sandys White Paper "introduces no basic
revolution in policy, but merely rationalizes and (probably
for the first time) explains in admirably intelligible form tendencies which have long been obvious and policies most of
which successive British Governments have accepted and
urged upon their Allies for some years."[6]

What Suez did was not to chart an entirely new course in
defense policy, but rather to confirm and extend existing
trends. Economic pressures would have militated in favor of
reduced military spending, despite Suez; doctrinal inconsistencies would have had to be resolved, regardless of the crisis
in the Middle East. There was already an observable tendency
to put greater emphasis upon global forces and less upon conventional and cold war forces. And even in these realms,
Sandy's policies were less thoroughgoing than they might
have been. The Navy's carrier force was left untouched.
Fighter Command earned a reprieve. Sandys's decisions were
less drastic curtailments of conventional capability than those
of Denis Healey, a decade later.

[4] *House of Commons Debates,* Vol. 537 (March 2, 1955), col. 2069.
[5] Eden, p. 374.
[6] "British Defense Policy," *Foreign Affairs,* Vol. 35 (July, 1957),
p. 551.

What Suez did was not to transform the direction of defense thinking, but rather to alter the political and international context in which it was carried on. The defeat in November, 1956, radically challenged British purposes in world affairs. It made it much more difficult for Britain to think of independent classical military operations when her major allies were opposed to their direction and intent. Before Suez it had automatically been assumed that the United States would support its British ally on a *quid pro quo* basis even in areas where U.S. and U.K. interests diverged. In return, America would receive corresponding support from Britain. Given American sensitivities, this bargain had partially become unstuck at the time of Indo-China and the French rejection of the European Defense Community. Particularly in the Far East, where British and American interests were not identical, London had refused support. In somewhat similar fashion during the prolonged Suez base negotiations, Washington had been of little if any help, and its actions had probably encouraged Colonel Nasser. Neither country then had acted in accord with presumed alliance obligations, though the issues had never been fundamental. At Suez, America not only did not offer military support to its already committed ally, it acted directly to frustrate British military and political ambitions. There was no doubt at all that many members of the British military and political establishment regarded America's actions as akin to treachery.[7]

The deductions which were drawn by the new Conservative leadership were twofold. First, Britain had to work even more closely with the United States to produce alliance harmony in those regions of the world where British and American interests partly diverged. Thus, Quemoy, Lebanon-

[7] See Martin, p. 27.

Jordan, and the Congo were handled completely differently from their counterparts in the early 1950s. Britain actively sought agreement on combined attitudes and policies, particularly as she was aware that these cases, like Suez, might lead to a rupture between Washington and London. Second, Britain had to have a symbol of military independence from the United States. Suez, understandably, had produced great disenchantment with America; it had given rise, not only to pro-Gaullist sentiment in Britain, but also to the Campaign for Nuclear Disarmament, equally critical of major aspects of American policy. An "independent deterrent" would not only help to reestablish the British position in world politics, it would also be a factor in rebuilding British morale at home, badly shaken by Suez.[8]

Suez also increased the urgency with which Britain sought viable strategic weapons. Always before, the British nuclear weapons and delivery system program had been relatively modest. Her plutonium and U-235 facilities had not been geared to large-scale military production. The V-bombers were not a trifling expense, but neither were they a great burden, and the government had chosen to produce only a limited number of them. Guided missile work had begun in the United Kingdom in 1947, but a real focusing of resources awaited the agreement on exchange of information with the United States in 1953. Until 1957 or thereabouts it seemed possible to get deterrence with manageable additional expense.

---

[8] There was doubt that the British public actually supported a British deterrent developed through hydrogen bomb tests. During most of the period of controversy over British strategic weapons, the public neither supported Conservative policy nor the demands of the unilateral disarmers.

Though from about 1954–55 on, a great deal was spent on Blue Streak, a liquid-fueled intermediate range strategic missile to be fired from underground implacements, it was not clear whether future deterrent weapons would be supersonic bombers or missiles. The unit costs of Blue Streak, moreover, might conceivably have been reduced by strategic longevity. A technological generation of missiles might last as long as a generation of bombers.

Still, it was not until 1957 that independent strategic weapons were viewed as all-important; it was therefore not until 1957 that Britain had to take seriously the possibility of escalating costs for research and development for these weapons. In this sense there was a difference between the period after 1952 and the period after 1957. After 1952 Britain had resolved on nuclear and delivery capabilities befitting her station as a Great Power; she had continued these automatically, adjusting them from time to time, and she believed that nuclear deterrent status would eventually be hers. After 1957, however, there could be no doubt that Britain had to continue her deterrent efforts and bring them to fruition. After 1952, nuclear deterrence had been a relatively unquestioned accompaniment to the British position in world affairs; it was well-nigh automatic. After 1957, however, deterrence was necessary, and it had to be consciously sought.

Research and development costs, which were previously tolerable because they were not excessive, now had to be borne whether they were excessive or not. Of course, officials told their masters that expenditures could be held within bounds. And the 1958 White Paper codified the optimism: "On the basis of present plans and estimates, it does not seem likely that these costs will increase significantly over the next few years." [9] But that pronouncement was the last of its genre in British history; since then, research and development costs for new strategic weapons have been seen to be beyond British resources.

In retrospect it is difficult to understand how Suez could possibly have occurred. It was not merely that it was badly executed at a time when world opinion had turned against Britain; it was also that it represented a colossal failure of the Anglo-American alliance. Ever since 1947 British policy had been based on a military *rapprochement* with the United States. Bevin's diplomacy had rested on the involvement of the United States in European affairs; American support would counterbalance continental weakness. A defensive alliance with the United States would also underwrite British security and compensate for American abstention in 1914 and 1939. At the time of the Korean War, Britain had made great sacrifices to maintain that alliance and to guarantee continuing American support.

In 1956, on the other hand, American support no longer seemed necessary. Britain was resolved to act without it. This was at best a dubious venture; even the United States had refrained from going into Indo-China in 1954 when British agreement was not forthcoming. But the United Kingdom was ready to act, not only in the absence of U.S. help, but also directly against her wishes. By October 3, Eden had concluded that America could not be brought 'round and that France and Britain would have to use force willy-nilly.

This was a surprising conclusion in light of the fact that the United States had made it perfectly clear that she opposed a

---

[9] Cmnd. 363, *Report on Defence: Britain's Contribution to Peace and Security* (February, 1958), p. 6.

military solution. On September 8 President Eisenhower wrote to Sir Anthony: "The use of military force under present circumstances might have consequences even more serious than causing the Arabs to support Nasser. It might cause a serious misunderstanding between our two countries because I must say frankly that there is as yet no public opinion in this country which is prepared to support such a move, and the most significant public opinion that there is seems to think that the United Nations was formed to prevent this very thing. It is for reasons such as these that we have viewed with some misgivings your preparations for mounting a military expedition against Egypt." In his messages to Eden, Eisenhower stressed that a resort to force would open the Middle East to Soviet influence, an eventuality which the United States could scarcely take lightly. Eden doubtlessly believed that the London Conference, the User's Association, and final submission to the United Nations would show that Britain had exhausted all peaceful recourse before embarking on war. In this he was misled by Eisenhower's early statement that "there should be no thought of military action before the influences of the UN are fully explored." [10]

But the United States never gave any grounds for believing that peaceful means of settlement had been exhausted. When Eden decided to implement the invasion plan after October 3, he did so knowing that America had not been squared and that she remained opposed to military measures. In fact, Eden committed himself to two conflicting principles: 1) force should be used against Nasser; and 2) the United States should be brought to accept that result. Nowhere did he realistically face the consequences of failure on the second

[10] Dwight D. Eisenhower, *Waging Peace* (Garden City, N.Y., 1965), pp. 669–70, 667, 666.

count. Finally, it was American opposition and intransigence, particularly as expressed in Mr. Dulles' press conference of October 2, that tipped the balance in favor of war. No thought seems to have been given to the ways in which the United States might obstruct the Suez operation. This oversight was an egregious error in British military planning.

A second critical fault was to misunderstand the role the Anglo-French invasion would play within Egyptian internal politics. Certain R.A.F. officers believed that Nasser would fall with the bombing of Egyptian air fields; others believed that the occupation of Port Said and the canal would be necessary to bring a political upheaval in Cairo. Yet it was not clear that these events would in fact guarantee the desired result. Nothing short of the occupation of Cairo itself could certainly displace Nasser, and yet no rationale had been provided for any such action.[11] The seizure of the canal would clearly "insulate the canal from the politics of any one country," but it would not end the dispute between Egypt and Britain; nor would it terminate Nasser's influence in the Arab world. The British plan for a political transformation in Cairo was little more realistic than the American plan for Cuban insurrection in April, 1961.

The Suez operation itself reflected British conventional weakness. If the task had been carried out early in August, 1956, the United States would have had less justification for opposition, though even at that time Eisenhower stated U.S. doubts in no uncertain terms. "Public opinion here, and I am convinced, in most of the world, would be outraged should

[11] Until September the operative British plan for military action against Egypt had involved an invasion at Alexandria, aimed at the occupation of Cairo. Eden reverted to an occupation of the canal when he became convinced that the earlier plan could not be justified in terms of international mandates.

there be a failure to make [peaceful] efforts. Moreover, initial military success might be easy, but the eventual price might become far too heavy." [12]

Despite political pressures for early action, the British military could not be ready before September 15. There were shortages of landing craft; an armored brigade had to be called up to provide the specialist troops needed for the operation. The Navy's fighters were vastly inferior to Egyptian MIGs; there were no fighter-escorts for bombers in the Middle East. "There were no transport aircraft and none of the base organizations or specialists required for an amphibious operation were readily available." [13] In short Britain was incapable of rapid military operations against a nation possessing even Egypt's modest strength. That Cairo turned out to be an even less effective opponent than had been believed in no way detracts from the weakness of British capability.

The major impediment to the operation, however, was not military. In the early stages of the movement of the invasion force the American Sixth Fleet had tried to harrass the operation. U.S. airplanes tested British carrier defenses; un-identified submarines were detected on the floor of the Mediterranean, and the British naval commander had finally to ask his American counterpart to bring them to the surface for fear of sinking an American vessel. On at least one occasion an American ship appeared off the bow of a British carrier as it was landing its planes. The U.S. fleet was presumably under orders to offer peaceful obstruction to the invasion force. These efforts, however, did not alter the British timetable.

Of far greater importance were the political and economic measures resolved on by the United States. American strategy

[12] Eisenhower, p. 664.
[13] A. J. Barker, *Suez: The Seven Day War* (London, 1964), p. 26.

fundamentally was to delay British resort to force, hoping that the longer action could be postponed, the less likely it would be undertaken. If the "solutions" proposed did not stick because of Egyptian intransigence, at least time would be gained. The major miscalculation by the British (not shared by the French) was that Eisenhower and Dulles could eventually be brought to stand aside. The Americans' tactics were confused with their strategy.

When the Suez operation began, it therefore confronted the worst of both worlds. The United States had neither been neutralized nor pacified, and the rest of the world had been alarmed. Domestic opinion in Britain (in contrast to that in the month of July) had turned against Eden; Nasser had managed to recruit the necessary pilots and was on his way to proving that the canal could be insulated from domestic politics under Cairo's management. The invasion plan posed other imponderables. Since there was no naval base at Cyprus, the fleet had to proceed from Malta, but it could sail only after the Anglo-French ultimatum to Egypt had expired. At the same time, the Egyptian air force had to be hit at its bases forthwith. The result was an irreducible six-day lag between operations. The bombing began on October 31, but not until dawn on November 6 did the invasion fleet arrive.

By this date opposition to the venture was all but decisive. Late in the evening of November 5, London time, a note from Russian Premier Bulganin warned "we are fully determined to crush the aggressors . . . through the use of force." Eden and French Prime Minister Guy Mollet were not intimidated, but agreed to seek nuclear reassurances from the United States. The State Department's reply early the next morning merely observed: "The Government of the United States will respect its obligations under the North Atlantic Treaty arrangements."

Since the Middle East was not part of the North Atlantic area defined in the treaty, the reply was dangerously ambiguous. Eden tried to reach Eisenhower by telephone, but could not get through. He then sent a personal message to the President "asking for immediate assurance that the United States would retaliate if Britain and France were attacked," but no reply was given. Inquiries made elsewhere had the same result. The American embassy in Paris was equally uncommunicative, and in Washington the British Joint Services Mission was denied contact with the U.S. Joint Chiefs.

Two days before the landings at Port Said, the British mission in Washington had shown Admiral Arthur Radford, Chairman of the Joint Chiefs of Staff, a copy of the U.K. invasion plan. Radford had the plan photocopied and distributed among key American officials. After the invasion began, however, British military representatives in Washington were unable to reach their opposite numbers. The absence of contact was all the more portentous since overflights of Turkey were being reported from NATO headquarters on the morning of November 6, and later in the day the Russians asked permission to move a cruiser and three destroyers through the Dardanelles.[14]

The significance of the interruption in communications, of

[14] Terence Robertson, *Crisis: The Inside Story of the Suez Conspiracy* (London, 1964), pp. 252, 253, 254, 260, 263. Much of this account rests on the accuracy of the Robertson version of the Suez affair. While its veracity has not been confirmed in every detail, the author is convinced that it contains a generally valid narrative of the unfolding of the Suez operation. It seems, moreover, to be correct on certain crucial events affecting Anglo-American relations.

course, could be exaggerated. There was a Strategic Air Command alert at the time, and if the Soviets had moved to attack Western nations, America was ready to respond. Notwithstanding this, the Middle Eastern situation was dangerous, and it remained unclear what America would do if Egypt demanded and got conventional military assistance from the Soviet Union.

Economic sanctions were also in train. The greatest pressure on the pound stemmed from speculation in New York, and even the Federal Reserve Bank was involved in offloading sterling at a discount. These pressures cost the Bank of England $300 million on November 5; over even a short period such "dumping" would have forced devaluation. The British Treasury then applied for backing from the International Monetary Fund, but U.S. votes were used to block the transaction. As the British Cabinet was meeting just before noon on November 6, Harold Macmillan, then Chancellor of the Exchequer, received a call from Washington which pledged a U.S. loan of $1 billion if a cease-fire was effected by midnight. When the cease-fire was conceded, it was clearly the result, more than anything else, of pressure from the United States. If the British had proceeded, even for the forty-eight hours the French believed sufficient to occupy the canal (the British estimate was four to five days), devaluation might have been required. Eden was undoubtedly right in rejecting the view that the U.S. attitude would have been modified by a *fait accompli:* "The United States Government had engaged their authority in the lead against us and would not have been appeased had Anglo-French forces occupied more of the Canal or even the whole of it. In all probability they would only have been more indignant." [15]

[15] Eden, p. 559.

The failure at Suez was perhaps the most crucial national setback in modern British history. It was the sequel to a record of unrivaled success. It was a reversal so fundamental and far-reaching that it toppled Britain from the ranks of the premier nations of the world. In political and military terms it undermined bases of British prestige and policy that dated from World War II. For the first ten years of the cold war British credentials had been national military strength and cohesion on the one hand, and the link with the United States on the other. Defeated European nations had remembered the splendid British effort in World War II; if they could not be sure of American military assistance, they wanted to know that the United Kingdom was on their side. But Britain had been valuable not only as an end but also as a means. The Anglo-American alliance was the major reference point for U.S. policy; it was largely British urging that brought the United States to Western support in 1948 and 1949. In Korea and Indo-China it was British influence which prevented a redirection of American energies toward the Far East and maintained NATO resolve. Continental states were quick to believe that the United States had to be approached through Britain, and that American responses to continental entreaties were partly dependent upon advice from Whitehall.

But Suez destroyed all this. No longer could it be held that British power, in the sphere of its traditional application, was dominant. The Middle East had been a British preserve for more than a half century, and British intervention had always determined its course. After Suez, however, this was no longer true. Britain could no longer be regarded as a world power; she could scarcely be viewed as a major regional power. The Europeans had believed that British intervention on the continent, to be effective, would have to be much more

formidable than British intervention overseas. Successes overseas, then, were uncertain testimony to British military efficacy in Europe. Failure overseas, on the other hand, showed
how far London had fallen from its high estate. Britain no
longer had to be courted in Europe; her strength could add
little to that already in existence.

The failure of the Anglo-American alliance was an equivalent demotion. Continentals were always suspicious of Anglo-
Saxon ties, but they did not deny their durability and force. If
Britain could be brought around, America would be more
likely to cooperate. In the Brussels pact negotiations, in the
commitment of American troops and the naming of an American Supreme Commander, in the Korean rearmament, and in
acceptance of Western European Union, London was a
means to Washington. If Bevin or Eden agreed, Acheson and
even Dulles were more likely to.

But Suez questioned all such relationships. It turned out
that London had no special influence on Washington, that it
could not act in the traditional preserves of British interest
without American interference. The division between Britain
and America was so great that British support was no longer
an asset. Individual European countries might do better in
bilateral negotiations with Washington.

None of these consequences affected the French. A fall in
national fortunes depended upon a high position to begin
with. Very little was expected of Paris; its government was
chaotic; its military had already suffered several important
setbacks in Indo-China and North Africa. It had no preten-
sions to close ties with the United States. It was neither a
Great Power, nor did it presume to be. Defeat at the canal
added few blemishes to the already tarnished French escutch-
eon. In the French case, however, the deductions drawn were

much more radical than those in Britain. France had yet to make herself into a major postwar power. She recognized that it was necessary to start at the bottom. Nuclear weapons, a stable internal structure, and freedom from overseas commitments had to be achieved.

In Britain, on the other hand, where the defeat was much more catastrophic, much less was done about it. If the defect was a lack of British power, the "independent deterrent" would remedy it; if the fault was estrangement from America, Britain would seek a new Anglo-American solidarity. British policies did not have to be refashioned, they merely needed refurbishing. These were not surprising conclusions to draw. The decisiveness of the Suez venture could only be seen after the fact. Coming on the heels of signal diplomatic and military achievement, it could be viewed as a minor anomaly, and one that could be quickly corrected. Diplomatic and military progress would be rapidly resumed. Since multiple capabilities had been borne previously without shortfall, they might be disposed once again.

Overseas, European and strategic capabilities might be deployed. Indeed, in one sense, Suez militated in the precisely wrong direction. Since triple capacities had been maintained at the peak of British prestige, they merely needed to be regained. The resulting disadvantage was that Britain would be tempted to cut too little, not too much. Prestige is a very variable quantity. It relates in part to the ratio between commitment and success. A nation with few commitments might discharge them effectively. A nation with many burdens might not be able to handle them all. In the past Britain had derived kudos from victories on all fronts. Suez was a vital setback on one front, but it did not alter British commitments; it merely changed Britain's approach to them. France, on the other hand, improved her position, not by rebalancing her forces, but by reducing her commitments. She resolved to do fewer things, but to do them well. Britain convinced herself that she might still do the same number of things, do them well, and with fewer forces.

Thus, one of the real tragedies of Suez was that it was an international and military setback of the first order; but it only produced changes in British force structure. The external deductions from the operation were fundamental; the internal deductions were peripheral. It was not at all surprising that Suez, in its military manifestations, was little but an extension of preexisting trends. In many respects it may be argued that new conclusions about British commitments should have been drawn by Duncan Sandys, but in fact they awaited Denis Healey.

Military planning after Suez was nonetheless different from previous years. Duncan Sandys, the Minister of Defence under Prime Minister Harold Macmillan, benefited from a conflict among service Chiefs. Because of dissension he was able to impose uncompromising policies, policies the like of which would not have been tolerated in 1947 or 1952. In so doing he remedied inconsistencies in British doctrine and force structure that had existed since 1955. If the government really believed that nuclear weapons would deter even smaller wars, it was irrational to plan for large classical or limited war forces. Mr. Churchill had been justly criticized in that year for trying to get something of everything and succeeding in getting enough of nothing.[16]

But there were still two routes that the Defence Minister

[16] By John Strachey, *House of Commons Debates,* Vol. 537 (March 2, 1955), col. 2072.

might choose. He might opt for the deterrent and do away with conscription; or he might emphasize conventional forces and rely on the United States for strategic nuclear support. This choice was not foredestined, despite the factors that militated in favor of British nuclear deterrence. Captain B. H. Liddell Hart argued forcefully that Britain's most important task was to deal with local threats abroad, and that while overseas bases were pared, the United Kingdom could still afford to make cuts in the Royal Navy's antisubmarine forces, in the R.A.F.'s Coastal and Fighter Commands, and in Army manpower. Eventually conscription could be abolished.[17] Conventional forces, of course, were at a discount in military planning after Suez: "The nuclear force was firmly believed by ministers—and, indeed, by the Chiefs of Staff Committee —to enhance national prestige and preserve an independence of action regarded as particularly desirable in view of what many regarded as America's treacherous abandonment of her allies during the Suez affair." [18]

Classical forces also had the disadvantage of making the abolition of national service more difficult and therefore of accentuating the labor shortage. If manpower was necessary to fight inflation, conventional preparedness would be unlikely to furnish it. It was also true that nuclear deterrent weapons were already in production. Research and development had been completed on all three V-bombers; the procurement stage would not add unmanageable extra costs. Even guided missile development was very far advanced. Blue Streak would be expensive when attained, but many of the initial expenditures had already been funded.

An enlarged conventional preparedness, on the other hand,

[17] See his articles in the *Daily Mirror*, January 23, 24, and 25, 1957.
[18] Martin, p. 27.

would demand new forces, greater stocks of equipment, new barracks, clubs, quarters for the married, greater service pay, and higher expenses all 'round. In the context of Suez, greater carrier strength, new carrier-borne jet fighters, commando ships, landing craft, and greater bombing capacity would all have been necessary. One informed observer pointed out that conventional increments which would have allowed Britain to deploy her forces two weeks early would have been of little avail. What was needed was a capability of acting two months early, and that would be very expensive.

It could also not be denied that the cost of meeting a high standard of conventional preparedness was greater than the cost (as then understood) of paying for the nuclear deterrent. Costs for the later marks of the V-bombers and for the Blue Streak missile turned out to be far higher than had been estimated in 1956–57.[19] The great acceleration of spending at the time of Korea was to be accounted to conventional items; the inclusion of bomber reequipment a year later added relatively little to the defense estimates. As late as 1958 the Minister for Defence could claim: "Britain's expenditure on the strategic bomber force and its nuclear bombs, and on related research and development (including work on ballistic rockets) represents less than one-tenth of the Defence Estimates."[20] Again, the deterrent seemed the better alternative.

Of course, Britain might conceivably had decided to concentrate on both conventional and nuclear forces. But this would have required a restriction in consumption and new taxes. Instead, taxes were cut by £100 million in 1958 and an

[19] See William P. Snyder, *The Politics of British Defence Policy, 1945–1962* (London, 1964), p. 28.

[20] Cmnd. 363, p. 6.

overall 9 percent reduction in the income tax was decreed for 1959. The result was pressure on the defense sector. One observer put it this way: "On the one hand, the share of the national output available to the central government declined between 1949 and 1954 from 37 percent of the GNP to about 29 percent, the approximate level of revenues in the early 1960s. On the other hand, alternative revenue outlets—debt charges and those social and economic services for which responsibility was largely assumed by the national government after World War II—have remained fairly stable. The result has been great pressure for reductions elsewhere in government. This pressure, particularly strong after the Korean War, fell largely on defense, the largest single category of expenditures."[21]

The process of arriving at the 1957 White Paper, which embodied the new emphasis upon the deterrent was one of acrimony and delay. The Minister of Defence, Duncan Sandys, never pushed his proposals so far as to elicit the resignation of one of the service Chiefs, though at one time or another he alienated each of them. Despite the emphasis upon nuclear deterrence, the R.A.F. was scarcely pleased. It had been deprived of any supersonic successor to the V-bombers, and fighter development was halted with the Lightning (P-1). The Air Staff did not object greatly to the cancellation of a new bomber, but they were upset about the prohibition on future fighters. There was even a strong initiative, generated in the office of the Chief Scientist of the Ministry of Defence, to reduce Fighter Command to two squadrons of "air police" designed to keep out "nosey intruders," and to save a large fraction of Fighter Command's £80 million annual cost. Even

[21] Snyder, pp. 194–95.

though the Air Staff recognized that Fighter Command could no longer take a decisive toll of enemy nuclear bombers, it was argued that ten squadrons would still have to be available for reinforcement overseas in cold war operations and that fighters still had a role in defending British bomber bases. If these arguments had not been accepted, the Chief of the Air Staff would have resigned.

The War Office had even more obvious grievances. Brigadier Antony Head, the Minister of Defence at the time of Suez, had refused to serve under Prime Minister Harold Macmillan because of the latter's known intention to abolish conscription and reduce Army manpower. A study conducted by a committee under General Hull concluded in 1956 that 210,000 troops were the minimum needed to fulfill the country's commitments. War Office acceptance of this figure "was based on use of Gurkhas in Asia, reductions of garrisons, severe weaknesses east of Suez and, in general, upon a number of optimistic assumptions as to capabilities and commitments." [22] An actuarial study done by the Central Statistical Office, on the other hand, estimated that the highest possible voluntary recruitment would produce an Army of 165,000, a shortfall of critical importance. NATO forces aside, such an Army would leave no more than "13,000 men for our world-wide commitments, excluding the strategic reserve." [23] When the Defence Minister accepted an Army of 165,000, he merely endorsed the estimates of government actuaries. Later, when recruitment seemed to hold out the possibility of a 180,000-man army, military requirements were adjusted accordingly. Faced with these policy determi-

[22] Martin, p. 28.
[23] See the arithmetic in Antony Head's statement in Parliament. *House of Commons Debates*, Vol. 592 (July 28, 1958), col. 991.

nations, the C.I.G.S. was disposed to resign, but refrained because his fellow Chiefs would not join him.[24]

The Navy also had its problems. Sandys had never been convinced of the effectiveness of the carrier in a global war. The Navy's strike capability on shore was minimal; it added little to the R.A.F.'s nuclear capacity. Navy leaders were disposed to accept this argument. Despite their tentative endorsement of the strike operations of NATO's Supreme Atlantic Command, they had doubts about sending their limited carrier fleet close to shore in the first days of a thermonuclear war.[25] The Admiralty, however, was disposed to fight for its role in antisubmarine warfare. There might be a period of limited war before global hostilities broke out, and even in the onset of all-out war, control of the sea lanes, and particularly communications with the United States, might still be important. As the White Paper argued: "There is the possibility that the nuclear battle might not prove immediately decisive; and in that event it would be of great importance to defend Atlantic communications against submarine attack." [26]

But defense against the undersea menace was not the only reason for retention of Navy carrier forces. The Navy would be of great utility in limited and cold war conflicts. Both Korea and Suez indicated that Britain might be confronted with non-nuclear challenges. As a means of meeting these, the chain of overseas bases, and strategic air-lift capacity, were quite inadequate. Suez would inevitably reduce the number of foreign bases available to Britain, and it would also complicate

[24] See Martin, p. 28.
[25] See the excellent account in W. J. Crowe Jr., "The Policy Roots of the Modern Royal Navy, 1946-1963," pp. 184-90. Unpublished dissertation, Princeton University, 1965.
[26] Cmnd. 124, *Defence: Outline of Future Policy* (April, 1957), p. 4.

the granting of overflight rights. If the United Kingdom relied only on the strategic reserve to fight brush-fire wars, its capabilities might be insufficient. The Navy pointed out that carrier task forces greatly augmented Army strength in this regard; they also provided a mobile complement "which could be moved from place to place to show the flag in areas evacuated by the Army." [27]

This did not mean that the Navy came out unscathed in the encounter with Sandys. The reserve fleet was pared; the cruiser force was let languish; both shore establishments and the naval personnel reserve were cut back. Still Sandys accepted the major navy contentions, and five carriers were to remain operational. One official commented that Sandys could only have canceled the carrier force, if he had been able to guarantee that Britain would never have to meet limited war commitments at great distances from the United Kingdom. Since he could not give such an undertaking, the case for carriers was unanswerable. The White Paper included the words: "On account of its mobility, the Royal Navy, together with the Royal Marines, provides another effective means of bringing power rapidly to bear in peacetime emergencies or limited hostilities. In modern conditions the role of the aircraft carrier, which is in effect a mobile air station, becomes increasingly significant." [28]

The 1957 White Paper actually contained a straightforward argument. It was by no means a novel case, but it was uncompromising in its force. The basic premise of the paper was that military planning had been fundamentally altered by recent scientific advances. The amount of allowable defense, moreover, had to be "considered in conjunction with the need

[27] Crowe, p. 188.   [28] Cmnd. 124, p. 6.

to maintain the country's financial and economic strength." [29]
Since 1951, defense expenditure had absorbed an undue
proportion of the Gross National Product, and thus impeded
the export effort. Bigger forces had been maintained than
were strictly necessary:

(i) to play their part with the forces of Allied countries in deterring and resisting aggression;

(ii) to defend British colonies and protected territories against
local attack, and undertake limited operations in overseas
emergencies.[30]

The first task required nuclear deterrent forces as well as
forces in Europe. The second required mobile limited and
brush-fire war forces for disposition overseas. As to the deterrent, the White Paper forthrightly stated:

It must be frankly recognized that there is at present no means
of providing adequate protecton for the people of this country
against the consequences of an attack with nuclear weapons.
Though in the event of war, the fighter aircraft of the Royal Air
Force would unquestionably be able to take a heavy toll of
enemy bombers, a proportion would inevitably get through.
Even if it were only a dozen, they could with megaton bombs
inflict widespread devastation. This makes it more than ever clear
that the overriding consideration in all military planning must be
to prevent war rather than to prepare for it. [While the larger
burden of deterrence rested with the United States], there is a
wide measure of agreement that [Britain] must possess an appreciable element of nuclear deterrent power of her own.[31]

For this purpose British megaton bombs had been developed and would be put into production. Initially these
would be delivered by British V-bombers. Later the Blue
Streak missile, to be fired from underground implacements,
would become the main deterrent weapon. For the short run,

[29] *Ibid.*, p. 1.   [30] *Ibid.*, p. 2.   [31] *Ibid.*, pp. 2–3.

British V-bomber bases might be protected by fighter defenses; later these would be replaced by a ground-to-air missile system.

Nuclear air power, however, was not sufficient for all military purposes. Britain had to maintain ground forces in Europe to make clear "that aggression will be resisted." Outside Europe, she had to defend a range of conventional commitments. In Europe the British Army of the Rhine could be reduced substantially without reducing the credibility of a Western nuclear response. Overseas, the strategic reserve would supplement local garrisons and colonial forces. New airlift capacity would be added to Transport Command to dispatch reinforcements abroad at short notice. Since garrisons in Jordan, Libya, and other places were being reduced in the aftermath of the Suez failure, the air-lifted reserve was of great importance. These forces would be powerfully assisted by Royal Navy task forces, now even more significant in light of the existing and prospective loss of foreign bases.

The most controversial provision of the government's defense paper was the abolition of national service. Sandys contended that conscription was uneconomic; it required 150,000 men in training establishments, and involved constant turnover in personnel. If administrative cadres could be reduced, and base and depot maintenance staffs replaced by civilians, a considerable saving could be effected. In addition new incentives would be provided for regular recruitment. New barracks and married quarters would be built; scales of rations were to be increased. Still, the 165,000-man regular army would not provide the strength deemed minimally necessary by Army Chiefs. Over a period of time, the ending of national service in Britain inevitably meant that overseas and European commitments would have to be reduced.

Perhaps the most unique feature of Britain's defense, underscored in the 1957 White Paper, was the emphasis upon cold war involvements. A case can be made that Britain would be far stronger without its overseas empire than confronted with its manifold challenges. Nuclear and NATO forces would have been far more easily sustained if Britain had not been required to disperse its strength overseas. And, in other contexts, constant pressure upon the defense budget had been avoided. France's great failures internationally after World War II occurred when she was striving to maintain the semblance of empire; her great successes occurred after that empire had been dissolved. Even the United States did not normally devote such a large proportion of its military resources to overseas political commitments. Aside from Korea and Vietnam, American garrisons overseas went largely to support an international network of U.S. bases, not to render political stiffening to dependent or vulnerable allies. They were, moreover, lodged within independent national states, not colonial territories.

America had no obligation to protect a nation merely because it was a part of an historic geographic legacy. As a consequence political evolutions within host countries were of far less concern than in the British instance. Despite the multitude of U.S. allies, the obligations undertaken were not as great as might be thought. And, for the most part, and again excepting Vietnam, bases were located in areas of relative stability where nascent political tendencies already had been given a wide latitude of expression. British involvements, contrastingly, were not just military, but also political; they were in areas groping for national identity and cohesion; they were largely situations of weakness, not situations of strength. As a result, British cold war commitments were checks which frequently had to be cashed; American commitments were drafts which only occasionally had to be honored. As a proportion of military spending, cold war burdens have always occupied a far greater share of British than they have of American energies. As long as they continue to do so, British military imbalance will be a constant feature of the strategic environment.

In the end, it was the failure to recognize these relationships that spelled failure to the Sandys White Paper. Forces might be cut; headquarters establishments reduced; conscription abolished. But as long as the range of commitments which these forces were to serve remained approximately the same, no real saving could be effected. In 1957, 1961, and 1964, Britain had to make extraordinary military expenditures because her conventional forces were inadequate. In 1961, despite all Sandys's good intentions, National Service had to be used to meet the Berlin crisis. It is interesting to observe that the strategic dialogue of the 1960s has been very different from the strategic dialogue of the 1950s. Ten years ago one wondered whether it was proper to stress nuclear or conventional forces; today one asks not about the balance of forces, but about the realms they will be asked to defend. The Sandys White Paper was the most sophisticated attempt to rebalance and reduce British forces to meet *existing* commitments in the postwar period. The ultimate failure of that attempt has concentrated new attention on the commitments themselves.

Suez and the deductions for British military planning were certainly not implausible responses to the challenge to British interests in 1956. The canal was vital for British trade; it was a crucial link with the oil of the Persian Gulf. It was only too easy to imagine the circumstances which might lead an unstable Middle Eastern leader like Colonel Nasser to regulate its traffic according to political whim. The Suez nationalization was also a political "last straw"; Eden had been very tolerant and patient in the negotiations leading to the transfer of the Suez base in 1954 to the discomfiture of many in his own party. It was all the more difficult to tolerate a peremptory and obviously malevolent seizure of the canal.

The justifications for British acquiescence were different in the two cases. At one stage at least the Suez base was thought of in terms of influence on the course of a new world war, and it was therefore subject to the "thermonuclear revolution." The Suez Canal, on the other hand, was useful, nay, vital, during conditions of peace. It was far easier to discard a military instrument whose usefulness depended upon a very improbable future event than to lose an economic instrument whose utility was confirmed day by day. The British government's decision to use force, if need be, was an understandable reflex response to Egyptian nationalization. It was, however, not a calculated response; nor was it modified when international conditions made its implementation more and more doubtful.

The aftermath showed how incompletely the basic import of the Suez reversal had been grasped by political and military leaders. The Sandys White Paper presumably was designed to reemphasize British strategic independence, while politically Prime Minister Macmillan strove to shore up the foundations of the Anglo-American alliance. Military autonomy was to accompany a new political solidarity and interdependence. Yet, as we have seen, the Sandys "revolution" turned out to be little more than a "pronunciamento." The Conservative Defence Minister may have been a parliamentary "revolutionary," but his policies could easily be defended in terms of legitimacy and historic wont. He did little but extend and confirm military tendencies that existed long before. And the twofold program on which the Conservatives relied to rebuild British prestige and influence turned out to have but one leaf. Partially because the government insisted on carrying the same burdens it had always done, military independence was not achieved. Classical forces turned out to be woefully inadequate; their insufficiency could be easily foretold at the time.[32]

Less expected was the inadequacy of strategic nuclear forces. Blue Streak was a failure and was canceled in 1960. Its successor system, the Skybolt air-launched ballistic missile, to be delivered by the V-bombers, was not procured by the United States, and therefore not made available to the British. In December, 1962, at Nassau, Britain accepted the Polaris missile and thereby ratified her strategic dependence on America. In partial consequence, Britain is no longer viewed as a separate factor in political or military affairs. The concomitant attempt to repair the breach with the United States, though completely successful, also paradoxically undermined British political credentials. The Anglo-American alliance was now seen as an American affair; the very closeness of its bonds diluted British political independence. The greatest British influence in the postwar period occurred when the link with the United States was buttressed by political autonomy and a tradition of military success. The Anglo-American alliance was then reflective of a wartime partnership to which each nation had made essential contributions. To undercut the British military position while maintaining the alliance, however, was not simply to earn the proverbial half a

[32] It was in fact predicted by Antony Head, the previous Minister of Defence.

loaf. It was to transform the significance of the Anglo-American alliance itself. The partnership was no longer one of equals.

The significance of 1957 defense planning was failure to provide a military foundation on which the Anglo-American alliance could be reconstructed. The alliance was reestablished, and its intimacy enhanced, but this did little to recoup the British position in world affairs. First in Europe and then overseas, Britain lost the primacy she had once maintained. In 1967 she was far from regaining it.

CHAPTER NINE

BRITISH DEFENSE IN TRANSITION, 1956–1966

THE DECADE which has passed since the Suez imbroglio has witnessed no fundamental evolutions in British defense policy. The major landmarks in the past ten years have been cancellations of weapons projects and the growing enfeeblement of cold war forces. Doctrinal issues have continued much as before with the repeated insistence that any serious conflict in Europe would rapidly develop into all-out war. Mr. Denis Healey's statements in 1966 could have been made by Duncan Sandys in 1957: "Once nuclear weapons were employed in Europe, on however limited a scale, it is almost certain that, unless the aggressor quickly decided to stop fighting, the conflict would escalate rapidly to a general nuclear exchange, in which the whole of America's nuclear forces would be engaged." [1] Nor was there optimism that a large ground attack could be dealt with in conventional terms. The nuclear deterrent was downplayed in appropriate regard for the sen-

[1] Cmnd. 2901, *Statement on the Defence Estimates, 1966:* Part I (February, 1966), p. 6.

sitivities of Labour government supporters, but it was maintained all the same. There was ample evidence that Labour ministers found it had some utility after all. The financial limitations on defense spending were even more clearly evident in 1966 than they had been a decade previously.

In 1957 the issue had been partly one of electoral appeal: an abolition of conscription and a cutting of defense costs would either return monies to the private sector or finance greater expenditure on welfare. In 1966 Britain was in a massive financial crisis: the balance of payments was under constant assault; prices and inflationary wage demands were undercutting the pound sterling. Industrial modernization was an imperative need. The government not only had to spend less to avert disaster, it also had to spend on different things, switching resources from relatively unproductive areas like defense to the export industries.[2]

If there has been an important shift in British defense thinking, it concerns relations with the United States. Until 1957, and aside from the collaboration on ballistic missiles, Britain's deterrent had been largely her own creation. The reactor programs, the gaseous diffusion plant, the bombs, the delivery vehicles all had been British, though they had benefited from the knowledge Britain acquired during the war. After Suez, however, a new Anglo-American cooperation in weapons ensued. In 1958 the U.S. McMahon Act was amended, permitting Britain to share in U.S. atomic secrets, and making

[2] The 1966 White Paper put the matter straightforwardly: "As we emphasized in the National Plan (Command 2764) to continue spending 7 per cent tof the Gross National Product on defence would be seriously damaging to Britain's economy, at a time when we need a rapid increase in production so that we can export more and import less; when industry must be re-equipped and modernised; and when we are running into a shortage of manpower." *Ibid.*, p. 1.

BRITISH DEFENSE, 1956-1966

change occurred, moreover, at a time when both countries
were seeking to repair damage to the alliance and thus were
all the more willing to seal a new military interdependence. In
the aftermath of Suez, the United States was prepared to
make the very information available that it had denied in
1946, 1951 and 1954. When the curtain went up, Britain was
given data on nuclear propulsion, warheads, and missilery,
and Britain made no insignificant contribution in return.
American scientists were apparently amazed at British progress on weapons designs and later made use of certain British
concepts. To underscore the point, the British exploded their
first hydrogen bomb in May, 1957.

In one sense it was an enormous tribute to the durability of
the Anglo-American alliance that it could survive the shock
of Suez and go on to a new level of cooperation and cordiality. The premise of nuclear exchange under the amendments
of the McMahon Act was that the information shared could
never be used against the United States. Yet, in the Suez
debacle, the divergence of interests between the United States
and Britain had approximated contrariety. It was difficult to
understand how the United States could have refused such
information to the United Kingdom when relations were at
their most friendly, and then proffer it when the political
climate had greatly worsened. On the British side the new
Prime Minister Macmillan's efforts at *rapprochement* were
also difficult to grasp. The British view of the alliance had
been that a major cleavage with the United States was inconceivable; such assumptions had sustained all British attempts at
cooperation since 1945.

But Suez provided just such an issue. Since divergence was
now seen to be possible, why shouldn't the British Prime

Minister accept the fact and seek a more independent position in world affairs? Macmillan's successful endeavors to rebuild the alliance, however, meant that Britain had partially to curb its accustomed positions on Quemoy and Matsu, and in the Congo. Only in Lebanon-Jordan did the American President do essentially British bidding. Thus in the end the Anglo-American alliance became closer, with Britain more dependent than she had ever been before.[3]

This dependency had certain advantages for the Conservative and also for the succeeding Labour government. If American weapons were used, development costs might be saved. Britain would either buy output from U.S. production (the F-111A) or she would use the fruits of American research and development to build her own weapons (Polaris submarines). In either case the military path would be smoothed for Britain. But more or less dependent collaboration with the United States had costs as well as benefits. If Whitehall could not generate its own system, its strategic fortunes lay in the hands of the United States. While the closeness of the trans-Atlantic tie disposed Washington to meet British strategic requests, it might not do so for all time. An avowedly dependent deterrent could be terminated at the outset of a new generation of weapon systems. This was not an idle danger. In 1962 when the United States finally decided to offer Polaris as a substitute for the canceled Sky Bolt, it did so only at the last minute. The State Department was resolutely against such an offer, both because it was discriminatory and because it extended the life of the British deterrent. It was far

---

[3] For a more complete study of the vicissitudes of the Anglo-American relationship, see Raymond Dawson and Richard Rosecrance, "Theory and Reality in the Anglo-American Alliance," *World Politics*, Vol. 19, No. 1 (October, 1960), pp. 21–51.

from clear that Britain had a renewal option on U.S. hardware, to be taken up after 1975 when Polaris submarines
would become vulnerable. A dependent deterrent might be
fired at British option, but it could not be sustained by British
alone. As we shall see later, moreover, challenges to its
efficacy are now on the short-term horizon.

The growing reliance on the United States for strategic
weapons systems and, more recently, for help in cold war
engagements reinforces a basic fact about present-day British
defense: London is far less a factor in the worldwide balance
of military and diplomatic power than she used to be. Nor is
this result merely a reflection of a fall in fortunes at the close
of World War II. British military prowess in the 1950s did
not compare to that of the United States or the Soviet Union,
but the influence which the United Kingdom exerted was not
greatly less. In Europe, in the Far East, and in summit confer-
ences, the British cut an imposing figure. After Suez, and in
the revised conditions of the Anglo-American tie, however,
British influence around the world and particularly in Europe
quickly declined. The attempt to undo the damage of Suez
put British fates, perhaps for the first time, into the hands of
the United States.

This new relationship undermined the British initiative in
Europe. As long as the Anglo-American bond was an alliance
of nations endowed with relatively equal influence in world
affairs, London would be listened to on the continent. Since
Whitehall had the ear of the State Department, the Europeans
often acted through a British intermediary. Since Britain had
an independent capacity in military affairs, British support
was wanted even when that of America could not be obtained. Further, as long as it was possible that Britain would
seek to increase her role in the evolution of European eco-

nomic and political institutions, she was a factor that could not be neglected. Regardless of her world prestige, Britain would clearly be able to play a major role in Europe if she chose to seek a permanent association with the European Six.

Indeed, the strength of Foreign Office diplomacy in the mid-1950s had been the maintenance of options, continental and trans-Atlantic. London had been the decisive fulcrum in bringing about the Paris agreements of 1954; in so doing she had pledged to station troops on the continent for fifty years, subject to majority vote in the Western European Union. It was not yet clear that she would refuse to associate herself more closely with all movements toward European integration. After 1957, however, British and continental paths diverged. The British placed first emphasis on rebuilding links with the United States; the French decided to build the bomb and to breathe new life into supranational economic arrangements. For the first, the gulf dividing America from Europe was so great it had to be bridged; for the second, the gulf was so great that it could not be bridged.

Between 1957 and 1959, then, Britain was forced to a choice. With the McMahon Act, the acceptance of U.S. Thor missiles, and the free-trade zone proposal, London opted for Washington. When the Common Market was proposed, Whitehall temporized, finally offering a purely economic device that would have given Britain the benefits of a customs union without sacrificing the Commonwealth or involving political constraints. In a series of negotiations, ending in 1959, Britain sought unsuccessfully to delay and dilute the Common Market and to make it amenable to British purposes. It had been one of the pillars of British policy since the beginning of the 1950s that London would maintain maximum freedom and influence, both in Europe and in America, if the continent did not too closely unite. Since Britain would retain greater primacy than any single European power, a division among the Six would preserve the British influence in Washington. If the Six came together in a truly supranational arrangement, on the other hand, the continental superpower was bound to supplant Britain in the "special relationship." At that stage, the United Kingdom's only alternative lay with Europe. When the free-trade zone plan failed, it was a fore-destined conclusion that Britain would seek to join the Common Market, and the Outer Seven of the European Free-Trade Area became bargaining counters to facilitate this entry. In 1961 Britain swallowed her pride and made application, only to be rebuffed by President de Gaulle two years later.

This result was not difficult to understand. The British reaction to Suez had been almost diametrically opposed to that of France. With the Nassau Agreements affording Polaris to the British, De Gaulle became finally convinced that the United Kingdom sought to have the best of both worlds, and interposed a French veto on British membership. The consequence was that London lost ground on both sides of the Atlantic. The American tie reduced British wherewithal in Europe; British weakness and dependency ultimately undercut the British reception in Washington. Indeed, as time wore on, it became clear that London would have greater influence upon American policy-makers as a member of Europe than as an outside observer.

The last point was not intuitively obvious. If Britain joined the continent, would not Washington treat her merely as a continental *primus inter pares?* Would not the British fear of relegation to a secondary status then come true? Traditional answers to these questions overlooked the fact that Washington had regarded London as a lever to influence continental outcomes. If Britain were excluded from Europe she could no longer shape its course, and it would be better to deal with Europe directly. Given the French defection from the alliance after 1958, it was not surprising that Bonn became the focus for the formulation of U.S. European policy, first under Secretary Dulles, and later under the Kennedy and Johnson administrations.

But it was not only that Britain should place herself in a position to wield influence in Europe; it was also that the European situation gave great potential scope to British initiative. General de Gaulle saw correctly that the Common Market would not greatly circumscribe French political policy, and he did not permit the Brussels institutions to run away with themselves. London need hardly have feared for her own independent role. More important than this, the Gaullist posture in Europe was inherently divisive: it sought to use the Franco-German pact as a means of gaining German adherence to French positions; these might then be mandated to the remaining four through the Brussels machinery. In this way France would chart the course of Europe. Washington, particularly, would be disadvantaged. But French presumption brought a discordant response. West Germany did not want to choose between Atlantic and European orientations, and many remembered that it was the United States which carried the ultimate burden of German security. Other nations of the Common Market resented the French *poseur* and the constant use of the Brussels institutions for French political ends. They were also disturbed at the veto on British entry. The test of will between the five and the one in E.E.C. and the fourteen and one in NATO meant that Europe was at loggerheads regardless of the character of its economic and political institutions. London could scarcely lose influence in such a system.

It might even gain a greater kudos. German politics was riven in 1966 because of the conflict between partisans of France on the one hand and NATO on the other. As long as no makeweight existed, Germany seemed destined to tremble on a knife-edge, the ensuing political uncertainty giving scope to previously submerged extremists. Impossible international demands foment their own nationalist reaction. If a nation cannot meet outside standards, it is likely to set its own. In these circumstances the British abstention has had a peculiarly unfortunate impact on European politics. A strong British presence in Europe would not only help remedy the British financial plight, it would also move Europe and Germany off dead-center. Within the Community of the Six, British membership would clearly offset French primacy and predominance; it would also give West Germany a new confidence. British participation would help to recast the Common Market as an outward looking trading arrangement in ways congenial to German thinking. It would help to remold European attitudes in ways congenial to the United States. But most important of all, it would commence the rebuilding of British power and influence in the world environment and without placing intolerable strains on British resources. That power which is able to break the intra-European deadlock will automatically gain in political stature and prestige.

If Britain joins she will reinforce the Atlantic element in European counsels. She will strengthen those factions relying on the U.S. guarantee, and weaken those who believe that the guarantee is suspect. For those nations interested in embarking upon a national nuclear program, her experience will convey important lessons. Aside from the Russians, the British (with the consummation of the Polaris program) will have the most potent nuclear force in Europe; yet, that force has not been an unmitigated boon. It will not be clearly viable against Russian countermeasures, and because it derived from the "special relationship" it will not be forthcoming to other states. Since it originated abroad, moreover, it must depend upon renewable technology controlled from outside. Because warhead components have to be provided by the United States every few years, it is only an "independent deterrent" between times.[4] The lesson drawn may be that the best of European national forces is still not good enough. This precept may reduce the incentive to further proliferation. Real British participation in Europe then may not only reinforce an Atlantic orientation; it may also provide clearer guidance on the merits and disadvantages of a national nuclear role.

In the United States, a British option for Europe would be warmly welcomed. In *de facto* terms London had the greatest leverage on America when it could speak on behalf of a European consensus. More than any other, Ernest Bevin sensed this interdependence. Though his object was to draw Washington into military alliance, he knew that Europe would have to cohere politically and militarily before American power could be brought to bear. He sought a Europe which was united in terms of a common overture to the United States, and NATO was virtually his personal creation. In those days the United Kingdom was the keystone of the arch uniting Europe with America. It could be so again, but only if the British regain their foothold on the continent. The real strength of the Anglo-American accord was not simply

---

[4] See *Times*, December 19, 1964; *Sunday Times*, December 20, 1964.

sentimental; it was founded on the centrality of the British position.

It remains true, therefore, that concrete British policies have changed little since Suez: the same military doctrines are advanced, the same cooperation with the United States is sought. British weapons are more crucially dependent on the United States than they used to be, but that has not greatly changed British policy. What has changed is the American and the continental attitude toward Britain. Britain used to be a major reference point for both American and continental diplomatic calculations; she is no longer a major focus for either. In part this has been due to British aloofness in the one case and dependency in the other. In part it has been due to a succession of military and economic reversals that have occurred since 1957.

There were two basic decisions in the Sandys White Paper of 1957. First, there was the decision to maintain and upgrade the deterrent through a new generation of weapon systems; second, there was the decision to carry on with the same cold war and conventional commitments as before, though to defend them with regular forces. However sound these choices were in principle, they could not be implemented by British resources. Thus, the government opened itself to a series of reverses. Since, at various times, cabinets either would not increase defense spending because they believed it would be electorally unpopular, or could not increase spending because it would bring on financial crisis, military budgets were held to a bare minimum. Welfare and social service expenditures had a tendency to grow, while tax rates remained the same, and the defense sector was under constant pressure. As inflationary trends mounted in the domestic economy, the pound plummeted in international markets, and only a series of international rescue operations conjoined with austerity averted devaluation. By 1966 these pressures had produced a price and wage freeze and rigid governmental retrenchment. Defense spending not only could not increase; it had to be reduced in real terms. By the end of 1966 then it had become amply clear that Britain had military autonomy in neither strategic nor conventional realms. But while British strategic independence had been questioned early on, her conventional preparedness seemed to suffice until quite recently.

In this respect the revolutionary quality of the Duncan Sandys Paper had been misapprehended. To many it revolved around the insistence upon an "independent deterrent"; to a discerning few, it concerned the attempt to man the full range of British commitments with reduced forces. The inadequacy of the "independent deterrent" became clear in 1960 when the government had to cancel the Blue Streak missile, which was the lineal successor to the V-bombers. The missile was to be fired from underground, but not from hardened emplacements, and it was to be liquid-fueled. On both grounds it was vulnerable to attack by Soviet intermediate range missiles. Unlike the V-bombers, approximately one quarter of which might have gotten off the ground within four-minutes warning of a Soviet strike, the Blue Streak would neither be ready nor sufficiently invulnerable to ride out an attack. After receipt of warning, its fueling procedures would have taken about twenty minutes. The yield and accuracy of Soviet missiles rendered the Blue Streak as impotent as the American-provided Thors.

The cancellation of Blue Streak, however, represented the end of an epoch in British military policy. Though Britain had relied on the United States during World War II to provide the final punch needed for victory in the West, both Britain and the United States had made separate national contributions to the Allied cause. Britain's forces had been smaller, but they had not depended vitally upon American weapons. After the war it had been assumed that both countries would meet their needs through national military production, and in atomic warheads and delivery systems, the presumption had proved true. The cancellation of Blue Streak and the decision to rely on the U.S. Sky Bolt air-launched ballistic missile to augment the range and penetration of the V-bombers meant that Britain would for the first time be dependent on another country for weapons in her own armory. The Anglo-American alliance was now not merely a device to add American to British military efforts, it was decisive for British national forces.

The cancellation of Sky Bolt in 1962 and its replacement by Polaris submarines carried the transformation even further. The V-bombers, at least, were British weapons, developed nationally. Sky Bolt was to be an extension to their range and strategic longevity; it was simply an increment to a national system. The U.S. decision against the production of Sky Bolt left Britain even more dependent. At Nassau in December, 1962, the United States agreed to furnish Polaris missiles for British nuclear submarines which were themselves original products of U.S. design. The missile compartment of the submarines had virtually to be built by the United States, and even the warheads for the missiles, which technically were to be a British responsibility, depended upon U.S. assistance in design and in provision of required fissionable components. The British Polaris system is little more than an American system once removed. Since there are no immediate plans for a British successor system to the Polaris, British participation in the strategic nuclear business will depend upon continuing grants of technology and hardware from the United States. Initially, moreover, the British seem to have rejected Poseidon, a larger missile disposing multiple warheads, as a follow-on to the Polaris.

The question takes on some urgency with the announcement of Russia's creation of a ballistic missile defense system to ring its major cities. A smaller nuclear country, lacking the ability to saturate the missile defense system of a large opponent may find that its deterrent preparations have been nullified. Submarine-launched missiles of limited range and size of warhead will be more vulnerable to defensive measures than certain other weapon systems. In the next few years it is quite doubtful that the United Kingdom will possess a strategic force capable of doing "unacceptable damage" to the Soviet Union. In the circumstances Britain may have got the worst of both possible worlds: a "deterrent" which is neither independent nor a deterrent.

If the British record in strategic weapons systems is scarcely exemplary, that in conventional and cold war forces is little better. The 1957 target of 165,000 in the Army was based on official actuarial figures concerning likely recruitment under an all-regular system. This was later changed to 180,000 when recruiting exceeded expectations. The British Army rose to 181,000 active strength, but remained less capable than before of meeting its commitments around the world. In 1966, 56,000 effectives were stationed in Germany and Berlin, 41,000 in the Far East, 11,000 in the Middle East, 9,000 in the Mediterranean, and 1,000 in other overseas areas. At home, aside from headquarters and forces in training, the United Kingdom had 42,000 troops in the strategic reserve. The great proportion of these were manpower to flesh out the NATO

commitment, however, and were not available for use elsewhere in the world, nor were they organized in self-contained
units. Of course there were a small number of battalions left
over, and the reserves could always be called out in an
emergency. As Britain's response to the 1961 Berlin crisis
showed, however, new military challenges required Whitehall
to depart from its established policies, and resort to measures
it had not planned to use.

But if existing regular forces were inadequate to cope with
new threats around the world, even their small numbers
would not be maintained. Defence Minister Healey made it
quite clear in his reply to the defense debate in March, 1966,
that the additional £100 million that had to be saved to reduce
defense spending to £2,000 million in real terms by 1969–70
would be found by "reductions in equipment and manpower"
following an end to the Indonesian confrontation of Malaysia.[5] Since it would only save foreign exchange costs to return
these forces to home bases, a substantial number would be
demobilized. At the same time the size of the Cyprus garrison
would be considerably reduced, with a consequent saving of
defense expenditure. Though the future size of the British
Army could not be forecast with accuracy, the plans the
government now apparently has in train could reduce it to
165,000 men over the next several years. In these circumstances Britain simply will not be able to care for its actual
and potential commitments in the Persian Gulf, East Africa,
and the Far East.

The cancellation for the proposed aircraft carrier also
underlined weaknesses in British conventional strength. As
Mr. Healey pointed out, a three-carrier force for the early
and middle 1970s was little better than the two-carrier force
that would exist in the absence of new construction. Even

[5] *House of Commons Debates*, Vol 725 (March 8, 1966), col. 2064.

a three-carrier force would permit only one carrier to be stationed permanently east of Suez, "and that ship would not always be in the right place at the right time." [6] Another would be able to be transferred east of Suez on fifteen days notice, nine or ten months of the year, but the combined total did not add up to an overpowering capability. The one carrier permanently to be stationed in the Eastern area had only seven strike aircraft and was capable of only four days intensive operation. The cost of sea-based air strength, moreover, was about 2½ times that of comparable strength based on land. The Labour Defence Minister made a good case that the proposed new carrier added little to British capability, while contributing greatly to the cost of conventional forces. But the situation in the absence of the CVA 01 is even more parlous. Since only two British carriers will be able to operate the F-4 Phantom, the third carrier will be obsolescent well before its planned phase-out in 1971. A force of two Phantom-capable carriers will certainly not permit one on permanent station east of Suez. For most emergencies, Britain will have to rely on land-based aircraft to perform fighter, bomber, and ground support roles in the Far East.

The weakness of the British carrier force and its termination in 1975 meant that the R.A.F. had for practical purposes inherited the Navy's limited war functions. These, however, could not be carried out in all situations and against all opponents. The Minister of Defence argued:

If we were to take seriously the possibility of landing troops on a hostile shore, without allies, outside the range of our land-based aircraft, we would have to have a force of at least five or six carriers so as to be certain of having two permanently available,

[6] *Ibid.* (March 7, 1966), col. 1791.

but such a force, besides costing very large sums far beyond our means, would be far beyond the capacity of the Royal Navy to man. We therefore decided not to keep the capability for such operations, and I regard this as a small sacrifice since we could not afford it anyway, and it is difficult to imagine circumstances in which it would be politically wise to use it.[7]

The opponent against whom such operations had at least theoretically to be planned was Indonesia. It had sophisticated bombing and fighter-interceptor capability, and British land-based aircraft had therefore to be kept nearby. When the fifty American F-111A's become available after 1968, the great proportion of them will be based in Singapore, within reach of Indonesian targets.[8] When the Singapore base later becomes untenable, they will be moved to Australia, and based in Darwin and the Cocos Islands. Together with Gan, and the possibility of another base off the coast of East Africa, these facilities would also make possible a considerable role in the Indian Ocean. Since Australia will be acquiring two squadrons of F-111A's, Australian basing arrangements will make some provision for British planes as well.

The decision to phase-out the British carrier force after 1975 (if it can even be maintained until that date) affects not only support for amphibious and land operations, but anti-submarine warfare, and the protection of ships at sea. Later on these functions are to be discharged by helicopters operating from cruisers, destroyers, and frigates, and by land-based air power coordinating with naval vessels. A small surface-to-surface missile is to be developed to counter the challenge of

[7] *Ibid.*, col. 1792.

[8] *Ibid.* (March 8, 1966), col. 2041. How long they will remain in Singapore in light of the government's decision to halve its Singapore garrison in 1971 and withdraw by 1977 is still unclear. See *Supplementary Statement of Defence Policy*, Cmnd. 3357 (July, 1967).

missile-firing destroyers. The anti-submarine warfare function will be facilitated by the construction of five hunter-killer nuclear submarines.

The net result of the changes in British conventional forces, however, was severely to deplete British capability. In recent years, the greatest problem in the rapid movement of troops to areas threatened by attack was the denial of overflight rights by a series of countries. The route to the Persian Gulf depended upon consent by Turkey and Iran; Turkish consent was held up in the Kuwait operation of 1961 and is likely to be even less dependable in the future. The route to Aden depended on overflight of Libya and the Sudan or upon an elaborate and costly detour through central Africa, including Nigeria, the Central African Republican, the Congo, Uganda, and Ethiopia. The first route has been vetoed by the Sudan, and the second could not be counted on in an emergency. Aside from local opposition from Adeni leaders, one of the major reasons for the initial decision to leave Aden in 1968 was unquestionably the uncertainty of getting planes and men there in a crisis.

An alternative has been the west-about route through North America, via the chain of U.S. bases in the Pacific, Singapore, and Australia. These certainly make possible reinforcement as far west as the Indian Ocean; the long ferry-range of F-111A is well suited to the distances involved. If operations are to be sustained from the Indian Ocean into East Africa, or the Persian Gulf, however, a major base must be sought as a replacement for Aden. Gan is acceptable as a staging base so long as Singapore is available with stocking and repair facilities. After Singapore is vacated, however, new installations will have to be constructed in Australia or somewhere in the Indian Ocean. If British garrisons are to be ready to act on short notice, barracks, training fields, and equipment stockpiles must also be provided. This either means starting *de novo* in the Indian Ocean or developing Australian facilities at not inconsiderable cost. It also must mean, since Commando ships and carriers can no longer be counted on for emergency operations, that there must be means of transporting men and equipment on short notice from the United Kingdom. Despite the air barrier problem, this could be done by air transport over the west-about route, but then Britain would have to procure additional transport capacity.

The conclusion is inescapable: either Britain will have to develop facilities elsewhere in the region, after Singapore's lease runs out, to house, train, and maintain British garrisions and equipment, or she will have to provide for much more adequate means of transporting men, equipment, and supplies from the United Kingdom. Developments in 1967 suggest the latter, while acknowledging that the Cabinet is "planning to maintain a military capability for use, if required, in the area, even when we no longer have forces permanently based there." In either event, Britain's position in the Far East will be largely dependent on the United States. It will also incur costs that were not budgeted in the 1966 and 1967 White Papers.

In one sense the 1966 defense review made a final disposition of issues raised in the Duncan Sandys White Paper in 1957. Sandys refused to cut British commitments, but reduced the forces that were to cover them. The deficiency was only gradually revealed: in Kuwait, East Africa, and Malaysia; then the question became whether forces would be increased or commitments reduced. Healey has given a partial answer on both counts. Commitments would be reduced as in the planned evacuation of Singapore, Malaysia, and Aden, but so would forces. And the East of Suez reductions were subject to political constraint: "We shall have dependencies and other obligations there for the foreseeable future." The termination of the British carrier program ended the original hopes of the Royal Navy for five new carriers, later pared to one new carrier by Conservative Defence Minister Peter Thorneycroft in July, 1963. The Navy, despite Nassau, increasingly saw its future in terms of conventional and cold war forces.[9] The carrier might be outmoded in strategic terms, but it was still extremely useful in conventional conflicts, and was not dependent upon a fixed base structure or foreign approval. At the very time, however, when conventional doctrines were being developed, the resources to support them were undercut.

The phenomenon was the same in Germany as in the Mediterranean and east of Suez. Denis Healey was the most learned of all British defense spokesmen on contemporary strategy and doctrine. He was most impressed of parliamentary leaders of the virtues of conventional warfare as a means to avoid the choice between Armageddon and inaction. In the Far East and on the Elbe, his predilections were in favor of conventional reinforcement and the "pause." He was also personally committed to the defense of Malaysia and saw clearly the unique role Britain could fill in the Commonwealth countries of Asia and Africa, a role which America had little chance of assuming. But the triumph of conventional doctrine occurred at a time of enormous financial stringency. In the Far East, Britain could not even afford one

[9] See W. J. Crowe Jr., "The Policy Roots of the Modern Royal Navy, 1946–1963," p. 218 ff. Unpublished dissertation, Princeton University, 1965.

of the two or three new carriers that she needed to make conventional doctrines effective. On the Rhine she could not increase her forces to permit a sustained conventional or limited nuclear resistance; indeed, those forces and stockpiles had to be reduced. Paradoxically British conventional forces have been least adequate as the rationale for them has grown.

The continued disparity between commitments and capabilities has been met by reliance on the United States. The strategic relationship between the United States and Britain requires no highlighting. But the 1966 White Paper carried British dependence into an area in which London had previously been independently successful: that of cold war conflicts. Denis Healey wrote:

> We have decided that, while Britain should retain a major military capability outside Europe, she should in future be subject to certain general limitations. First, Britain will not undertake major operations of war except in co-operation with allies. Secondly, we will not accept an obligation to provide another country with military assistance unless it is prepared to provide us with the facilities we need to make such assistance effective in time. Finally, there will be no attempt to maintain defence facilities in an independent country against its wishes.[10]

The first and most important requirement meant essentially that Britain would not become engaged in a major cold war action without the help of the United States. This formulation extended the discretionary role of America in British defense planning. In the Malaysian confrontation of 1963–65, Washington had not wished to be involved, but had sympathized with British efforts to protect Malaysia. The Healey doctrine of 1966 suggested, however, that the anti-confrontation struggle could not be repeated. Benign ap-

[10] Cmnd. 2901, p. 7.

proval would not be enough; America should actively aid British forces or they could not engage in such "major operations of war." That admission reflected upon the straitened British position in Borneo. As long as the struggle was confined to several hundred casualties in encounters between terrorists and security forces, Britain could handle the conflict. If Indonesia had launched a major attack on Sarawak, however, the British would have been hard pressed to offer sufficient resistance locally. Without the United States, the help of Australia and New Zealand might not have been decisive in such a case. Far from Suez remaining a landmark in the history of British limited encounters, the defense of Malaysia probably sets a standard which will not subsequently be attained. The United States, as the main British ally, now helps to bridge the gap between capabilities and commitments. But as the government found at Suez, its policies and forces may not always be tailored to British requirements.

The essential problem of future British defense policy is a politico-military sleight of hand: to gain greater influence in the world international system as defense capabilities and supporting finance are reduced. In practical terms the problem may well be insoluble. If present trends continue Britain will steadily lose influence in the system and will be viewed increasingly as an appendage of the United States. Neither her nuclear deterrent nor her world role have commanded attention and prestige in recent years; both now seem as weak or weaker than before. Neither of these tendencies, however, is irreversible. And Britain still devotes a higher fraction of its Gross National Product to arms than any major power in the North Atlantic Alliance except the United States. It is puzzling that Britain spends more than the French, the Germans, or the Japanese and yet the last three nations seem to be regarded as more formidable powers. One can only conclude that Britain has not made maximum political use of its military resources, and this judgment focuses attention on means for acquiring greater influence. What can Britain do now to enhance her prestige and position in the world system?

Answers to this question are closely linked with developments in European and East Asian defense over the past decade. Powers defeated since World War II have on the whole maximized their influence. This has been for three reasons. First, defeat meant a loss of overseas defense commitments. Even France eventually disentangled itself from draining military responsibilities and Germany and Japan lost their foreign role directly at the end of the war. Second, because of the failure of military adventures, these countries, and particularly Japan and Germany, have been able to devote their main energies to internal economic development and industrial progress. Productivity rates have greatly increased; factories have been rebuilt or modernized; foreign trade patterns revived. The very devastation of World War II required new industrial construction, largely facilitated by outside aid. Third, the partially dependent status of defeated powers involved two favorable relationships. On the one hand, the United States and Britain were bound to help restore these countries, economically and politically, and this often required the major defense burden to be borne by the two guarantor powers. On the other hand, the reestablishment of political and economic momentum gave ground for further concessions from the guarantor states. As Germany and Japan resume their accustomed places, they may legitimately ask for total political, economic, and military equality. And the argument for parity of status is very difficult to resist. The result has been to regard Germany, Japan, and France as rising, even revisionist, nations, while Britain and even the United States are viewed as stable or possibly declining powers.

Of course, this record cannot be recapitulated by Britain, nor would such a course be desirable, even if it were possible. But the United Kingdom can derive some instructive lessons from its direction and force. The first has to do with overseas commitments. A nation is usually regarded as more powerful when it is not compelled continuously to expend its military capital. Unless concrete applications of force are overwhelming, constant expenditure of military resources only reveals weaknesses in national posture. If some endeavors are unsuccessful, the defeats absorbed reduce prestige and influence even further. Other things being equal, it is preferable to have a military capability which does not have to be tested, than one which is tested frequently and occasionally found wanting.

British commitments still make it likely that British forces will be engaged in combat in different parts of the globe. It is unthinkable that the commitment to the defense of Western Europe could be greatly hedged. Interests in Europe are fundamental; even the connection with the United States is partly dependent on the need to bring American power to bear in Europe. Troops might be cut from the British Army of the Rhine, but no major reductions would be justifiable in the light of British interests themselves. In current political conditions of *détente* with Russia and slackening effort in NATO, a fully conventional defense of Europe is completely out of the question. Britain will continue to maintain sufficient troops for at least a ten-day battle before resorting to strategic nuclear exchanges. Given the U.S. and Western military investment in Europe, and the probable incentives for a Soviet attack, this should suffice for the kind of unpremeditated or miscalculated incursion that could possibly occur. British commitments elsewhere may have to be pared, but they cannot be greatly diminished in Europe.

Reductions, therefore, will take place overseas. Singapore is the most exposed bastion currently, and the defense of Malaysia is a burden which Britain will not indefinitely carry. Indeed, it is the task of coping with Indonesia that requires substantial forces and technologically advanced British weapons. Withdrawal to Darwin or another Australian base would be only a partial substitute, and in terms of the new facilities needed for naval and ground forces, it might be very expensive. Further, it has practically been admitted that a major operation against Indonesia would require American support. As confrontation is gradually halted and Indonesian political orientations become more clear, the British will want to reduce their garrisons in the Far East, and they will not be likely to pay for expensive new installations in Australia. In Hongkong the British military presence is required for internal security; if China were to seize the colony it would lose its most important source of foreign exchange. It is possible, therefore, to imagine a complete British withdrawal from the Far East in the next five years, with the exception of small units stationed in Malaysia and Hong kong for internal security tasks. Most of the F-111A's could then be based in Britain for use in European defense. A British presence on a much reduced scale could remain in Bahrein and Masira, with the possibility of developing a new air base off the East African coast. Gan and Cocos would then provide a Western gateway to Darwin. Eventually, Britain might be able to reduce her commitments sufficiently so that they could be handled without strain. The protection of Kuwait and Bahrein, and even of certain East African nations is unlikely to occupy a fraction of the resources previously devoted to the defense of Malaysia. Nor will Britain maintain a major policing role in Cyprus. The laying-down of Far Eastern responsibilities and a refusal to accept new ones could decisively replenish Britain's military and political capital.

The reduction of military spending, made possible by retrenchment overseas, could help to stimulate economic advance in Britain. The transfer of resources from home consumption to export, resolute modernization of industry, an end to restrictive labor and business practices, and the acceptance of some unemployment could assist this objective. British membership in the Common Market would strengthen all these tendencies and make it imperative to keep a tight rein on domestic inflationary pressures. The competition of European industry and agriculture would stimulate and challenge their British counterparts.

But the most important point of all is the reestablishment of British diplomatic precedence. In previous years Britain served as a crucial link between Atlantic and European halves of the Western alliance. This central role was never based strictly on military competence. In the period in which Britain exerted the greatest influence (1946–50) her military forces were small and ill-equipped. Her nuclear effort had not yet reached fruition; relative to the Soviet Union she was much weaker than she is now. Her primacy depended upon the simultaneous heeding of her initiatives in Europe and in America. In the first case she helped to author the Council of Europe; in the second she was the initiator of the North Atlantic alliance. In 1966 her diplomatic position had been undermined by the formulation of a distinct European view and direct links between Washington and the continent; intermediaries were no longer necessary. The problem of reversing the decline of influence, then, is by no means easy; it may be impossible.

Given a further reduction in British commitments overseas, however, the United Kingdom may approach Europe with a new concentration of effort and resolve. To be sure, she can no longer serve as "broker" between alliance partners in Europe and America; the United States has too many bilateral contacts for that to be either useful or significant. But Britain remains one of the world's great trading nations; her links with Washington are still probably more intimate than that of any European power. As a member of the Common Market, she would inevitably exert pressure on behalf of open-ended trading relationships. A Europe with British participation would be more outward-looking, economically, politically, and militarily, than a Europe of the Six alone. Britain-in-Europe would be more likely to reinsure the Atlantic alliance for the indefinite future than an exclusive continental combination. Further, Britain could help to relieve Germany of the simultaneous and countervailing pressure of both the United States and France. Until the issue of Paris versus Washington is resolved, Germany will oscillate irregularly between them. British presence would help to settle this issue and solidify the Atlantic bond.

One of the surprising outcomes since 1958 has been the British disinclination to seek a closer relationship with the Federal Republic. In one sense it was not unexpected to find pro-Gaullist sentiment in reaction to American opposition over Suez. But Gaullism and maintenance of the Atlantic relationship were not ultimately compatible. If Paris was the alternative, then to enter Europe was to sacrifice the United States. And London has gone quite far to keep open its French option. The Concord, the strike trainer, and the now canceled variable geometry fighter were all manifestations of Anglo-French military cooperation. In the meantime relations with Bonn have been correct, but chilly. No military cooperation in production has developed; Britain, particularly under the Labour government, took a strong line against the possibly proliferative aspects of the multilateral force proposed by Washington and has been preoccupied with the need to press Bonn for a full offsetting of the foreign exchange costs of stationing the B.A.O.R. in Germany. The last has been temporarily solved in a tripartite agreement with the United States and the Federal Republic, but a residue of antagonism remains. British words about the perpetual retention of an American veto in any Atlantic nuclear force have rankled German feelings; in German opinion, British policy has been tailored completely to the mandates of nonproliferation and has shown little hospitality to continental views. The estrangement between London and Bonn is all the more difficult to understand in light of British interests on the continent. Always empirical, the British should wish to find a continental link which does not impair their freedom in regard to North America. An Anglo-German combination does not do so, because the need to strengthen trans-Atlantic ties is mutual. Britain has something to offer Germany as well, and German support in Common Market discussions would not be of negligible importance.

This does not mean that Britain will not have to reemphasize her European sentiments and play down her Atlantic links if she wishes to secure admission. Prime Minister Wilson has already espoused French views on the dangers of too great a level of U.S. investments in Europe. And it will probably be necessary to make a greater obeisance to Paris on sterling and Commonwealth relationships if membership is to be finally achieved. Ultimate British policy and interests, however, would seem to lie much more largely with Germany-in-Europe than with France-in-Europe. As the United States reduces its military forces in Germany and becomes increasingly preoccupied with Vietnam, the British option might have certain advantages for Germany. British participation could also be crucial for a post-Gaullist France. Indeed, British strategic bargaining powers are not negligible even against current French intransigence. Not only does the British market open vistas for continental manufacturers, British technology and British military hardware make it conceivable that a greater Western Europe could offer more than token opposition to American industrial penetration. In strict military terms Britain's notions of rapid escalation of any major European conflict accord much more with continental doctrines than those of the United States. Atlantic nuclear sharing schemes have foundered, and Secretary McNamara's Select Committee is apparently not fully satisfactory to Bonn, because it does not deal with the really important matters of nuclear policy and choice.[11] Today, the prospect of a nonproliferation treaty makes it even less likely that Bonn will ever acquire national control of strategic nuclear weapons.

At this point the British may conceivably have something to contribute. Their Polaris force, equipped with A.3 missiles, may not credibly penetrate Soviet ABM defenses. The Poseidon, of greater range and disposing multiple warheads, however, could redress the balance. A small force, like that of the British or French, must be technologically more advanced to be a credible deterrent than a large force like that of the

[11] See Theo Sommer, "The Objectives of Germany," in Alastair Buchan, ed., *A World of Nuclear Powers* (Englewood Cliffs, N.J., 1966), p. 46.

United States. The Poseidon missile may still be available to Britain under the terms of the Nassau Accords, even though the British government has not yet sought to ascertain precise terms. Costs clearly would not be insignificant. As the *Times* defense correspondent recently pointed out:

> Britain, under the terms of the (Nassau) agreement, would have to share the development costs of the missile, which will be at least £300 million.
> The cost of fitting existing submarines with the (Poseidon) C3 has not been calculated, even in America. But it would involve installing a new range of missile equipment as well as widening the missile tubes.
> Poseidon has a new warhead which would not be supplied by the United States and which would require an extensive nuclear development programme—including a new series of underground tests—which is not contemplated at present.[12]

One of the questions for Britain, then, is to find a means under which Poseidon can be furnished on better technical and financial terms. The British calculate, rightly, that the United States is unlikely to make new grants of technology to what is essentially a national deterrent force, and thus do not expect to receive such terms. A British approach to Europe, however, might redefine the British force in American eyes. If the British force were to be conceived as in trust for the European allies, and particularly for the Germans, it might be more favorably viewed.

There is a major question, however, of the conditions on which Britain would act as a trustee of Europe. Under U.S.–U.K. nuclear agreements, the British would have to keep custody and control of nuclear warheads. The delivery vehicle might be in the hands of Europeans as well as Britons, though

[12] *Times*, September 26, 1966.

the complex associated technology perhaps might not be produced under license by European firms. The exact application of the nonproliferation treaty draft is unclear, but one interpretation could allow Europeans—Germans, French, Italians, Belgians, and others—a major role in planning the operation, targeting, and rules of engagement for such a force. Decisions to fire might also be taken jointly. While General de Gaulle might be expected to resist such an arrangement, the result would mark the furthest pooling of British arms with continental counterparts. If Frenchmen believe in developing a real alternative to American military predominance, they can scarcely hope to do so, today or ultimately, without British support. Further, such a sharing scheme would have the advantage, from the standpoint of U.S. critics, of functioning without American participation.

Such an arrangement might not be a satisfactory long-term solution of the problems associated with Europe's strategic defense. But no panaceas are now in sight. All designs come up against the fundamental difficulty that they either give insufficient national control and therefore fail to meet minimum concerns for national security, or they are tantamount to nuclear dissemination and therefore impinge upon international security. A genuinely supranational European deterrent would avoid the problem of the credibility of the U.S. guarantee, but it would also create another nuclear power. A British nuclear trusteeship involves no further proliferation, but it would add reinsurance that strategic nuclear weapons would be used in Europe's defense. In this respect it would be completely compatible with long-established trends in British defense thinking.

It would be insufficient merely to tell European nations

that British weapons would be used to protect their interests. Since 1954, no British military or economic initiative has really come to grips with the integrative principles of continental planning. Short of a constitutional decision-making role, European nations would scarcely consider their participation in the British deterrent as either influential or decisive. If they were given such a role, however, the way might be open for a new British leverage on the continent. As the British Polaris submarines become operational in 1968, the British force will certainly be the most potent nuclear deterrent aside from those of the United States and Russia.

America might welcome such a force, and her policy toward it could well be different from that toward a deterrent to be used for national purposes. As long as information on weapons designs was not passed to European nations, the relationship with Europe would not violate restrictions of the McMahon Act. If certain information had to be provided to the Europeans on weapons effects and other characteristics of the British deterrent system, the United States might well be willing to construe or amend the Atomic Energy Act. In the circumstances of a new British strategic initiative toward Europe, it is possible that the United States might renew its offer of weapons systems and assist Britain to acquire Poseidon missile technology at much less cost than presently estimated. Exchanges of information and materials, of course, would have to be limited to those permissible under prohibitions on proliferation. They would accord with the restriction: "Each nuclear weapon state party to this Treaty undertakes not to transfer to any recipient whatsoever nuclear weapons or other nuclear explosive devices." At the same time such agreements would bypass Russian objections to MLFtype arrangements which might be held to involve transfer-ring "control over such weapons or explosive devices directly or indirectly" [13] through multilateral nuclear sharing.

From the American point of view, continuing assistance to a British deterrent conceived as European trustee would not only strengthen London's bargaining position in European negotiations, it would also reassure continentals that nuclear weapons would be used in their defense and not tactical nu-clears only. It would accomplish some of the objectives of the MLF-ANF proposals, without the creation of a new and probably vulnerable force, complicated by international own-ership and cumbersome mixed-manning. It would keep the British in the nuclear business while compelling them to a constitutional association with the continent. America would presumably have to pledge continuing help beyond the next generation of weapons systems, if the Europeans were to place any credence in the enduring qualities of the British strategic guarantee.

If reliance on Britain might not satisfy the Europeans in the long run, it should at least be as attractive an alternative as re-liance on France. France has made no moves towards the con-stitutional internationalization of her deterrent, and when it finally emerges it is likely to be far less formidable than the British force. It is sometimes forgotten that France had failed to detonate a hydrogen bomb as late as 1967 when the British achieved their first explosion, entirely without American help, ten years previously. Participation in such a force would also be open to the successors of General de Gaulle. A similar and linked arrangement for the French force at some later time

[13] *U.S. Draft Treaty to Prevent the Spread of Nuclear Weapons* (Washington, 1967), Article I.

would add further credibility to use of strategic weapons in a war in Europe. It would therefore additionally reassure the Germans.

Concentration upon Europe in both economic and military fields, however, will still not reestablish the British position of yesteryear. Europe has grown in material strength and also in cohesion relative to Britain in the intervening period. In the old days Britain easily sustained her overseas and continental roles. Now she scarcely has resources for the second. Her response to the political failure of Suez was realistic, but misguided in some respects. London accepted her fall from grace with remarkable equanimity and placed ever greater stress on the U.S. connection. But the success in restoration of the trans-Atlantic link took place at the expense of Britain's world and European position. Whether she is or not, Britain is now desperately in need of being seen as independent of the United States. To the end of 1966, the Wilson government even more than its predecessor had cultivated and depended upon American good will. Britain was almost beginning to be taken for granted in Washington.

The British record in defense policy has been unique. In many respects London has made more sacrifices to sustain her role in world affairs than any other modern nation. The continuing expenditure of 7 to 10 percent of her GNP on arms has had its social costs. Modernization, exports, and social welfare have all suffered while the defense bill mounted. Though her recent efforts have not been proportionate to those of the United States, the industrial base from which she operates has been much weaker, and the real sacrifices much more significant. It is an enormous tribute to the responsibility of the British people that the retreat from empire was not more precipitate. It is also testimony to the desire of British policy makers to bear their fair share of Western defense burdens. Compared to nations of similar industrial strength, the British defense effort has been remarkable.

Year-to-year changes in defense spending from this relatively high plateau of international responsibility, however, have usually been occasioned by economic factors. Though Britain avoided this hasty demobilization of her forces at the end of the war, her military budgets up to 1950 bore little relation to probable enemy threats. As the threat increased, British forces declined. It was not until Korea that the British military machine gave a galvanic response, and even the enormous rearmament then agreed on was cut back when finance supervened. When the Conservatives returned to power they maintained expenditure at a relatively high level initially, despite the perceptible decline in the Soviet threat. The British deterrent was doubtlessly responsible for a large fraction of this cost. And as cold war and conventional doctrines became more important after 1957, the forces to implement them were steadily whittled down. Domestic inflation and the trade balance again were governing.

In fact, it is not inaccurate to claim that financial limitations have helped to determine preferred strategies. Had it not been for the constricting influence of the Treasury, British doctrine under the Wilson government would probably have embraced notions of flexible response and a conventional build-up in Europe. Denis Healey had criticized his Conservative predecessors for relying on rapid escalation of a European conflict, and yet he paraded the very same arguments. This was not because he accepted for all time the mandates of the 1952 global strategy paper; even if nuclear weapons would be used in any large-scale conflict in Europe, there still was need to provide political reassurance of sensitive European populations. Beyond this, it was desirable to extend the range of options in a crisis and avoid immediate commitment to a nuclear chain reaction. This was a desideratum which the British Chiefs had overlooked in 1952. If any war in Europe would necessarily be total, large ground forces were not needed and the Lisbon plans suspect. If limited war in Europe, at least for a short period, was not a contradiction in terms, then forces had to be raised to fight it. It is striking to recollect that British ground forces were larger when the strategy was automatic escalation than when graduated deterrence became the order of the day. The first inconsistency was political and reflected obeisance to outdated alliance doctrines. The second was financial and reflected doctrinal concessions by Labour defense spokesmen. The primacy of economics was again demonstrated, even though it sanctioned a larger defense budget than that of comparable powers.

Strategically the British have both been ahead of and behind their American counterparts. Their vision of the probable course of a nuclear war was initially more realistic than NATO doctrine in point. If weapons of massive retaliation would be used, and used effectively, there was no need for a mighty shield in Europe. When doctrines of limited war arose after 1957, however, they evoked little response in Whitehall. It was still maintained that a conventional encounter in Europe would escalate to all-out war, and that conventional preparedness was of only limited efficacy or interest. Eventually British experts were persuaded of the case for flexible response and the "pause" only to find that the resources to implement them were lacking. In 1967, however, they may be right in contending that the probability of a Soviet attack has declined sufficiently to risk dealing with it in largely unconventional terms. They are certainly right in arguing that Europeans will not spend more on conventional forces and that the net impact of the flexible response doctrine has been to engender political uncertainty in West Germany. In this sense, their strategy has political appeal and validity, even if it is not what they would doctrinally prefer. And in a general sense, it is possible to argue that British strategists most recently have taken more account of political realities on the European continent than their American brethren. This is a good omen for the rebuilding of British prestige and influence in the system.

Perhaps the most interesting aspect of British strategic experience has had to do with the acquisition of nuclear weapons. At the end of World War II a decision was taken to carry the British nuclear effort to a final conclusion. This was not an unexpected evolution. Even during the war, Britain had made clear that she wanted bombs for the postwar period. At the same time, when the decision was actually made, the war was over; the Soviet Union was not yet an enemy, and at least ten years of peace were foreseen. The future policy of the United States, however, was uncertain. American isolationism was a distinct possibility, and Britain viewed the bomb as protection against a series of unspecified future contingencies. Britain's nuclear program was not hurried, not did it have overriding priority on financial resources. When the Labour government left office it was still unclear whether a new bomber fleet would be built to carry British atomic bombs or London would continue to rely on the U.S. Strategic Air Command. Churchill took the necessary decision, and the V-bombers were procured.

Until 1957, however, there was no urgency in the British

deterrent effort, and there was certainly no insistence that strategic weapons be "independent." Labour's offer in 1949 would have produced a genuine atomic pooling with America, Britain deriving her bombs from a joint effort culminating in the production of warheads in the United States. Even Churchill conceived the British force as supplementary to that of the United States. After 1957, on the other hand, the deterrent had to be brought to national fruition. Britain had to produce her bombs and carry them in British delivery vehicles. The paradox was that as Britain insisted upon "independence" her weapons actually became more "dependent"; when she was unworried by "dependence," her weapons were in fact "independent." Since 1960 it can scarcely be claimed that British strategic preparedness is not largely the result of collaboration with the United States.

The British nuclear effort underscores the role of alliance calculations in strategic policy. National nuclear weapons have not shattered the Anglo-American alliance; in some respects they have made Britain even more reliant on the United States. After 1946 the British nuclear effort was related to an Atlantic context. The nuclear program was designed to elicit more U.S. cooperation, not to obviate the need for cooperation. Until Suez there was no questioning of the American willingness to use its strategic forces in defense of British interests. After Suez, there were doubts of American nuclear credibility in all circumstances, but the practical necessities forced Britain into an even closer association with the United States. Again, British nuclear weapons offered no obstacle to alliance cohesion. In balance of power terms, the Anglo-American alliance should have foundered long ago. Traditional theory would have us believe that where interests are contrary, alliance must give way. But the Suez episode proved that where alliance was primary, British interests would yield.

This result is more difficult to understand in the light of the moderation of Soviet policy in recent years, the growing power of the West, and the advent of nuclear abundance. As Western military strength has prospered, the requirement—in power terms—for a cohesive Western alliance has become less necessary. British dependence on U.S. military guarantees has also decreased. Suez, then, could well have provided a justification for the termination of the alliance. It did not. From another point of view, the relative shift in the power positions of the United States and Britain could have occasioned a reorientation in British thinking about the alliance. When it was forged, both countries were weak militarily; now the United States is enormously stronger. But that power has not repelled—Britain has not sought ties elsewhere to offset American predominance.

Nor is it true that there has been no alternative to an American connection for Britain. Europe has always represented such a choice; but it has been one, as we have seen, that Britons have hesitated to select. In economic, military, and other realms, Europe, or even several individual European countries, might offer Britain what it now obtains from the United States in military terms. A European *démarche* would also be consistent with the diminution of Soviet hostility and the growth in the autarchic power of America. Yet Labour, for all of its left-wing credentials, has been a more fervent proponent of the alliance than have its Conservative colleagues. The government wants the United States to exert a strong influence in European political and economic evolutions. This hardly smacks of a desire to offset or dilute American strength; rather, it is an almost transparent effort to augment it.

The British experience in strategic affairs also violates traditional aphorisms about national nuclear development. According to certain theorists, nuclear countries evince successively three reactions to weapons development.[14] In the first phase, they neglect the drastic change which nuclear firepower makes in strategic and tactical terms. They then become mesmerized with the advantages of nuclear posture, and seek to make an atomic strategy relevant to every level of conflict. Finally, they come to recognize that total reliance on a strategy of nuclear retaliation paralyzes the will; since the decision is cataclysmic, it cannot be made. At this point doctrines of limited war evolve as a viable surrogate for all-out conflict; the ultimate sanction of thermonuclear war is reserved for the most vital challenges.

Along with this triple evolution, it is often held that antinuclear or "ban the bomb" movements will be generated coevally with hydrogen weapons and that their political force will diminish the dependence on nuclear weapons and perhaps even culminate in a withering away of nuclear capabilities. None of these outcomes, however, has emerged in the British context. Far more than the United States, Britain understood the role of conventional and cold war operations and never permitted a thermonuclear strategy to usurp the role of limited warfare. Massive retaliation was possible for the United States which had few garrison-commitments in politically sensitive areas; it was not feasible for the United Kingdom which was continually engaged in counter-insurgency operations.

At the same time Britain saw earlier than the United States that if all-out war was to be fought in Europe it should be fought with primary reliance on strategic weapons. The

[14] See Henry Kissinger, *Nuclear Weapons and Foreign Policy* (New York, 1957).

irrealism of the Lisbon Plans was that they superimposed a conventional upon an atomic strategy. The conventional option was supposed to be adequate for all tasks; the nuclear option was supposed to be adequate for all tasks; but it was then decided to use both simultaneously. It was partly at British urging and initiative that more realistic contingency plans were drawn at NATO Supreme Headquarters.

It is true, thus, that Britain never realistically entertained the possibility of fighting a prolonged conventional war over the body of Western Europe. When the "pause" and flexible response came into vogue after 1962, Britain expressed reservations. It might have been strategically desirable to fight a land war in Europe rather than escalate to all-out war, but the forces to implement that conception simply were not available; nor would they be provided. More than the United States, perhaps, Britain continued to emphasize limited forces for peripheral encounters in less than central geographic areas; more than the United States, she emphasized an unlimited response to attack in areas that were absolutely vital. But in none of the three "stages" of nuclear development did London derive univocal lessons. She never underestimated the impact of nuclear weapons; she did not overestimate the role of nuclear forces; nor did she succumb to the temptations of a conventional strategy more or less across the board. Flexible response might have been a useful option in Europe, but it was expensive politically and economically, and the need for it strategically was at least open to question.

The "ban the bomb" movement and the Campaign for Nuclear Disarmament also failed to have their predicted effects on British defense and politics. If pressure for unilateral nuclear disarmament was a function of the British bomb program, then Labour should have spurred a return to innocence and a divestment of nuclear capability. But neither outcome occurred. Despite the C.N.D., British unilateralism is now weaker than it has ever been. British ministers no longer trumpet the blessings of the "independent deterrent," but there is no move to extract Britain from the nuclear military business. Oddly enough left-wing criticism of the government has had greatest effect in forcing an even closer *rapprochement* with the United States. If Britain cannot be self-sufficient strategically, she must depend ever more on America. Perversely, the left-wing has made the British government even more right-wing, and the Wilson government has been at pains to show that Britain's nuclear system is not "independent" in that it is closely interwoven with that of the United States. Unilateralism in Britain has been very far from causing a national renunciation of weapons.

Partly as a result the supposed dangers of nuclear "proliferation" have not appeared in the British instance. The United Kingdom is probably now less disposed to use her weapons independently than was previously the case. Her adherence to the Western alliance and to Anglo-American ties is even greater than before. In one sense the very logic of national nuclear weapons has compelled a return to the founts of strategic expertise and knowledge to keep those weapons up to date. Britain provides no exemplar of immanent trends toward world multipolarity. Indeed, if the consequences of the spread of bombs are as moderate in other cases as they have been in Britain, the rationale against proliferation disappears.

At the same time, the United Kingdom holds no favorable portents about stopping the spread. If any nation might have been expected to curtail or halt its program, Britain provided the most likely case. The devotion to the United States and

Western Europe in international terms, the distaste for provocative or suicidal military postures in domestic terms—these might theoretically have combined to put an end to weapons development. In one sense Britain did not need national strategic weapons; in another, she could not abide them; yet they were built and carefully sustained. It is scarcely to be anticipated that nations lacking such favorable international and domestic balances will stay their hand. This does not mean that nuclear weapons will spread ineluctably; it does mean that the case against their dispersion is far from persuasive.

Britain enters the third decade of the nuclear epoch with uncertain economic and military credentials. She has developed the most formidable nuclear force outside of the Soviet Union and the United States, but has lost influence in the international system. Unless the British economy can show stable growth without a chronic deficit in international payments, her prestige will slip even further. Even if her economic problems are surmounted, with or without devaluation, political and international problems will remain. International prestige is an evanescent phenomenon, and it depends as much on the presentation of policy as on its quality. When Britain was as strong in the counsels of Europe as she was in America, her position was at its apex. This central role depended less upon her concrete military preparations than upon diplomatic posture. Britain, paradoxically, was taken more seriously by other powers when she was less strong relatively than she is today. Since then the insistence upon a certain *de facto* capability has occasioned London to gain that capability by whatever means; if it could not be obtained nationally, it would be acquired through alliance arrangements. But the acquisition, even of a larger capability, through the

Anglo-American alliance has lessened independent British influence. A slightly weaker Britain with a secure foothold in Europe would be a more potent international factor that the Britain of 1966. Somewhat surprisingly, a more independent Britain would probably have even greater influence in Washington that the present regime.

British defense arrangements in the nuclear era have functioned satisfactorily on the whole, and the British record in world affairs has been generally successful. London has devolved responsibility and autonomy upon a succession of independent polities previously part of the British empire. She has fought successfully in practically every corner of the globe. It is remarkable in a way that Britain turned over an empire far larger than the French, with a fraction of the social and political cost. She remains a factor of great importance in world politics. British failures have largely represented the defects of a virtue. Her solidarity with Washington has been far more than tactical; it has also been moral. But "balance of power" has been the traditional empirical interest in international affairs. The United Kingdom should not force itself to emulate discredited nineteenth-century policies at this late date. But influence can never be a function of dependency. A discerning historian, commenting on the last century of British diplomacy, might be tempted to point out contrasting errors in the expression of British diplomacy and strategy. Before both world wars Britain was too neutral and lost influence in the system; after World War II, Britain was too committed and lost influence in the system. The latter is a defect which can still be remedied.

APPENDIX

TABLE I.

DEFENSE EXPENDITURE
(ooo omitted)

	Gross National Product [1]	Total Ordinary Government Expenditure [2]	Total Public Expenditure [3]
1946	8,646	3,910.3	3,979
1947	9,210	3,209.5	3,509
1948	10,368	3,175.6	3,630
1949	11,055	3,375.3	3,837
1950	11,637	3,257.3	3,897
1951	12,790	4,053.6	4,337
1952	13,940	4,350.6	4,938
1953	14,910	4,274.0	5,147
1954	15,937	4,304.7	5,316
1955	16,945	4,496.0	5,475
1956	18,421	4,868.1	5,861
1957	19,516	4,919.6	6,132
1958	20,375	5,102.5	6,536
1959	21,376	5,243.9	6,942
1960	22,768	5,786.6	7,657
1961	24,335	6,234.8	8,152
1962	25,409	6,441.3	8,672
1963	27,003	6,817.3	9,295
1964	28,910	7,712.9	10,557
1965	30,997	8,445.7	10,791
1966	32,371	9,177.0	
1967			

[1] Gross National Product
1946–53: *Annual Abstract of Statistics*, No. 94, HMSO 1957.
1954–64: *Ibid.*, No. 102, HMSO 1965.
1965–66: *Ibid.*, No. 104, HMSO 1967 (forthcoming).

[2] Total Ordinary Government Expenditure
A. Base Year runs from April 1 to March 31; 1946–47 is considered as 1946 in table, and so on.
B. 1946–55: *Annual Abstract of Statistics*, No. 93, HMSO 1956.
1956–64: *Ibid.*, No 102, HMSO 1965.
1965–66: *Whitaker Annual Volume*, No 99, 1967 (1966 estimated figures).

TABLE I (*continued*)

Defense Total [4]	Defense Total × 100 / Total Public Expenditure	Defense Total × 100 / Total Ordinary Government Expenditure	Defense Total × 100 / Gross National Product
1,736	43.6	44.4	20.1
974	27.8	30.4	10.6
770	21.2	24.2	7.4
777	20.3	23.0	7.0
829	21.3	25.5	7.1
1,110	25.6	27.4	8.7
1,489	30.2	34.2	10.7
1,573	30.6	37.0	10.6
1,566	29.5	36.4	9.8
1,508	27.5	33.5	8.9
1,585	27.0	32.6	8.6
1,556	25.4	31.6	8.0
1,501	23.0	29.4	7.4
1,548	22.3	29.5	7.2
1,612	21.6	27.9	7.1
1,715	21.0	27.5	7.1
1,837	21.2	28.5	7.2
1,915	20.6	28.1	7.1
1,921	18.2	24.9	6.6
2,060	19.1	24.4	6.6
2,172		23.7	6.7
2,205			6.6 [5]

[3] Total Public Expenditure
1946–63: *The British Economy Key Statistics, 1900–1964* (London School of Economics and Cambridge University edition), Table E.
1964: *Britain: An Official Handbook, 1966* (Central Office of Information).
1965: *Ibid., 1967.*

[4] Defense Total
1946–63: *The British Economy Key Statistics*, Table E.
1964: *Britain: An Official Handbook, 1966*, p. 252.
1965: *Ibid.*, p. 238.
1966–67: Cmnd. 3203, *Statement on the Defence Estimates 1967*, HMSO 1967 (estimates).

[5] Estimated in *Statement on the Defense Estimates 1967*, February, 1967.

TABLE 2.

MILITARY STRENGTH
(000 omitted)

	Royal Navy	Military Strength [1] Army	Royal Air Force
1946	350.0	1,128.9	438.5
1947	189.6	773.5	284.5
1948	135.3	450.0	222.2
1949	136.9	395.4	205.1
1950	129.4	354.0	182.7
1951	135.8	426.8	241.4
1952	141.2	445.0	262.2
1953	138.0	435.1	268.2
1954	127.7	436.5	251.9
1955	122.1	415.7	245.7
1956	116.1	393.0	236.1
1957	110.1	361.1	215.9
1958	101.8	318.2	180.1
1959	96.7	287.4	165.9
1960	93.4	251.8	158.1
1961	91.4	217.4	149.6
1962	90.6	192.8	141.3
1963	92.7	181.1	135.0
1964	94.3	185.5	127.7
1965	95.0	187.1	125.9
1966	94.2	187.1	121.6
1967	93.4	190.8	118.5
1968	92.5	191.3	116.5

[1] Military Strength

1946–55: *Annual Abstract of Statistics*, No. 93, HMSO 1956.
1956–64: *Ibid.*, No. 102, HMSO 1965.
1965:   Cmnd. 2902, *Statement on the Defence Estimates 1966*, HMSO 1966.
1966:   Cmnd. 3203, *Statement on the Defence Estimates 1967*, HMSO 1967.
1967–68: *Ibid.*, estimated figures.

TABLE 2 (*continued*)

Total Military Strength	Total Working Males [2]	Total Military Strength × 100 / Total Working Males
1,917.4	14,638	13.1
1,247.6	14,628	8.5
807.5	15,657	5.2
737.4	15,641	4.7
666.1	15,678	4.2
804.0	15,791	5.1
848.4	15,864	5.3
841.3	15,883	5.3
816.1	15,974	5.1
783.5	16,084	4.9
745.2	16,188	4.6
687.1	16,225	4.2
600.1	16,160	3.7
550.1	16,137	3.4
503.3	16,239	3.1
458.4	16,369	2.8
424.8	16,528	2.6
408.8	16,588	2.5
407.5	16,605	2.5
408.0	16,682	2.4
402.9	16,637	2.4
402.7		
400.3		

[2] Total Working Males (June each year)

1946–47: *Monthly Digest of Statistics*, No. 39 (March, 1949). Figures not strictly comparable with future data.

1948–51: *Ibid.*, No. 91 (July, 1953).

1952–54: *Ibid.*, No. 121 (January, 1956).

1955–58: *Ibid.*, No. 169 (January, 1960).

1959–60: *Ibid.*, No. 193 (January, 1962).

1961–65: *Ibid.*, No. 253 (February, 1967).

1966: *Ministry of Labor Gazette*, Vol. LXXV, No. 2 (February, 1967).

TABLE 3.

DEPLOYMENT FIGURES

	1964 [1]	1965 [2]	1966 [3]
United Kingdom	241,000	238,900	243,300
Germany	62,000	64,800	63,460
Mediterranean	23,000		
Mediterranean and Near East		22,200	20,300
East of Suez	58,000 + 14,000 Gurkhas		
Middle and Far East		80,900	72,650
Elsewhere	9,000	45,000	43,290
TOTAL	393,000 + 14,000 Gurkhas	451,800	443,000

[1] Cmnd. 2592, 1964 *Statement on Defence Estimates 1965*, February, 1966.

[2] Cmnd. 2902, 1965 *Statement on Defence Estimates 1966*, February, 1966.

[3] Cmnd. 3203, 1966 *Statement on Defence Estimates 1967*, February, 1966.

INDEX